Houghton Mifflin

Math Expressions

Volume 2

Developed by
The Children's Math Worlds
Research Project

PROJECT DIRECTOR AND AUTHOR

Dr. Karen C. Fuson

This material is based upon work supported by the
National Science Foundation
under Grant Numbers
ESI-9816320, REC-9806020, and RED-935373.

Any opinions, findings, and conclusions or recommendations expressed in this
material are those of the author and do not necessarily reflect the views of the
National Science Foundation.

HOUGHTON MIFFLIN   BOSTON

T80402

MATH
H8146
2006
3
wbk
v. 2

Teacher Reviewers

Kindergarten
Patricia Stroh Sugiyama
Wilmette, Illinois

Barbara Wahle
Evanston, Illinois

Grade 1
Sandra Budson
Newton, Massachusetts

Janet Pecci
Chicago, Illinois

Megan Rees
Chicago, Illinois

Grade 2
Molly Dunn
Danvers, Massachusetts

Agnes Lesnick
Hillside, Illinois

Rita Soto
Chicago, Illinois

Grade 3
Jane Curran
Honesdale, Pennsylvania

Sandra Tucker
Chicago, Illinois

Grade 4
Sara Stoneberg Llibre
Chicago, Illinois

Sheri Roedel
Chicago, Illinois

Grade 5
Todd Atler
Chicago, Illinois

Leah Barry
Norfolk, Massachusetts

Special Thanks
Special thanks to the many teachers, students, parents, principals, writers, researchers, and work-study students who participated in the Children's Math Worlds Research Project over the years.

Credits
Cover art: (scale) © HMCo./Richard Hutchings. (elephant) © Art Wolfe/Stone/Getty Images. (chipmunk) © David W. Hamilton/The Image Bank/Getty Images.

Illustrative art: Robin Boyer/Deborah Wolfe, LTD
Technical art: Nesbitt Graphics, Inc.
Photos: Nesbitt Graphics, Inc.

ISBN-13: 978-0-618-50985-0
ISBN-10: 0-618-50985-2

6 7 8 9 CK 14 13 12 11 10 09 08

VOLUME 2 CONTENTS

Mini Unit E Time

Unit 6 Exploring Fractions, Probability, and Division with Remainders

Fraction Concepts

Equivalent Fractions

* This lesson consists only of activities from the Teacher's Guide.

Name _____ Date _____

Class Activity

▶ Explore Patterns with 5s

What patterns do you see below?

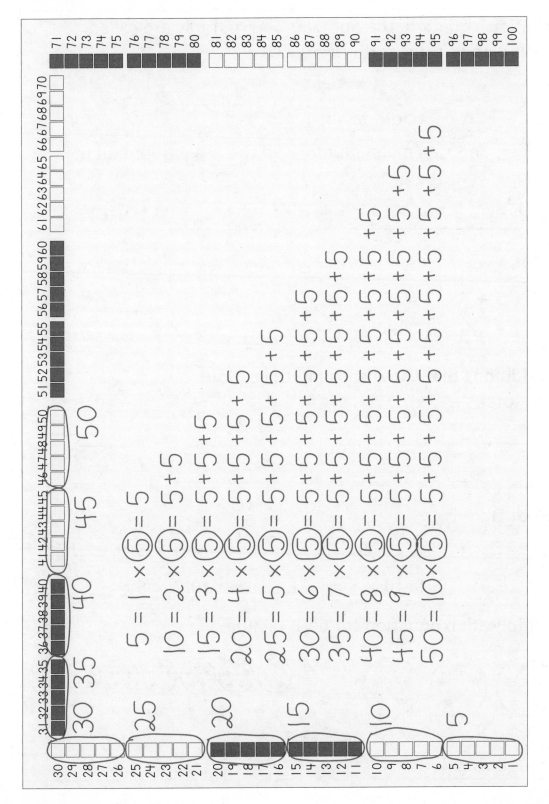

Multiply with 5 **193**

Class Activity

Name _____   **Date** _____

Vocabulary

multiplication
factor
product

▶**Practice Multiplications with 5**

In a **multiplication** equation, the numbers you multiply are called **factors**. The answer, or total, is the **product**.

$$3 \times 5 = 15$$

factor   factor   product

The symbols ×, *, and • all mean *multiply*. So these equations all mean the same thing.

$$3 \times 5 = 15 \qquad\qquad 3 * 5 = 15 \qquad\qquad 3 \bullet 5 = 15$$

Write each total.

1. $4 \times \boxed{5} = 5 + 5 + 5 + 5 =$ _____

2. $7 \bullet \boxed{5} = 5 + 5 + 5 + 5 + 5 + 5 + 5 =$ _____

**Write the 5s additions that show each multiplication.
Then write the total.**

3. $6 \times \boxed{5} =$ _____ = _____

4. $9 * \boxed{5} =$ _____ = _____

Write each product.

5. $8 \times 5 =$ _____   6. $2 \times 5 =$ _____   7. $5 \times 5 =$ _____

8. $4 \times 5 =$ _____   9. $10 \times 5 =$ _____   10. $7 \times 5 =$ _____

Write a 5s multiplication equation for each picture.

11.

12.

_____   _____

Multiply with 5

Dear Family,

In this unit and the next, your child will be practicing basic multiplications and divisions. *Math Expressions* incorporates studying, practicing, and testing of the basic multiplications and divisions in class. Your child is also expected to practice at home.

Study Plans Each day your child will fill out a study plan, indicating which basic multiplications and divisions he or she will study that evening. When your child has finished studying (practicing), his or her Homework Helper should sign the study plan.

4–1	Name		Date
Homework			

Study Plan

5s count bys
5s multiplications

_____
Homework Helper

Practice Charts Each time a new number is introduced, students' homework will include a practice chart. To practice, students can cover the products with a pencil or a strip of heavy paper. They will say the multiplications, sliding the pencil or paper down the column to see each product after saying it. Students can also start with the last problem in a column and slide up. It is important that your child studies count-bys and multiplications at least 5 minutes every night. Your child can also use these charts to practice division on the mixed up column by covering the first factor.

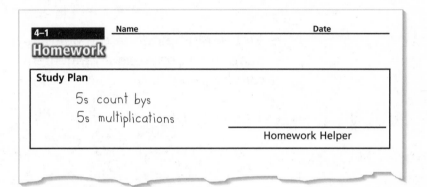

	In Order	Mixed Up
5s	1 x 5 = 5	9 x 5 = 45
	2 x 5 = 10	5 x 5 = 25
	3 x 5 = 15	2 x 5 = 10
	4 x 5 = 20	7 x 5 = 35
	5 x 5 = 25	4 x 5 = 20
	6 x 5 = 30	6 x 5 = 30
	7 x 5 = 35	10 x 5 = 50
	8 x 5 = 40	8 x 5 = 40
	9 x 5 = 45	1 x 5 = 5
	10 x 5 = 50	3 x 5 = 15

To help students understand the concept of multiplication, the *Math Expressions* program presents three ways to think about multiplication. They are described on the back of this letter.

- **Repeated groups:** Multiplication can be used to find the total in repeated groups of the same size. In early lessons, students circle the group size in repeated-groups equations to help keep track of which factor is the group size and which is the number of groups.

4 groups of bananas

$4 \times ③ = 3 + 3 + 3 + 3 = 12$

- **Arrays:** Multiplication can be used to find the total number of items in an *array*—an arrangement of objects into rows and columns.

5 columns

2 rows   2-by-5 array

2 rows of pennies = $2 \times 5 = 10$

- **Area:** Multiplication can be used to find the area of a rectangle.

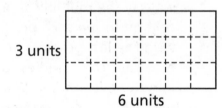

3 units

6 units

Area: 3 units $\times$ 6 units = 18 square units

Please call if you have any questions or comments.

Thank you.

Sincerely,
Your child's teacher

Estimada familia:

En esta unidad y la unidad que sigue, su niño va a practicar las multiplicaciones y divisiones básicas. *Math Expressions* incorpora en la clase el estudio, la práctica y la evaluación de las multiplicaciones y divisiones básicas. También se espera que su niño practique en casa.

Planes de estudio Todos los días su niño va a completar un plan de estudio, que indica cuáles multiplicaciones y divisiones debe estudiar esa noche. Cuando su niño haya terminado de estudiar (practicar), la persona que lo ayude debe firmar el plan de estudio.

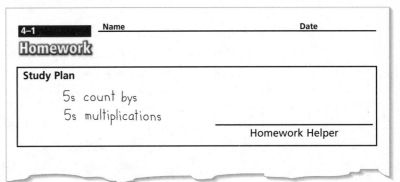

Tablas de práctica Cada vez que se presente un número nuevo, la tarea de los estudiantes incluirá una tabla de práctica. Para practicar, los estudiantes pueden cubrir los productos con un lápiz o una tira de papel grueso. Los niños dicen la multiplicación y deslizan el lápiz o el papel hacia abajo para revelar el producto después de decirlo. También pueden empezar con el último problema de la columna y deslizar el lápiz o el papel hacia arriba. Es importante que su niño practique el conteo y la multiplicación por lo menos 5 minutos cada noche. Su niño también puede usar estas tablas para practicar la división en la columna de productos desordenados cubriendo el primer factor.

	En orden	Desordenados
5	1 × 5 = 5	9 × 5 = 45
	2 × 5 = 10	5 × 5 = 25
	3 × 5 = 15	2 × 5 = 10
	4 × 5 = 20	7 × 5 = 35
	5 × 5 = 25	4 × 5 = 20
	6 × 5 = 30	6 × 5 = 30
	7 × 5 = 35	10 × 5 = 50
	8 × 5 = 40	8 × 5 = 40
	9 × 5 = 45	1 × 5 = 5
	10 × 5 = 50	3 × 5 = 15

Para ayudar a los estudiantes a comprender el concepto de la multiplicación, el programa *Math Expressions* presenta tres maneras de pensar en la multiplicación. Éstas se describen a continuación.

- **Grupos repetidos:** La multiplicación se puede usar para hallar el total con grupos del mismo tamaño que se repiten. Cuando empiezan a trabajar con ecuaciones de grupos repetidos, los estudiantes rodean con un círculo el tamaño del grupo en las ecuaciones, para recordar cuál factor representa el tamaño del grupo y cuál representa el número de grupos.

4 grupos de bananas

$4 \times ③ = 3 + 3 + 3 + 3 = 12$

- **Matrices:** Se puede usar la multiplicación para hallar el número total de objetos en una *matriz,* es decir, una disposición de objetos en filas y columnas.

5 columnas

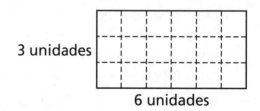

2 filas   matriz de 2 por 5

2 filas de monedas de un centavo = $2 \times 5 = 10$

- **Área:** Se puede usar la multiplicación para hallar el área de un rectángulo.

3 unidades

6 unidades

Área: 3 unidades × 6 unidades = 18 unidades cuadradas

Si tiene alguna duda o comentario, por favor comuníquese conmigo. Gracias.

Atentamente,
El maestro de su niño

Multiply with 5

Class Activity

Name _____

Date _____

Vocabulary

repeated groups

►Explore Repeated Groups

You can use multiplication to find the total when you have repeated groups of the same size.

$2 \times \text{⑤} = 5 + 5 = 10$

►Write Multiplication Equations

Write a multiplication equation to find the total number.

1. How many bananas?

_____

2. How many toes?

_____

3. How many wheels?

_____

Name _____ **Date** _____

Class Activity

▶Make a Math Drawing to Solve Problems

**Make a drawing for each problem. Label your
drawing with a multiplication equation. Then
write the answer to the problem.**

Show your work.

4. Sandra bought 4 bags of lemons. There were
   6 lemons in each bag. How many lemons did
   she buy in all?

   _____

5. Batai baked 2 peach pies. He used 7 peaches per
   pie. How many peaches did he use in all?

   _____

6. The Fuzzy Friends pet store has 3 rabbit cages.
   There are 5 rabbits in each cage. How many
   rabbits does the store have in all?

   _____

7. The Paws Plus pet store has 5 rabbit cages.
   There are 3 rabbits in every cage. How many
   rabbits does the store have in all?

   _____

Multiplication as Repeated Groups

►Explore Equal-Shares Drawings

Here is a problem with repeated groups. Read the problem, and think about how you would solve it.

> Ms. Thomas bought 4 bags of oranges. Each bag contained 5 oranges. How many oranges did she buy in all?
>
> You could also find the answer to this problem by making an **Equal-Shares Drawing**.

Think:

⑤ ⑤ ⑤ ⑤

bags of oranges

$4 \times ⑤ = \square$

Equal-Shares Drawing

20

$4 \times$

⑤ ⑤ ⑤ ⑤

bags of oranges

$4 \times ⑤ = 20$

Make an Equal-Shares Drawing to solve each problem.

8. Ms. Gonzales bought 6 boxes of pencils. There were 5 pencils in each box. How many pencils did she buy in all?

_____

9. Mr. Franken made lunch for his 9 nieces and nephews. He put 5 carrot sticks on each of their plates. How many carrot sticks did he use in all?

_____

Show your work.

Name _____ **Date** _____

Going Further

►Function Tables

Complete each function table.

1.

Number of Tricycles	Number of Wheels
1	
2	
3	
4	
5	

2.

Number of Rabbits	Number of Ears
1	
2	
3	
4	
5	

3.

Number of Cars	Number of Wheels
1	
2	
3	
4	
5	

4.

Number of Spiders	Number of Legs
1	
2	
3	
4	
5	

Multiplication as Repeated Groups

Signature Sheet

	Count-Bys Partner	Multiplications Partner	Divisions Partner	Multiplications Sprint	Divisions Sprint
0					
1					
2					
3					
4					
5					
6					
7					
8					
9					
10					

Signature Sheet

Study Sheet A

2s

Count-bys	Mixed Up ×	Mixed Up ÷
$1 \times 2 = 2$	$7 \times 2 = 14$	$20 \div 2 = 10$
$2 \times 2 = 4$	$1 \times 2 = 2$	$2 \div 2 = 1$
$3 \times 2 = 6$	$3 \times 2 = 6$	$6 \div 2 = 3$
$4 \times 2 = 8$	$5 \times 2 = 10$	$16 \div 2 = 8$
$5 \times 2 = 10$	$6 \times 2 = 12$	$12 \div 2 = 6$
$6 \times 2 = 12$	$8 \times 2 = 16$	$4 \div 2 = 2$
$7 \times 2 = 14$	$2 \times 2 = 4$	$10 \div 2 = 5$
$8 \times 2 = 16$	$10 \times 2 = 20$	$8 \div 2 = 4$
$9 \times 2 = 18$	$4 \times 2 = 8$	$14 \div 2 = 7$
$10 \times 2 = 20$	$9 \times 2 = 18$	$18 \div 2 = 9$

5s

Count-bys	Mixed Up ×	Mixed Up ÷
$1 \times 5 = 5$	$2 \times 5 = 10$	$10 \div 5 = 2$
$2 \times 5 = 10$	$9 \times 5 = 45$	$35 \div 5 = 7$
$3 \times 5 = 15$	$1 \times 5 = 5$	$50 \div 5 = 10$
$4 \times 5 = 20$	$5 \times 5 = 25$	$5 \div 5 = 1$
$5 \times 5 = 25$	$7 \times 5 = 35$	$20 \div 5 = 4$
$6 \times 5 = 30$	$3 \times 5 = 15$	$15 \div 5 = 3$
$7 \times 5 = 35$	$10 \times 5 = 50$	$30 \div 5 = 6$
$8 \times 5 = 40$	$6 \times 5 = 30$	$40 \div 5 = 8$
$9 \times 5 = 45$	$4 \times 5 = 20$	$25 \div 5 = 5$
$10 \times 5 = 50$	$8 \times 5 = 40$	$45 \div 5 = 9$

9s

Count-bys	Mixed Up ×	Mixed Up ÷
$1 \times 9 = 9$	$2 \times 9 = 18$	$81 \div 9 = 9$
$2 \times 9 = 18$	$4 \times 9 = 36$	$18 \div 9 = 2$
$3 \times 9 = 27$	$7 \times 9 = 63$	$36 \div 9 = 4$
$4 \times 9 = 36$	$8 \times 9 = 72$	$9 \div 9 = 1$
$5 \times 9 = 45$	$3 \times 9 = 27$	$54 \div 9 = 6$
$6 \times 9 = 54$	$10 \times 9 = 90$	$27 \div 9 = 3$
$7 \times 9 = 63$	$1 \times 9 = 9$	$63 \div 9 = 7$
$8 \times 9 = 72$	$6 \times 9 = 54$	$72 \div 9 = 8$
$9 \times 9 = 81$	$5 \times 9 = 45$	$90 \div 9 = 10$
$10 \times 9 = 90$	$9 \times 9 = 81$	$45 \div 9 = 5$

10s

Count-bys	Mixed Up ×	Mixed Up ÷
$1 \times 10 = 10$	$1 \times 10 = 10$	$80 \div 10 = 8$
$2 \times 10 = 20$	$5 \times 10 = 50$	$10 \div 10 = 1$
$3 \times 10 = 30$	$2 \times 10 = 20$	$50 \div 10 = 5$
$4 \times 10 = 40$	$8 \times 10 = 80$	$90 \div 10 = 9$
$5 \times 10 = 50$	$7 \times 10 = 70$	$40 \div 10 = 4$
$6 \times 10 = 60$	$3 \times 10 = 30$	$100 \div 10 = 10$
$7 \times 10 = 70$	$4 \times 10 = 40$	$30 \div 10 = 3$
$8 \times 10 = 80$	$6 \times 10 = 60$	$20 \div 10 = 2$
$9 \times 10 = 90$	$10 \times 10 = 100$	$70 \div 10 = 7$
$10 \times 10 = 100$	$9 \times 10 = 90$	$60 \div 10 = 6$

Study Sheet A

Name _____   Date _____

Vocabulary

array
row
column

▶ Explore Arrays

An **array** is an arrangement of objects in **rows** and **columns**. You can use multiplication to find the total number of objects in an array.

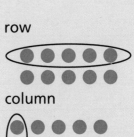

row

column

2-by-5 array

5 columns

2 rows of 5 = 2 × 5 = 10   2 rows

▶ Write Multiplication Equations

Write a multiplication equation for each array.

1. How many flowers?

_____

2. How many stamps?

_____

3. How many mugs?

_____

4. **On the Back** Write a problem that you can solve by using this array. Show how to solve your problem.

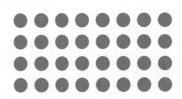

_____

_____

_____

_____

_____

_____

_____

_____

_____

Class Activity

▶Make a Math Drawing to Solve Problems

Make a drawing for each problem. Label your drawing with a multiplication equation. Then write the answer to the problem.

Show your work.

5. The clarinet section of the band marched in 6 rows, with 2 clarinet players in each row. How many clarinet players were there in all?

_____

6. Mali put some crackers on a tray. She put the crackers in 3 rows, with 5 crackers per row. How many crackers did she put on the tray?

_____

7. Ms. Shahin set up some chairs in 7 rows, with 5 chairs in each row. How many chairs did she set up?

_____

8. Zak has a box of crayons. The crayons are arranged in 4 rows, with 6 crayons in each row. How many crayons are in the box?

_____

▶Explore Commutativity

Multiplication is **commutative**. This means you can switch the order of the factors without changing the product.

Arrays: 4 × 5 = 5 × 4   **Groups:** 4 × ⑤ = 5 × ④

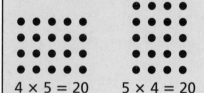

4 × 5 = 20   5 × 4 = 20

4 × ⑤ = 20   5 × ④ = 20

▶Solve Problems Using the Commutative Property

Make a math drawing for each problem. Write a multiplication equation and the answer to the problem.

9. Katie bought some stickers. She put the stickers on her folder in 6 rows of 2. How many stickers did she buy?

10. Marco also bought some stickers. He put the stickers on his folder in 2 rows of 6. How many stickers did he buy?

11. On Monday, Juan helped Ms. Chang clean the art cabinet. He packed jars of paint in 3 boxes, with 7 jars per box. How many jars of paint did Juan put away?

12. On Tuesday, Therese helped Ms. Chang. She packed jars of paint in 7 boxes, with 3 jars per box. How many jars of paint did Therese put away?

Dear Family,

In addition to practice charts for the basic multiplications and divisions for each of the numbers 1 through 10, your child will bring home a variety of other practice materials over the next several weeks.

- **Home Study Sheets:** A Home Study Sheet includes 3 or 4 practice charts on one page. Your child can use the Home Study Sheets to practice all the count-bys, multiplications, and divisions for a number or to practice just the ones he or she doesn't know for that number. The Homework Helper can then use the sheet to test (or retest) your child. The Homework Helper should check with your child to see which basic multiplications or divisions he or she is ready to be tested on. The helper should mark any missed problems lightly with a pencil.

  If your child gets all the answers in a column correct, the helper should sign that column on the Home Signature Sheet. When signatures are on all the columns of the Home Signature Sheet, your child should bring the sheet to school.

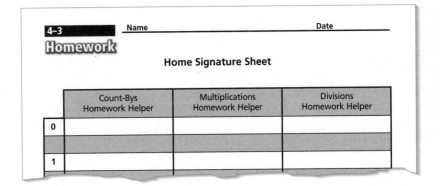

- **Home Check Sheets:** A Home Check Sheet includes columns of 20 multiplications and divisions in mixed order. These sheets can be used as a more challenging alternative to the Home Study Sheets.

- **Strategy Cards:** Students use Strategy Cards in class as flashcards, to play games, and to develop multiplication and division strategies.

Sample Multiplication Card   **Sample Division Card**

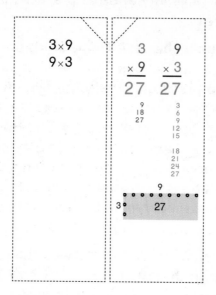   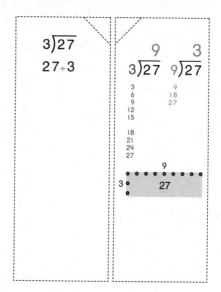

- **Games:** Near the end of this unit, students are introduced to games that provide multiplication and division practice.

Encourage your child to show you these materials and explain how they are used. Make sure your child spends time practicing multiplications and divisions every evening.

Please call if you have any questions or comments.

Thank you.

Sincerely,
Your child's teacher

Multiplication and Arrays

Estimada familia:

Además de las tablas de práctica para las multiplicaciones y divisiones básicas para cada número del 1 al 10, su niño llevará a casa una variedad de materiales de práctica en las semanas que vienen.

- **Hojas para estudiar en casa:** Una hoja para estudiar en casa incluye 3 ó 4 tablas de práctica en una página. Su niño puede usar las hojas para practicar todos los conteos, multiplicaciones y divisiones de un número, o para practicar sólo las operaciones para ese número que no domina. La persona que ayude a su niño con la tarea puede usar la hoja para hacerle una prueba (o repetir una prueba). Esa persona debe hablar con su niño para decidir sobre qué multiplicaciones o divisiones básicas el niño puede hacer la prueba. La persona que ayude debe marcar ligeramente con un lápiz cualquier problema que conteste mal. Si su niño contesta bien todas las operaciones de una columna, la persona que ayude debe firmar esa columna de la hoja de firmas. Cuando todas las columnas de la hoja de firmas estén firmadas, su niño debe llevar la hoja a la escuela.

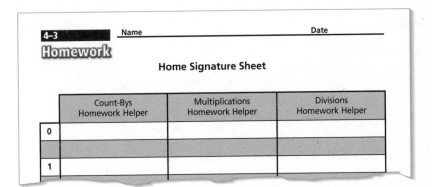

- **Hojas de verificación:** Una hoja de verificación consta de columnas de 20 multiplicaciones y divisiones sin orden fijo. Estas hojas pueden usarse como alternativa de mayor desafío que las hojas para estudiar en casa.

- **Tarjetas de estrategias:** Los estudiantes usan las tarjetas de estrategias en la clase como ayuda de memoria, en juegos y para desarrollar estrategias para hacer multiplicaciones y divisiones.

Ejemplo de tarjeta de multiplicación   **Ejemplo de tarjeta de división**

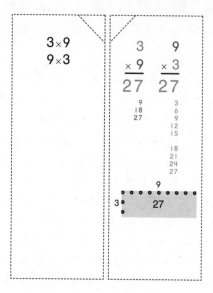
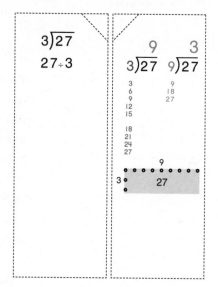

- **Juegos:** Hacia el final de esta unidad se les presentan a los estudiantes juegos para practicar la multiplicación y la división.

Anime a su niño a que le muestre a Ud. estos materiales y a que le explique cómo se usan. Asegúrese de que su niño practique la multiplicación y la división cada noche.

Si tiene alguna duda o pregunta, por favor comuníquese conmigo.

Atentamente,
El maestro de su niño

Multiplication and Arrays

Class Activity

Vocabulary	
division	divisor
dividend	quotient

▶ Explore Division

Solve each problem.

1. Marc bought some bags of limes. There were 5 limes in each bag. He bought 15 limes altogether. How many bags did he buy?

   _____

2. There were 10 photographs on one wall of an art gallery. The photographs were in rows, with 5 photographs in each row. How many rows were there?

   _____

The problems above can be represented by multiplication equations or by **division** equations.

Problem 1	**Multiplication**				**Division**			
	☐	×	⑤	=	15	15	÷	⑤	=	☐

Problem 1	**Multiplication**	**Division**
	$\square \times \boxed{5} = 15$	$15 \div \boxed{5} = \square$
	number of groups (factor) · group size (factor) · total (product)	total (product) · group size (factor) · number of groups (factor)
Problem 2	**Multiplication**	**Division**
	$\square \times 5 = 10$	$10 \div 5 = \square$
	number of rows (factor) · number in each row (factor) · total (product)	total (product) · number in each row (factor) · number of rows (factor)

Here are ways to write a division. The following all mean "15 divided by 5 equals 3."

$$15 \div 5 = 3 \qquad 15 / 5 = 3 \qquad \frac{15}{5} = 3$$

$$\begin{array}{r} 3 \leftarrow \text{quotient} \\ 5{\overline{)15}} \leftarrow \text{dividend} \end{array}$$
$\uparrow$
divisor

The number you divide into is called the **dividend**. The number you divide by is called the **divisor**. The number that is the answer to a division problem is called the **quotient**.

Class Activity

▶ Math Tools: Equal-Shares Drawings

You can use Equal-Shares Drawings to help solve division problems. Here is how you might solve problem 1 on Student Activity Book page 215.

Start with the total, 15.

$15 \div ⑤ = \square$

Draw groups of 5, and connect them to the total. Count by 5s as you draw the groups. Stop when you reach 15, the total. Count how many groups you have: 3 groups.

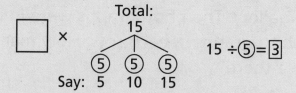

You can use a similar type of drawing to find the number of rows or columns in an array. Here is how you might solve problem 2.

Start with the total, 10.

$10 \div ⑤ = \square$

Draw rows of 5, and connect them to the total. Count by 5s as you draw the rows. Stop when you reach 10, the total. Count how many rows you have: 2 rows.

Solve each problem.

3. At a bake sale, Luisa bought a lemon square for 35¢. If she paid using only nickels, how many nickels did she spend? _____

4. Mr. Su bought a sheet of 20 stamps. There were 5 stamps in each row. How many columns of stamps were there? _____

The Meaning of Division

▶Relate Division and Multiplication Equations with 5

Find the unknown numbers.

5. $20 \div \text{⑤} = \boxed{}$ $\boxed{} \times \text{⑤} = 20$ $20 \div \text{④} = \boxed{}$ $\boxed{} \times \text{④} = 20$

6. $10 \div \text{⑤} = \boxed{}$ $\boxed{} \times \text{⑤} = 10$ $10 \div \text{②} = \boxed{}$ $\boxed{} \times \text{②} = 10$

7. $15 \div \text{⑤} = \boxed{}$ $\boxed{} \times \text{⑤} = 15$ $15 \div \text{③} = \boxed{}$ $\boxed{} \times \text{③} = 15$

8. $40 \div \text{⑤} = \boxed{}$ $\boxed{} \times \text{⑤} = 40$ $40 \div \text{⑧} = \boxed{}$ $\boxed{} \times \text{⑧} = 40$

9. $5 \div \text{⑤} = \boxed{}$ $\boxed{} \times \text{⑤} = 5$ $5 \div \text{①} = \boxed{}$ $\boxed{} \times \text{①} = 5$

10. $25 \div \text{⑤} = \boxed{}$ $\boxed{} \times \text{⑤} = 25$ $25 \div \text{⑤} = \boxed{}$ $\boxed{} \times \text{⑤} = 25$

11. $30 \div \text{⑤} = \boxed{}$ $\boxed{} \times \text{⑤} = 30$ $30 \div \text{⑥} = \boxed{}$ $\boxed{} \times \text{⑥} = 30$

12. $50 \div \text{⑤} = \boxed{}$ $\boxed{} \times \text{⑤} = 50$ $50 \div \text{⑩} = \boxed{}$ $\boxed{} \times \text{⑩} = 50$

13. $35 \div \text{⑤} = \boxed{}$ $\boxed{} \times \text{⑤} = 35$ $35 \div \text{⑦} = \boxed{}$ $\boxed{} \times \text{⑦} = 35$

14. $45 \div \text{⑤} = \boxed{}$ $\boxed{} \times \text{⑤} = 45$ $45 \div \text{⑨} = \boxed{}$ $\boxed{} \times \text{⑨} = 45$

▶Find the Number in Each Group

Solve each problem.

15. Aziz put 15 ice cubes in 5 glasses. He put the same number of ice cubes in each glass. How many ice cubes did he put in each glass?

_____

16. Lori's uncle gave her 20 stickers. She put the same number of stickers on each of 5 folders. How many stickers did she put on each folder?

_____

17. **On the Back** Write a word problem for $30 \div 5$ where the 5 is the size of the group. Write another word problem where 5 is the number of groups. Explain what multiplication equations the problems relate to and why.

The Meaning of Division

Class Activity

▶ Explore Patterns with 2s

What patterns do you see below?

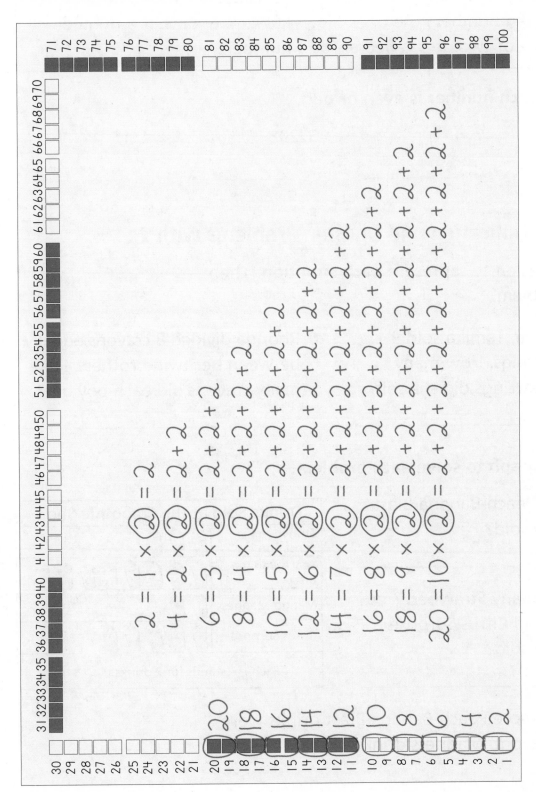

Multiply and Divide with 2 **219**

Class Activity

▶ Even and Odd Numbers

The 2s count-bys are called *even numbers* because they are multiples of 2. In an **even number**, the ones digit is 0, 2, 4, 6, or 8. If a number is not a multiple of two, it is called an **odd number**.

Tell whether each number is even or odd.

1. 7   2. 4   3. 20   4. 15

_____   _____   _____   _____

▶ Solve Multiplication and Division Problems with 2s

Write an equation to represent each situation. Then solve the problem.

5. At the art fair, Tamika sold 9 pairs of earrings. How many individual earrings did she sell?

_____

6. Rhonda divided 8 crayons equally between her twin brothers. How many crayons did each boy get?

_____

Use the pictograph to solve each problem.

7. How many Peach-Banana Blast drinks were sold?

_____

8. In all, how many Strawberry Sensation and Citrus Surprise drinks were sold?

_____

Drinks Sold at the Smoothie Shop	
Strawberry Sensation	🥤🥤🥤
Peach-Banana Blast	🥤🥤🥤🥤🥤🥤
Mango-Madness	🥤
Citrus Surprise	🥤🥤🥤🥤
Each 🥤 stands for 2 drinks.	

9. How many more Peach-Banana Blast drinks were sold than Mango Madness drinks?

_____

▶ **Check Sheet 1: 5s and 2s**

5s Multiplications	5s Divisions	2s Multiplications	2s Divisions
2 × 5 = 10	30 / 5 = 6	4 × 2 = 8	8 / 2 = 4
5 • 6 = 30	5 ÷ 5 = 1	2 • 8 = 16	18 ÷ 2 = 9
5 * 9 = 45	15 / 5 = 3	1 * 2 = 2	2 / 2 = 1
4 × 5 = 20	50 ÷ 5 = 10	6 × 2 = 12	16 ÷ 2 = 8
5 • 7 = 35	20 / 5 = 4	2 • 9 = 18	4 / 2 = 2
10 * 5 = 50	10 ÷ 5 = 2	2 * 2 = 4	20 ÷ 2 = 10
1 × 5 = 5	35 / 5 = 7	3 × 2 = 6	10 / 2 = 5
5 • 3 = 15	40 ÷ 5 = 8	2 • 5 = 10	12 ÷ 2 = 6
8 * 5 = 40	25 / 5 = 5	10 * 2 = 20	6 / 2 = 3
5 × 5 = 25	45 / 5 = 9	2 × 7 = 14	14 / 2 = 7
5 • 8 = 40	20 ÷ 5 = 4	2 • 10 = 20	4 ÷ 2 = 2
7 * 5 = 35	15 / 5 = 3	9 * 2 = 18	2 / 2 = 1
5 × 4 = 20	30 ÷ 5 = 6	2 × 6 = 12	8 ÷ 2 = 4
6 • 5 = 30	25 / 5 = 5	8 • 2 = 16	6 / 2 = 3
5 * 1 = 5	10 ÷ 5 = 2	2 * 3 = 6	20 ÷ 2 = 10
5 × 10 = 50	45 / 5 = 9	2 × 2 = 4	14 / 2 = 7
9 • 5 = 45	35 ÷ 5 = 7	1 • 2 = 2	10 ÷ 2 = 5
5 * 2 = 10	50 ÷ 5 = 10	2 * 4 = 8	16 ÷ 2 = 8
3 × 5 = 15	40 / 5 = 8	5 × 2 = 10	12 / 2 = 6
5 • 5 = 25	5 ÷ 5 = 1	7 • 2 = 14	18 ÷ 2 = 9

Check Sheet 1: 5s and 2s

Class Activity

▶ **Sprints for 5s**

As your teacher reads each multiplication or division, write your answer on the lines.

× 5	÷ 5
a. _____	a. _____
b. _____	b. _____
c. _____	c. _____
d. _____	d. _____
e. _____	e. _____
f. _____	f. _____
g. _____	g. _____
h. _____	h. _____
i. _____	i. _____
j. _____	j. _____

Class Activity

▶Explore Patterns with 10s

What patterns do you see below?

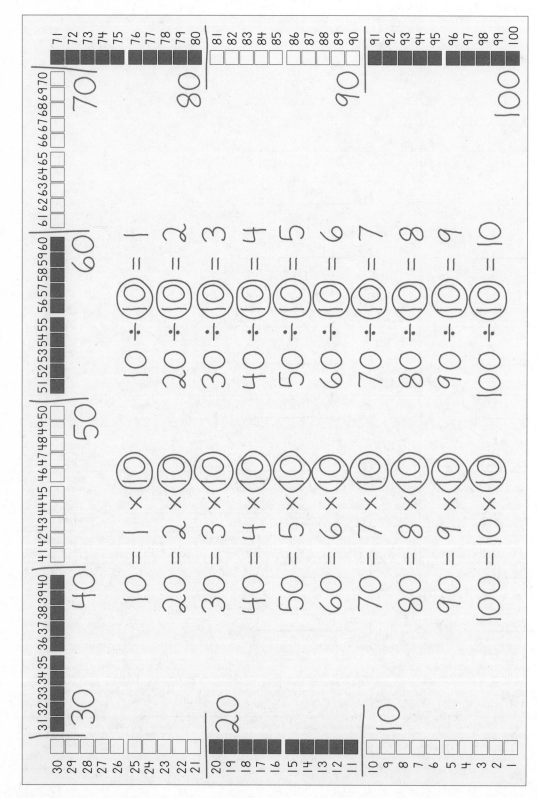

Multiply and Divide with 10

Class Activity

▶ Solve Problems with 10s

Solve each problem.

Show your work.

1. Raymundo has 9 dimes. How many cents does he have?

   _____

2. Yoko has some dimes in her pocket, and no other coins. She has a total of 70¢. How many dimes does she have?

   _____

3. Jonah picked 40 strawberries. He gave them to 10 of his friends. Each friend got the same number of strawberries. How many strawberries did each friend get?

   _____

4. There are 10 Space Command trading cards in each pack. Zoe bought 5 packs of cards. How many cards did she buy in all?

   _____

5. There were 80 students in the auditorium. There were 10 students in each row. How many rows of students were there?

   _____

6. **On the Back** Write a word problem that can be solved using the division 60 ÷ 10. Then write a related multiplication word problem.

▶ **Check Sheet 2: 10s and 9s**

10s Multiplications	10s Divisions	9s Multiplications	9s Divisions
9 × 10 = 90	100 / 10 = 10	3 × 9 = 27	27 / 9 = 3
10 • 3 = 30	50 ÷ 10 = 5	9 • 7 = 63	9 ÷ 9 = 1
10 * 6 = 60	70 / 10 = 7	10 * 9 = 90	81 / 9 = 9
1 × 10 = 10	40 ÷ 10 = 4	5 × 9 = 45	45 ÷ 9 = 5
10 • 4 = 40	80 / 10 = 8	9 • 8 = 72	90 / 9 = 10
10 * 7 = 70	60 ÷ 10 = 6	9 * 1 = 9	36 ÷ 9 = 4
8 × 10 = 80	10 / 10 = 1	2 × 9 = 18	18 / 9 = 2
10 • 10 = 100	20 ÷ 10 = 2	9 • 9 = 81	63 ÷ 9 = 7
5 * 10 = 50	90 / 10 = 9	6 * 9 = 54	54 / 9 = 6
10 × 2 = 20	30 / 10 = 3	9 × 4 = 36	72 / 9 = 8
10 • 5 = 50	80 ÷ 10 = 8	9 • 5 = 45	27 ÷ 9 = 3
4 * 10 = 40	70 / 10 = 7	4 * 9 = 36	45 / 9 = 5
10 × 1 = 10	100 ÷ 10 = 10	9 × 1 = 9	63 ÷ 9 = 7
3 • 10 = 30	90 / 10 = 9	3 • 9 = 27	72 / 9 = 8
10 * 8 = 80	60 ÷ 10 = 6	9 * 8 = 72	54 ÷ 9 = 6
7 × 10 = 70	30 / 10 = 3	7 × 9 = 63	18 / 9 = 2
6 • 10 = 60	10 ÷ 10 = 1	6 • 9 = 54	90 ÷ 9 = 10
10 * 9 = 90	40 ÷ 10 = 4	9 * 9 = 81	9 ÷ 9 = 1
10 × 10 = 100	20 / 10 = 2	10 × 9 = 90	36 / 9 = 4
2 • 10 = 20	50 ÷ 10 = 5	2 • 9 = 18	81 ÷ 9 = 9

Check Sheet 2: 10s and 9s

Class Activity

► **Explore Patterns with 9s**

What patterns do you see below?

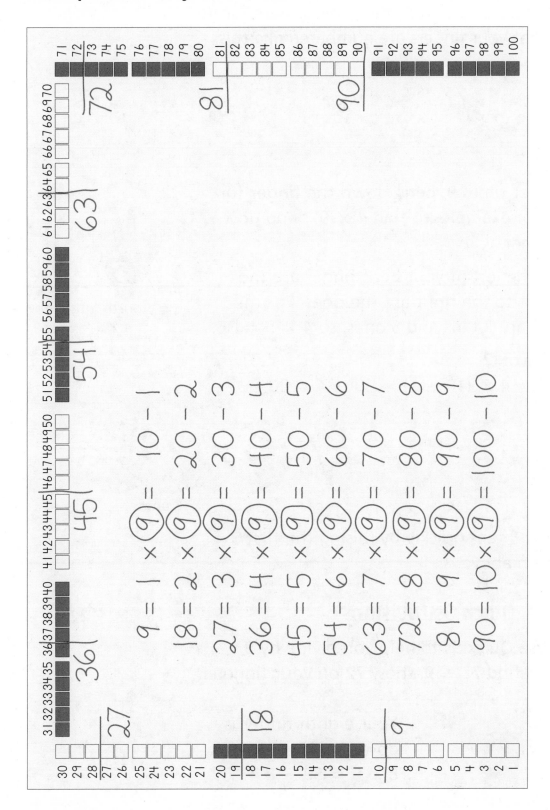

71 72 73 74 75 76 77 78 79 80 81 82 83 84 85 86 87 88 89 90 91 92 93 94 95 96 97 98 99 100

72

81

90

63

54

45

36

27

18

9

9 = 1 × 9 = 10 − 1
18 = 2 × 9 = 20 − 2
27 = 3 × 9 = 30 − 3
36 = 4 × 9 = 40 − 4
45 = 5 × 9 = 50 − 5
54 = 6 × 9 = 60 − 6
63 = 7 × 9 = 70 − 7
72 = 8 × 9 = 80 − 8
81 = 9 × 9 = 90 − 9
90 = 10 × 9 = 100 − 10

30 29 28 27 26 25 24 23 22 21 20 19 18 17 16 15 14 13 12 11 10 9 8 7 6 5 4 3 2 1

Class Activity

► Math Tools: Quick 9s Multiplication

You can use the Quick 9s method to help you multiply by 9. Open your hands and turn them so they are facing you. Imagine that your fingers are numbered like this.

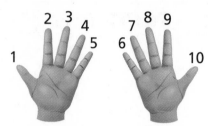

To find a number times 9, bend down the finger for that number. For example, to find 4×9, bend down your fourth finger.

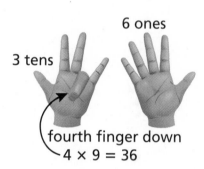

6 ones

3 tens

fourth finger down
$4 \times 9 = 36$

The fingers to the left of your bent finger are the tens. The fingers to the right are the ones. For this problem, there are 3 tens and 6 ones, so $4 \times 9 = 36$.

Why does this work?
Because $4 \times 9 = 4 \times (10 - 1) = 40 - 4 = 36$

3 tens   6 ones

You could show 3 tens quickly by raising the first 3 fingers as shown above.

► Math Tools: Quick 9s Division

You can also use Quick 9s to help you divide by 9. For example, to find $72 \div 9$, show 72 on your fingers.

7 tens   2 ones

Your eighth finger is down, so $72 \div 9 = 8$.
$8 \times 9 = 80 - 8 = 72$

Multiply and Divide with 9

Class Activity

► Sprints for 2s

As your teacher reads each multiplication or division, write your answer in the space provided.

× 2	÷ 2
a. _____	a. _____
b. _____	b. _____
c. _____	c. _____
d. _____	d. _____
e. _____	e. _____
f. _____	f. _____
g. _____	g. _____
h. _____	h. _____
i. _____	i. _____
j. _____	j. _____

Name _____   Date _____

▶Solve Word Problems with 2s, 5s, 9s, and 10s

**Write an equation to represent each problem.
Then solve the problem.**

1. Ian planted tulip bulbs in an array with 5 rows and 10 columns. How many bulbs did he plant?

_____

2. Erin gave 30 basketball cards to her 5 cousins. Each cousin got the same number of cards. How many cards did each cousin get?

_____

3. Martina bought 7 cans of racquetballs. There were 2 balls per can. How many racquetballs did she buy in all?

_____

4. The 27 students in the orchestra stood in rows for their school picture. There were 9 students in every row. How many rows of students were there?

_____

Class Activity

▶ Math Tools: Fast-Array Drawings

When you solve a word problem involving an array, you can save time by making a Fast-Array drawing. This type of drawing shows the number of items in each row and column, but does not show every single item.

Here is how you might use a Fast-Array drawing for problem 1 on Student Activity Book page 232.

Show the number of rows and the number of columns. Make a box in the center to show that you don't know the total.

Here are three ways to find the total.

- Find 5 × 10.
- Use 10s count-bys to find the total in 5 rows of 10: 10, 20, 30, 40, 50.
- Use 5s count-bys to find the total in 10 rows of 5: 5, 10, 15, 20, 25, 30, 35, 40, 45, 50.

Here is how you might use a Fast-Array drawing for problem 4.

Show the number in each row and the total. Make a box to show that you don't know the number of rows.

Here are two ways to find the number of rows.

- Find 27 ÷ 9 or solve ☐ × 9 = 27.
- Count by 9s until you reach 27: 9, 18, 27.

⬤ **On the Back** **Make a Fast-Array Drawing to solve each problem.**

5. Beth planted tulip bulbs in an array with 9 rows and 6 columns. How many bulbs did she plant?

6. The 36 students in the chorus stood in 4 rows for their school picture. How many students were in each row?

Fluency Day for 2s, 5s, 9s, and 10s

▶ Check Sheet 3: 2s, 5s, 9s, and 10s

2s, 5s, 9s, 10s Multiplications	2s, 5s, 9s, 10s Multiplications	2s, 5s, 9s, 10s Divisions	2s, 5s, 9s, 10s Divisions
$2 \times 10 = 20$	$5 \times 10 = 50$	$18 / 2 = 9$	$36 / 9 = 4$
$10 \cdot 5 = 50$	$10 \cdot 9 = 90$	$50 \div 5 = 10$	$70 \div 10 = 7$
$9 * 6 = 54$	$4 * 10 = 40$	$72 / 9 = 8$	$18 / 2 = 9$
$7 \times 10 = 70$	$2 \times 9 = 18$	$60 \div 10 = 6$	$45 \div 5 = 9$
$2 \cdot 3 = 6$	$5 \cdot 3 = 15$	$12 / 2 = 6$	$45 / 9 = 5$
$5 * 7 = 35$	$6 * 9 = 54$	$30 \div 5 = 6$	$30 \div 10 = 3$
$9 \times 10 = 90$	$10 \times 3 = 30$	$18 / 9 = 2$	$6 / 2 = 3$
$6 \cdot 10 = 60$	$3 \cdot 2 = 6$	$50 \div 10 = 5$	$50 \div 5 = 10$
$8 * 2 = 16$	$5 * 8 = 40$	$14 / 2 = 7$	$27 / 9 = 3$
$5 \times 6 = 30$	$9 \times 9 = 81$	$25 / 5 = 5$	$70 / 10 = 7$
$9 \cdot 5 = 45$	$10 \cdot 4 = 40$	$81 \div 9 = 9$	$20 \div 2 = 10$
$8 * 10 = 80$	$9 * 2 = 18$	$20 / 10 = 2$	$45 / 5 = 9$
$2 \times 1 = 2$	$5 \times 1 = 5$	$8 \div 2 = 4$	$54 \div 9 = 6$
$3 \cdot 5 = 15$	$9 \cdot 6 = 54$	$45 / 5 = 9$	$80 / 10 = 8$
$4 * 9 = 36$	$10 * 1 = 10$	$63 \div 9 = 7$	$16 \div 2 = 8$
$3 \times 10 = 30$	$7 \times 2 = 14$	$30 / 10 = 3$	$15 / 5 = 3$
$2 \cdot 6 = 12$	$6 \cdot 5 = 30$	$10 \div 2 = 5$	$90 \div 9 = 10$
$4 * 5 = 20$	$8 * 9 = 72$	$40 \div 5 = 8$	$100 \div 10 = 10$
$9 \times 7 = 63$	$10 \times 6 = 60$	$9 / 9 = 1$	$12 / 2 = 6$
$1 \cdot 10 = 10$	$2 \cdot 8 = 16$	$50 \div 10 = 5$	$35 \div 5 = 7$

Check Sheet 3: 2s, 5s, 9s, and 10s

Name _____ Date _____

▶ **Sprints for 10s**

As your teacher reads each multiplication or division, write your answer in the space provided.

× 10	÷ 10
a. _____	a. _____
b. _____	b. _____
c. _____	c. _____
d. _____	d. _____
e. _____	e. _____
f. _____	f. _____
g. _____	g. _____
h. _____	h. _____
i. _____	i. _____
j. _____	j. _____

Class Activity

▶ Explore Patterns with 3s

What patterns do you see below?

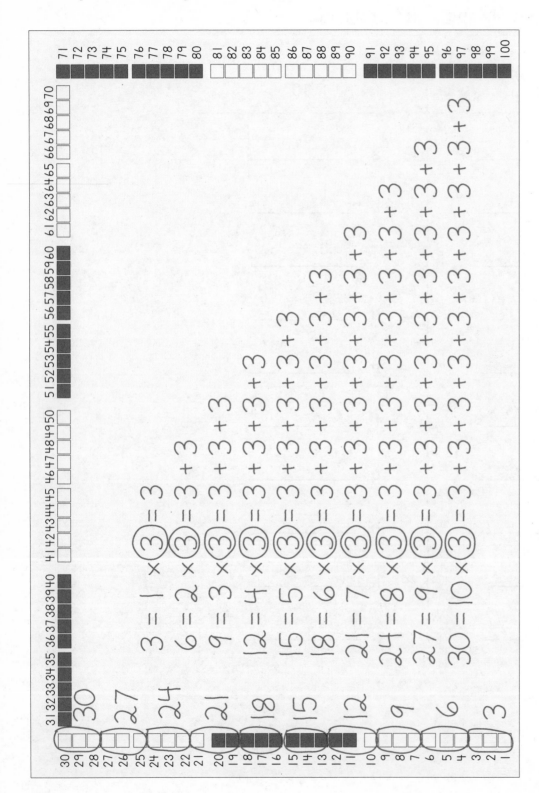

Multiply and Divide with 3

Name _____

Date _____

Class Activity

▶ **Use the 5s Shortcut for 3s**

Write the 3s count-bys to find the total.

1. How many sides are in 8 triangles?

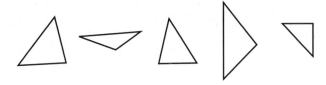

___ ___ ___ ___ ___   ___ ___ ___

2. How many wheels are on 6 tricycles?

___ ___ ___ ___ ___   ___

3. How many legs are on 7 tripods?

___ ___ ___ ___ ___   ___ ___

Multiply and Divide with 3

Class Activity

Find the total by starting with the fifth count-by and counting by 3s from there.

4. How many sides are in 7 triangles?

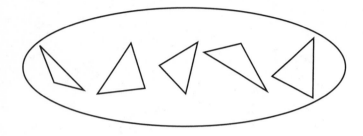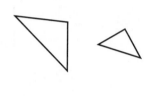

_____   _____

5. How many wheels are on 9 tricycles?

_____   _____ _____ _____ _____

6. How many legs are on 8 tripods?

_____   _____ _____ _____

Going Further

▶ **Solve Open-Ended Problems**

Back to School Sale!

Pencils – 4 for $1.00

Markers – $2.95 per box

Calculators – $3.00 each

Notebooks – $1.19 each

Pens – 60¢ each

Backpacks – $9.00 each

Crayons – $2.59 per box

1. Hilda has $20.00 to buy her school supplies. She needs 12 pencils, 2 pens, a box of crayons, and a backpack. She also needs either a box of markers or a calculator, but not both. How should Hilda spend her $20.00 to get everything she needs and still have money left over? Explain your thinking.

Party Favors on Sale!

6 for $1 Party Bags

4 for $3 High-Bounce Balls

3 for $2 Bubbles

4 for $1 Funny Glasses

6 for $2 Crazy Straws

6 for $4 Yo-Yo's

2. Ivan and his dad are planning to make 12 identical party bags with 3 different items in each bag for a total cost under $25.00. List the 3 items they should buy. Explain your thinking.

➡ 3. **On the Back** Find another combination of toys that Ivan and his dad could buy.

Multiply and Divide with 3

Study Sheet B

4s

Count-bys	Mixed Up ×	Mixed Up ÷
1 × 4 = 4	4 × 4 = 16	12 ÷ 4 = 3
2 × 4 = 8	1 × 4 = 4	36 ÷ 4 = 9
3 × 4 = 12	7 × 4 = 28	24 ÷ 4 = 6
4 × 4 = 16	3 × 4 = 12	4 ÷ 4 = 1
5 × 4 = 20	9 × 4 = 36	20 ÷ 4 = 5
6 × 4 = 24	10 × 4 = 40	28 ÷ 4 = 7
7 × 4 = 28	2 × 4 = 8	8 ÷ 4 = 2
8 × 4 = 32	5 × 4 = 20	40 ÷ 4 = 10
9 × 4 = 36	8 × 4 = 32	32 ÷ 4 = 8
10 × 4 = 40	6 × 4 = 24	16 ÷ 4 = 4

1s

Count-bys	Mixed Up ×	Mixed Up ÷
1 × 1 = 1	5 × 1 = 5	10 ÷ 1 = 10
2 × 1 = 2	7 × 1 = 7	8 ÷ 1 = 8
3 × 1 = 3	10 × 1 = 10	4 ÷ 1 = 4
4 × 1 = 4	1 × 1 = 1	9 ÷ 1 = 9
5 × 1 = 5	8 × 1 = 8	6 ÷ 1 = 6
6 × 1 = 6	4 × 1 = 4	7 ÷ 1 = 7
7 × 1 = 7	9 × 1 = 9	1 ÷ 1 = 1
8 × 1 = 8	3 × 1 = 3	2 ÷ 1 = 2
9 × 1 = 9	2 × 1 = 2	5 ÷ 1 = 5
10 × 1 = 10	6 × 1 = 6	3 ÷ 1 = 3

3s

Count-bys	Mixed Up ×	Mixed Up ÷
1 × 3 = 3	5 × 3 = 15	27 ÷ 3 = 9
2 × 3 = 6	1 × 3 = 3	6 ÷ 3 = 2
3 × 3 = 9	8 × 3 = 24	18 ÷ 3 = 6
4 × 3 = 12	10 × 3 = 30	30 ÷ 3 = 10
5 × 3 = 15	3 × 3 = 9	9 ÷ 3 = 3
6 × 3 = 18	7 × 3 = 21	3 ÷ 3 = 1
7 × 3 = 21	9 × 3 = 27	12 ÷ 3 = 4
8 × 3 = 24	2 × 3 = 6	24 ÷ 3 = 8
9 × 3 = 27	4 × 3 = 12	15 ÷ 3 = 5
10 × 3 = 30	6 × 3 = 18	21 ÷ 3 = 7

0s

Count-bys	Mixed Up ×
1 × 0 = 0	3 × 0 = 0
2 × 0 = 0	10 × 0 = 0
3 × 0 = 0	5 × 0 = 0
4 × 0 = 0	8 × 0 = 0
5 × 0 = 0	7 × 0 = 0
6 × 0 = 0	2 × 0 = 0
7 × 0 = 0	9 × 0 = 0
8 × 0 = 0	6 × 0 = 0
9 × 0 = 0	1 × 0 = 0
10 × 0 = 0	4 × 0 = 0

Study Sheet B

2×2

$$\begin{array}{r} 2 \\ \times 3 \\ \hline \end{array} \qquad \begin{array}{r} 3 \\ \times 2 \\ \hline \end{array}$$

$$2 \times 4$$
$$4 \times 2$$

$$\begin{array}{r} 2 \\ \times 5 \\ \hline \end{array} \qquad \begin{array}{r} 5 \\ \times 2 \\ \hline \end{array}$$

$$2 \times 6$$
$$6 \times 2$$

$$\begin{array}{r} 2 \\ \times 7 \\ \hline \end{array} \qquad \begin{array}{r} 7 \\ \times 2 \\ \hline \end{array}$$

$$2 \times 8$$
$$8 \times 2$$

$$\begin{array}{r} 2 \\ \times 9 \\ \hline \end{array} \qquad \begin{array}{r} 9 \\ \times 2 \\ \hline \end{array}$$

Multiplication Strategy Cards **245**

$10 = 2 \times 5$
$10 = 5 \times 2$
 	
5 2
10 4
   6
   8
  10
	$\begin{array}{r} 2 \\ \times 4 \\ \hline 8 \end{array}$ $\begin{array}{r} 4 \\ \times 2 \\ \hline 8 \end{array}$
	2 4
	4 8
	6
	8
		$6 = 2 \times 3$
		$6 = 3 \times 2$
		
		3 2
		6 4
		  6
			$\begin{array}{r} 2 \\ \times 2 \\ \hline 4 \end{array}$
			2
			4

$18 = 2 \times 9$
$18 = 9 \times 2$
 	
9   2
18 4
    6
    8
   10
   12
   14
   16
   18
	$\begin{array}{r} 2 \\ \times 8 \\ \hline 16 \end{array}$ $\begin{array}{r} 8 \\ \times 2 \\ \hline 16 \end{array}$
	8 2
	16 4
	6
	8
	10
	12
	14
	16
		$14 = 2 \times 7$
		$14 = 7 \times 2$
		
		7 2
		14 4
		    6
		    8
		   10
		   12
		   14
			$\begin{array}{r} 2 \\ \times 6 \\ \hline 12 \end{array}$ $\begin{array}{r} 6 \\ \times 2 \\ \hline 12 \end{array}$
			6 2
			12 4
			6
			8
			10
			12

Multiplication Strategy Cards

3×3

$\begin{array}{r} 3 \\ \times\, 4 \end{array}$ $\begin{array}{r} 4 \\ \times\, 3 \end{array}$

3×5
5×3

$\begin{array}{r} 3 \\ \times\, 6 \end{array}$ $\begin{array}{r} 6 \\ \times\, 3 \end{array}$

3×7
7×3

$\begin{array}{r} 3 \\ \times\, 8 \end{array}$ $\begin{array}{r} 8 \\ \times\, 3 \end{array}$

3×9
9×3

$\begin{array}{r} 4 \\ \times\, 4 \end{array}$

Multiplication Strategy Cards **247**

Card 1:

$18 = 3 \times 6$

$18 = 6 \times 3$

6	3
12	6
18	9
	12
	15
	18

6

3 ○ 18

Card 2:

$\begin{array}{r} 3 \\ \times 5 \\ \hline 15 \end{array}$ $\begin{array}{r} 5 \\ \times 3 \\ \hline 15 \end{array}$

5	3
10	6
15	9
	12
	15

3

5 ○ 15

Card 3:

$12 = 3 \times 4$

$12 = 4 \times 3$

4	3
8	6
12	9
	12

4

3 ○ 12

Card 4:

$\begin{array}{r} 3 \\ \times 3 \\ \hline 9 \end{array}$

3
6
9

3

3 ○ 9

Card 5:

$16 = 4 \times 4$

4
8
12
16

4

4 ○ 16

Card 6:

$\begin{array}{r} 3 \\ \times 9 \\ \hline 27 \end{array}$ $\begin{array}{r} 9 \\ \times 3 \\ \hline 27 \end{array}$

9	3
18	6
27	9
	12
	15
	18
	21
	24
	27

9

3 ○ 27

Card 7:

$24 = 3 \times 8$

$24 = 8 \times 3$

8	3
16	6
24	9
	12
	15
	18
	21
	24

3

8 ○ 24

Card 8:

$\begin{array}{r} 3 \\ \times 7 \\ \hline 21 \end{array}$ $\begin{array}{r} 7 \\ \times 3 \\ \hline 21 \end{array}$

7	3
14	6
21	9
	12
	15
	18
	21

7

3 ○ 21

Multiplication Strategy Cards

4×5
5×4

$$\begin{array}{r} 4 \\ \times\ 6 \end{array} \qquad \begin{array}{r} 6 \\ \times\ 4 \end{array}$$

4×7
7×4

$$\begin{array}{r} 4 \\ \times\ 8 \end{array} \qquad \begin{array}{r} 8 \\ \times\ 4 \end{array}$$

4×9
9×4

$$\begin{array}{r} 5 \\ \times\ 5 \end{array}$$

5×6
6×5

$$\begin{array}{r} 5 \\ \times\ 7 \end{array} \qquad \begin{array}{r} 7 \\ \times\ 5 \end{array}$$

Card 1

$32 = 4 \times 8$

$32 = 8 \times 4$

8	4
16	8
24	12
32	16
	20
	24
	28
	32

4

8 32

Card 2

4   7

$\times 7$ $\times 4$

28   28

7	4
14	8
21	12
28	16
	20
	24
	28

7

4 28

Card 3

$24 = 4 \times 6$

$24 = 6 \times 4$

6	4
12	8
18	12
24	16
	20
	24

4

6 24

Card 4

4   5

$\times 5$ $\times 4$

20   20

5	4
10	8
15	12
20	16
	20

5

4 20

Card 5

$35 = 5 \times 7$

$35 = 7 \times 5$

7	5
14	10
21	15
28	20
35	25
	30
	35

7

5 35

Card 6

5   6

$\times 6$ $\times 5$

30   30

6	5
12	10
18	15
24	20
30	25
	30

5

6 30

Card 7

$25 = 5 \times 5$

5
10
15
20
25

5

5 25

Card 8

4   9

$\times 9$ $\times 4$

36   36

9	4
18	8
27	12
36	16
	20
	24
	28
	32
	36

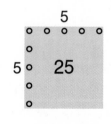

9

4 36

Multiplication Strategy Cards

5×8
8×5

5   9
×9   ×5

6×6

6   7
×7   ×6

6×8
8×6

6   9
×9   ×6

7×7

7   8
×8   ×7

Card 1

$42 = 7 \times 6$

$42 = 6 \times 7$

6	7
12	14
18	21
24	28
30	35
36	42
42	

7

6 | 42

Card 2

$$\begin{array}{r} 6 \\ \times\,6 \\ \hline 36 \end{array}$$

6
12
18
24
30

36

6

6 | 36

Card 3

$45 = 9 \times 5$

$45 = 5 \times 9$

5	9
10	18
15	27
20	36
25	45
30	
35	
40	
45	

9

5 | 45

Card 4

$$\begin{array}{r} 8 \\ \times\,5 \\ \hline 40 \end{array}$$ $$\begin{array}{r} 5 \\ \times\,8 \\ \hline 40 \end{array}$$

5	8
10	16
15	24
20	32
25	40
30	
35	
40	

5

8 | 40

Card 5

$56 = 7 \times 8$

$56 = 8 \times 7$

8	7
16	14
24	21
32	28
40	35
48	42
56	49
	56

8

7 | 56

Card 6

$$\begin{array}{r} 7 \\ \times\,7 \\ \hline 49 \end{array}$$

7
14
21
28
35

42
49

7

7 | 49

Card 7

$54 = 9 \times 6$

$54 = 6 \times 9$

6	9
12	18
18	27
24	36
30	45
36	54
42	
48	
54	

9

6 | 54

Card 8

$$\begin{array}{r} 6 \\ \times\,8 \\ \hline 48 \end{array}$$ $$\begin{array}{r} 8 \\ \times\,6 \\ \hline 48 \end{array}$$

6	8
12	16
18	24
24	32
30	40
36	48
42	
48	

8

6 | 48

Multiplication Strategy Cards

7 × 9
9 × 7

8
× 8

9 × 8
8 × 9

9
× 9

Multiplication Strategy Cards **253**

Card 1

$$81 = 9 \times 9$$

9
18
27
36
45

54
63
72
81

9

9 · 81

Card 2

$$\begin{array}{r} 9 \\ \times\,8 \\ \hline 72 \end{array} \qquad \begin{array}{r} 8 \\ \times\,9 \\ \hline 72 \end{array}$$

8   9
16 18
24 27
32 36
40 45

48 54
56 63
64 72
72

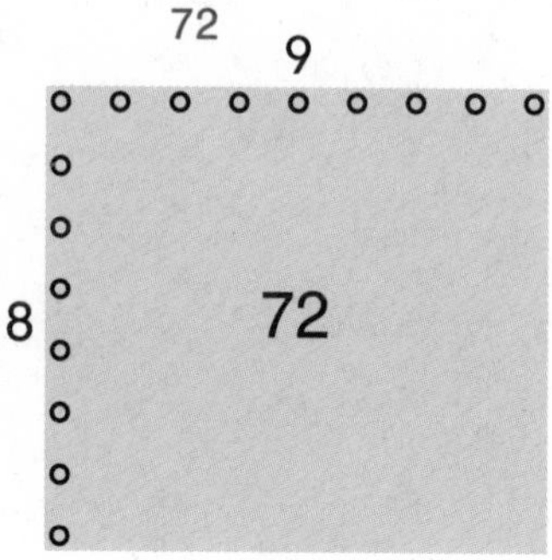

9

8 · 72

Card 3

$$64 = 8 \times 8$$

8
16
24
32
40

48
56
64

8

8 · 64

Card 4

$$\begin{array}{r} 7 \\ \times\,9 \\ \hline 63 \end{array} \qquad \begin{array}{r} 9 \\ \times\,7 \\ \hline 63 \end{array}$$

9   7
18 14
27 21
36 28
45 35

54 42
63 49
     56
     63

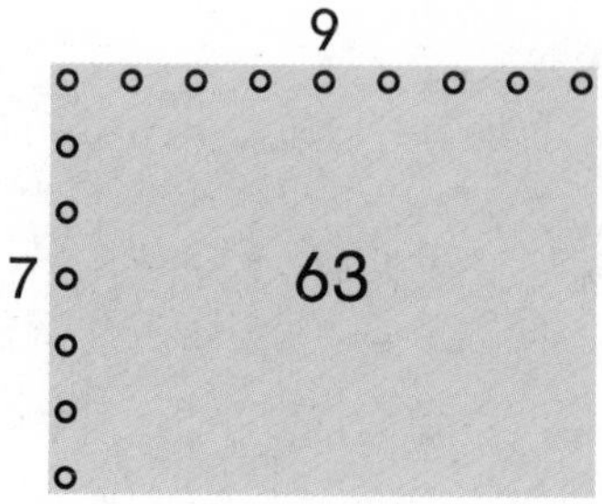

9

7 · 63

Multiplication Strategy Cards

$2\overline{)4}$

$4 \div 2$

$2\overline{)6}$

$6 \div 2$

$2\overline{)8}$

$8 \div 2$

$2\overline{)10}$

$10 \div 2$

$2\overline{)12}$

$12 \div 2$

$2\overline{)14}$

$14 \div 2$

$2\overline{)16}$

$16 \div 2$

$2\overline{)18}$

$18 \div 2$

Division Strategy Cards

Card 1

$$5 \atop 2\overline{)10}$$ $$2 \atop 5\overline{)10}$$

2
4
6
8
10

5
10

5
2 o o o o o
  o   10

Card 2

$$4 \atop 2\overline{)8}$$ $$2 \atop 4\overline{)8}$$

2
4
6
8

4
8

4
2 o o o o
  o 8

Card 3

$$3 \atop 2\overline{)6}$$ $$2 \atop 3\overline{)6}$$

2
4
6

3
6

3
2 o o o
  o 6

Card 4

$$2 \atop 2\overline{)4}$$

2
4

2
2 o o
  o 4

Card 5

$$9 \atop 2\overline{)18}$$ $$2 \atop 9\overline{)18}$$

2
4
6
8
10

12
14
16
18

9
18

9
2 o o o o o o o o o
  o   18

Card 6

$$8 \atop 2\overline{)16}$$ $$2 \atop 8\overline{)16}$$

2
4
6
8
10

12
14
16

8
16

8
2 o o o o o o o o
  o   16

Card 7

$$7 \atop 2\overline{)14}$$ $$2 \atop 7\overline{)14}$$

2
4
6
8
10

12
14

7
14

7
2 o o o o o o o
  o   14

Card 8

$$6 \atop 2\overline{)12}$$ $$2 \atop 6\overline{)12}$$

2
4
6
8
10

12

6
12

6
2 o o o o o o
  o   12

Division Strategy Cards

$3\overline{)6}$

$6 \div 3$

$4\overline{)8}$

$8 \div 4$

$5\overline{)10}$

$10 \div 5$

$6\overline{)12}$

$12 \div 6$

$7\overline{)14}$

$14 \div 7$

$8\overline{)16}$

$16 \div 8$

$9\overline{)18}$

$18 \div 9$

$3\overline{)9}$

$9 \div 3$

| 2 6$\overline{)12}$ | 6 2$\overline{)12}$ | | 2 5$\overline{)10}$ | 5 2$\overline{)10}$ | | 2 4$\overline{)8}$ | 4 2$\overline{)8}$ | | 2 3$\overline{)6}$ | 3 2$\overline{)6}$ |

Card 1:
2 6)12   6 2)12
6 / 12   2 4 6 8 10 12
2 
6 ∘ 12

Card 2:
2 5)10   5 2)10
5 / 10   2 4 6 8 10
2 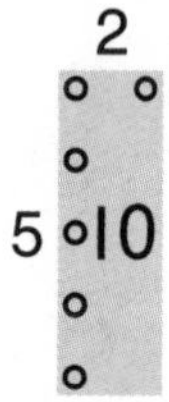
5 ∘ 10

Card 3:
2 4)8   4 2)8
4 / 8   2 4 6 8
2 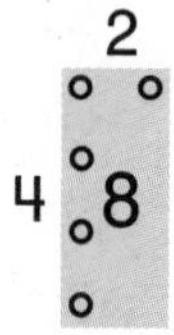
4 ∘ 8

Card 4:
2 3)6   3 2)6
3 / 6   2 4 6
2 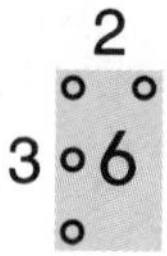
3 ∘ 6

Card 5:
3 3)9
3 6 9
3 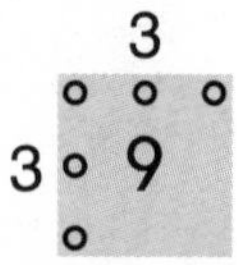
3 ∘ 9

Card 6:
2 9)18   9 2)18
9 / 18   2 4 6 8 10 12 14 16 18
2 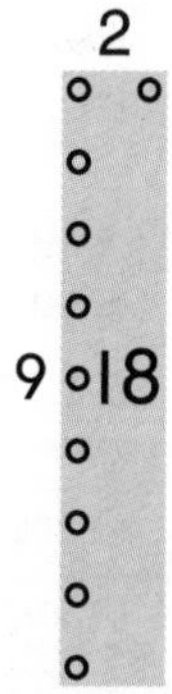
9 ∘ 18

Card 7:
2 8)16   8 2)16
8 / 16   2 4 6 8 10 12 14 16
2 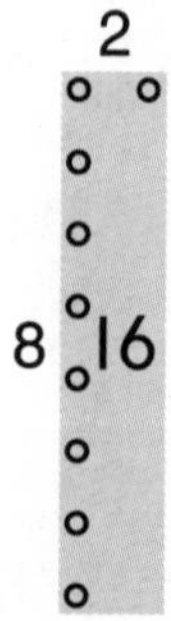
8 ∘ 16

Card 8:
2 7)14   7 2)14
7 / 14   2 4 6 8 10 12 14
2 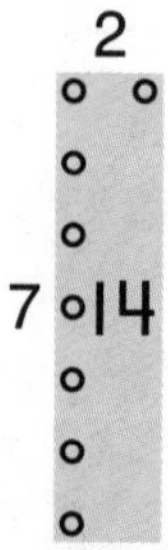
7 ∘ 14

Division Strategy Cards

$3\overline{)12}$

$12 \div 3$

$3\overline{)15}$

$15 \div 3$

$3\overline{)18}$

$18 \div 3$

$3\overline{)21}$

$21 \div 3$

$3\overline{)24}$

$24 \div 3$

$3\overline{)27}$

$27 \div 3$

$4\overline{)12}$

$12 \div 4$

$5\overline{)15}$

$15 \div 5$

Top Row

Card 1

$$7 \quad 3$$
$$3\overline{)21} \quad 7\overline{)21}$$

3	7
6	14
9	21
12	
15	
18	
21	

```
      7
  o o o o o o o
3 o        21
  o
```

Card 2

$$6 \quad 3$$
$$3\overline{)18} \quad 6\overline{)18}$$

3	6
6	12
9	18
12	
15	
18	

```
      6
  o o o o o o
3 o       18
  o
```

Card 3

$$5 \quad 3$$
$$3\overline{)15} \quad 5\overline{)15}$$

3	5
6	10
9	15
12	
15	

```
      5
  o o o o o
3 o     15
  o
```

Card 4

$$4 \quad 3$$
$$3\overline{)12} \quad 4\overline{)12}$$

3	4
6	8
9	12
12	

```
      4
  o o o o
3 o   12
  o
```

Bottom Row

Card 5

$$3 \quad 5$$
$$5\overline{)15} \quad 3\overline{)15}$$

5	3
10	6
15	9
	12
	15

```
    3
  o o o
  o
5 o 15
  o
  o
```

Card 6

$$3 \quad 4$$
$$4\overline{)12} \quad 3\overline{)12}$$

4	3
8	6
12	9
	12

```
    3
  o o o
  o
4 o 12
  o
```

Card 7

$$9 \quad 3$$
$$3\overline{)27} \quad 9\overline{)27}$$

3	9
6	18
9	27
12	
15	
18	
21	
24	
27	

```
      9
  o o o o o o o o o
3 o          27
  o
```

Card 8

$$8 \quad 3$$
$$3\overline{)24} \quad 8\overline{)24}$$

3	8
6	16
9	24
12	
15	
18	
21	
24	

```
      8
  o o o o o o o o
3 o         24
  o
```

Division Strategy Cards

$6\overline{)18}$

$18 \div 6$

$7\overline{)21}$

$21 \div 7$

$8\overline{)24}$

$24 \div 8$

$9\overline{)27}$

$27 \div 9$

$4\overline{)16}$

$16 \div 4$

$4\overline{)20}$

$20 \div 4$

$4\overline{)24}$

$24 \div 4$

$4\overline{)28}$

$28 \div 4$

Card 1

$$3 \qquad 9$$
$$9\overline{)27} \qquad 3\overline{)27}$$

9   3
18   6
27   9
     12
     15

     18
     21
     24
     27

3
9 · 27

Card 2

$$3 \qquad 8$$
$$8\overline{)24} \qquad 3\overline{)24}$$

8   3
16   6
24   9
     12
     15

     18
     21
     24

3
8 · 24

Card 3

$$3 \qquad 7$$
$$7\overline{)21} \qquad 3\overline{)21}$$

7   3
14   6
21   9
     12
     15

     18
     21

3
7 · 21

Card 4

$$3 \qquad 6$$
$$6\overline{)18} \qquad 3\overline{)18}$$

6   3
12   6
18   9
     12
     15

     18

3
6 · 18

Card 5

$$7 \qquad 4$$
$$4\overline{)28} \qquad 7\overline{)28}$$

4   7
8   14
12   21
16   28
20

24
28

7
4 · 28

Card 6

$$6 \qquad 4$$
$$4\overline{)24} \qquad 6\overline{)24}$$

4   6
8   12
12   18
16   24
20

24

6
4 · 24

Card 7

$$5 \qquad 4$$
$$4\overline{)20} \qquad 5\overline{)20}$$

4   5
8   10
12   15
16   20
20

5
4 · 20

Card 8

$$4$$
$$4\overline{)16}$$

4
8
12
16

4
4 · 16

Division Strategy Cards

$4 \overline{)32}$

$32 \div 4$

$4 \overline{)36}$

$36 \div 4$

$5 \overline{)20}$

$20 \div 5$

$6 \overline{)24}$

$24 \div 6$

$7 \overline{)28}$

$28 \div 7$

$8 \overline{)32}$

$32 \div 8$

$9 \overline{)36}$

$36 \div 9$

$5 \overline{)25}$

$25 \div 5$

Top Row

Card 1

$$\frac{4}{6\overline{)24}} \qquad \frac{6}{4\overline{)24}}$$

6	4
12	8
18	12
24	16
	20
	24

4
6 | 24

Card 2

$$\frac{4}{5\overline{)20}} \qquad \frac{5}{4\overline{)20}}$$

5	4
10	8
15	12
20	16
	20

4
5 | 20

Card 3

$$\frac{9}{4\overline{)36}} \qquad \frac{4}{9\overline{)36}}$$

4	9
8	18
12	27
16	36
20	
24	
28	
32	
36	

9
4 | 36

Card 4

$$\frac{8}{4\overline{)32}} \qquad \frac{4}{8\overline{)32}}$$

4	8
8	16
12	24
16	32
20	
24	
28	
32	

8
4 | 32

Bottom Row

Card 5

$$\frac{5}{5\overline{)25}}$$

5
10
15
20
25

5
5 | 25

Card 6

$$\frac{4}{9\overline{)36}} \qquad \frac{9}{4\overline{)36}}$$

9	4
18	8
27	12
36	16
	20
	24
	28
	32
	36

4
9 | 36

Card 7

$$\frac{4}{8\overline{)32}} \qquad \frac{8}{4\overline{)32}}$$

8	4
16	8
24	12
32	16
	20
	24
	28
	32

4
8 | 32

Card 8

$$\frac{4}{7\overline{)28}} \qquad \frac{7}{4\overline{)28}}$$

7	4
14	8
21	12
28	16
	20
	24
	28

4
7 | 28

Division Strategy Cards

$5 \overline{)30}$

$30 \div 5$

$5 \overline{)35}$

$35 \div 5$

$5 \overline{)40}$

$40 \div 5$

$5 \overline{)45}$

$45 \div 5$

$6 \overline{)30}$

$30 \div 6$

$7 \overline{)35}$

$35 \div 7$

$8 \overline{)40}$

$40 \div 8$

$9 \overline{)45}$

$45 \div 9$

Card 1

9   5

5)45 9)45

5	9
10	18
15	27
20	36
25	45
30	
35	
40	
45	

9
5 45

Card 2

8   5

5)40 8)40

5	8
10	16
15	24
20	32
25	40
30	
35	
40	

8
5 40

Card 3

7   5

5)35 7)35

5	7
10	14
15	21
20	28
25	35
30	
35	

7
5 35

Card 4

6   5

5)30 6)30

5	6
10	12
15	18
20	24
25	30
30	

6
5 30

Card 5

5   9

9)45 5)45

9	5
18	10
27	15
36	20
45	25
	30
	35
	40
	45

5
9 45

Card 6

5   8

8)40 5)40

8	5
16	10
24	15
32	20
40	25
	30
	35
	40

5
8 40

Card 7

5   7

7)35 5)35

7	5
14	10
21	15
28	20
35	25
	30
	35

5
7 35

Card 8

5   6

6)30 5)30

6	5
12	10
18	15
24	20
30	25
	30

5
6 30

Division Strategy Cards

$6\overline{)36}$

$36 \div 6$

$6\overline{)42}$

$42 \div 6$

$6\overline{)48}$

$48 \div 6$

$6\overline{)54}$

$54 \div 6$

$7\overline{)42}$

$42 \div 7$

$8\overline{)48}$

$48 \div 8$

$9\overline{)54}$

$54 \div 9$

$7\overline{)49}$

$49 \div 7$

Card 1

$9 \quad 6$

$6\overline{)54} \quad 9\overline{)54}$

6	9
12	18
18	27
24	36
30	45
36	54
42	
48	
54	

9

6 | 54

Card 2

$8 \quad 6$

$6\overline{)48} \quad 8\overline{)48}$

6	8
12	16
18	24
24	32
30	40
36	48
42	
48	

8

6 | 48

Card 3

$7 \quad 6$

$6\overline{)42} \quad 7\overline{)42}$

6	7
12	14
18	21
24	28
30	35
36	42
42	

7

6 | 42

Card 4

6

$6\overline{)36}$

6
12
18
24
30
36

6

6 | 36

Card 5

7

$7\overline{)49}$

7
14
21
28
35
42
49

7

7 | 49

Card 6

$6 \quad 9$

$9\overline{)54} \quad 6\overline{)54}$

9	6
18	12
27	18
36	24
45	30
54	36
	42
	48
	54

6

9 | 54

Card 7

$6 \quad 8$

$8\overline{)48} \quad 6\overline{)48}$

8	6
16	12
24	18
32	24
40	30
48	36
	42
	48

6

8 | 48

Card 8

$6 \quad 7$

$7\overline{)42} \quad 6\overline{)42}$

7	6
14	12
21	18
28	24
35	30
42	36
	42

6

7 | 42

Division Strategy Cards

$7 \overline{)56}$

$56 \div 7$

$7 \overline{)63}$

$63 \div 7$

$8 \overline{)56}$

$56 \div 8$

$9 \overline{)63}$

$63 \div 9$

$8 \overline{)64}$

$64 \div 8$

$8 \overline{)72}$

$72 \div 8$

$9 \overline{)72}$

$72 \div 9$

$9 \overline{)81}$

$81 \div 9$

Card 1

$$7 \quad 9$$
$$9\overline{)63} \quad 7\overline{)63}$$

9	7
18	14
27	21
36	28
45	35
54	42
63	49
	56
	63

7

9 | 63

Card 2

$$7 \quad 8$$
$$8\overline{)56} \quad 7\overline{)56}$$

8	7
16	14
24	21
32	28
40	35
48	42
56	49
	56

7

8 | 56

Card 3

$$9 \quad 7$$
$$7\overline{)63} \quad 9\overline{)63}$$

7	9
14	18
21	27
28	36
35	45
42	54
49	63
56	
63	

9

7 | 63

Card 4

$$8 \quad 7$$
$$7\overline{)56} \quad 8\overline{)56}$$

7	8
14	16
21	24
28	32
35	40
42	48
49	56
56	

8

7 | 56

Card 5

$$9$$
$$9\overline{)81}$$

9
18
27
36
45
54
63
72
81

9

9 | 81

Card 6

$$8 \quad 9$$
$$9\overline{)72} \quad 8\overline{)72}$$

9	8
18	16
27	24
36	32
45	40
54	48
63	56
72	64
	72

8

9 | 72

Card 7

$$9 \quad 8$$
$$8\overline{)72} \quad 9\overline{)72}$$

8	9
16	18
24	27
32	36
40	45
48	54
56	63
64	72
72	

9

8 | 72

Card 8

$$8$$
$$8\overline{)64}$$

8
16
24
32
40
48
56
64

8

8 | 64

Division Strategy Cards

▶Find the Area

The area of a rectangle is the number of square units that fit inside of it.

Write a multiplication equation to represent the area of each rectangle.

1.

_____

2.

_____

3.

_____

Make a rectangle drawing to represent each problem. Then give the product.

4. 5 × 3 = _____

5. 7 * 2 = _____

6. 2 • 9 = _____

Class Activity

▶Different Ways to Find Area

The large rectangle has been divided into two small rectangles. You can find the area of the large rectangle in two ways:

- Add the areas of the two small rectangles:

  $5 \times 3 = 15$ square units

  $2 \times 3 = \underline{6}$ square units

  $\overline{21}$ square units

- Multiply the number of rows in the large rectangle by the number of square units in each row:

  $7 \times 3 = 21$ square units

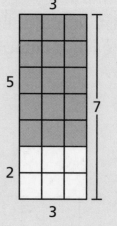

Complete.

7. Find the area of the large rectangle by finding the areas of the two small rectangles and adding them.

   _____

   _____

8. Find the area of the large rectangle by multiplying the number of rows by the number of square units in each row.

   _____

   _____

9. Find this product: $5 \times 4 =$ _____

10. Find this product: $2 \times 4 =$ _____

11. Use your answers to exercises 9 and 10 to

    find this product: $7 \times 4 =$ _____

Multiplication and Area

Class Activity

▶ **Sprints for 9s**

As your teacher reads each multiplication or division, write your answer in the space provided.

× 9	÷ 9
a. _____	a. _____
b. _____	b. _____
c. _____	c. _____
d. _____	d. _____
e. _____	e. _____
f. _____	f. _____
g. _____	g. _____
h. _____	h. _____
i. _____	i. _____
j. _____	j. _____

Class Activity

Name _____ Date _____

► Identify Types of Problems

Read each problem and decide what type of problem
it is. Write the letter from the list below. Then write
an equation to solve the problem.

a. Array Multiplication
b. Array Division
c. Repeated-Groups Multiplication
d. Repeated-Groups Division with an Unknown Group Size
e. Repeated-Groups Division with an Unknown Multiplier (number of groups)
f. None of the above

1. Mrs. Ostrega has 3 children. She
wants to buy 5 juice boxes for
each child. How many juice
boxes does she need?

_____

2. Sophie picked 15 peaches from
one tree and 3 peaches from
another. How many peaches did
she pick in all?

_____

3. Zamir brought 21 treats to the
dog park. He divided the treats
equally among the 7 dogs that
were there. How many treats did
each dog get?

_____

4. Art said he could make 12
muffins in his muffin pan. The
pan has space for 3 muffins in a
row. How many rows does the
muffin pan have?

_____

5. Bia is helping with the lights for
the school play. Each box of light
bulbs has 6 rows, with 3 bulbs in
each row. How many light bulbs
are in each box?

_____

6. Tryouts were held to find triplets
to act in a commercial for Triple-
Crunch Peanut Butter. If 24
children tried out for the
commercial, how many sets of
triplets tried out?

_____

Going Further

▶Multiply Using Patterns

Use mental math and patterns to complete.

1. $3 \times 4 =$ _____
   $3 \times 40 =$ _____

2. $10 \times 2 =$ _____
   $100 \times 2 =$ _____

3. $9 \times 8 =$ _____
   $9 \times 80 =$ _____

4. $2 \times 9 =$ _____
   $2 \times 90 =$ _____
   $2 \times 900 =$ _____

5. $5 \times 5 =$ _____
   $5 \times 50 =$ _____
   $5 \times 500 =$ _____

6. $3 \times 4 =$ _____
   $3 \times 40 =$ _____
   $3 \times 400 =$ _____

7. $1 \times 1 =$ _____
   $10 \times 1 =$ _____
   $100 \times 1 =$ _____

8. $2 \times 3 =$ _____
   $20 \times 3 =$ _____
   $200 \times 30 =$ _____

9. $5 \times 6 =$ _____
   $5 \times 60 =$ _____
   $5 \times 600 =$ _____

10. $2 \times 4 =$ _____
    $2 \times 40 =$ _____
    $2 \times 400 =$ _____

11. $5 \times 3 =$ _____
    $5 \times 30 =$ _____
    $3 \times 300 =$ _____

12. $9 \times 2 =$ _____
    $9 \times 20 =$ _____
    $9 \times 200 =$ _____

13. $2 \times 30 =$ _____

14. $5 \times 40 =$ _____

15. $9 \times 60 =$ _____

16. $3 \times 80 =$ _____

17. $2 \times 70 =$ _____

18. $5 \times 90 =$ _____

19. $9 \times 500 =$ _____

20. $5 \times 200 =$ _____

21. $3 \times 300 =$ _____

22. $5 \times 800 =$ _____

23. $9 \times 900 =$ _____

24. $5 \times 600 =$ _____

25. **On the Back** Describe a pattern you can use to find 4×200.

Solve and Create Word Problems

▶Check Sheet 4: 3s and 4s

3s Multiplications	3s Divisions	4s Multiplications	4s Divisions
$8 \times 3 = 24$	$9 / 3 = 3$	$1 \times 4 = 4$	$40 / 4 = 10$
$3 \cdot 2 = 6$	$21 \div 3 = 7$	$4 \cdot 5 = 20$	$12 \div 4 = 3$
$3 * 5 = 15$	$27 / 3 = 9$	$8 * 4 = 32$	$24 / 4 = 6$
$10 \times 3 = 30$	$3 \div 3 = 1$	$3 \times 4 = 12$	$8 \div 4 = 2$
$3 \cdot 3 = 9$	$18 / 3 = 6$	$4 \cdot 6 = 24$	$4 / 4 = 1$
$3 * 6 = 18$	$12 \div 3 = 4$	$4 * 9 = 36$	$28 \div 4 = 7$
$7 \times 3 = 21$	$30 / 3 = 10$	$10 \times 4 = 40$	$32 / 4 = 8$
$3 \cdot 9 = 27$	$6 \div 3 = 2$	$4 \cdot 7 = 28$	$16 \div 4 = 4$
$4 * 3 = 12$	$24 / 3 = 8$	$4 * 4 = 16$	$36 / 4 = 9$
$3 \times 1 = 3$	$15 / 3 = 5$	$2 \times 4 = 8$	$20 / 4 = 5$
$3 \cdot 4 = 12$	$21 \div 3 = 7$	$4 \cdot 3 = 12$	$4 \div 4 = 1$
$3 * 3 = 9$	$3 / 3 = 1$	$4 * 2 = 8$	$32 / 4 = 8$
$3 \times 10 = 30$	$9 \div 3 = 3$	$9 \times 4 = 36$	$8 \div 4 = 2$
$2 \cdot 3 = 6$	$27 / 3 = 9$	$1 \cdot 4 = 4$	$16 / 4 = 4$
$3 * 7 = 21$	$30 \div 3 = 10$	$4 * 6 = 24$	$36 \div 4 = 9$
$6 \times 3 = 18$	$18 / 3 = 6$	$5 \times 4 = 20$	$12 / 4 = 3$
$5 \cdot 3 = 15$	$6 \div 3 = 2$	$4 \cdot 4 = 16$	$40 \div 4 = 10$
$3 * 8 = 24$	$15 \div 3 = 5$	$7 * 4 = 28$	$20 \div 4 = 5$
$9 \times 3 = 27$	$12 / 3 = 4$	$8 \times 4 = 32$	$24 / 4 = 6$
$2 \cdot 3 = 6$	$24 \div 3 = 8$	$10 \cdot 4 = 40$	$28 \div 4 = 7$

Check Sheet 4: 3s and 4s

►Explore Patterns with 4s

What patterns do you see below?

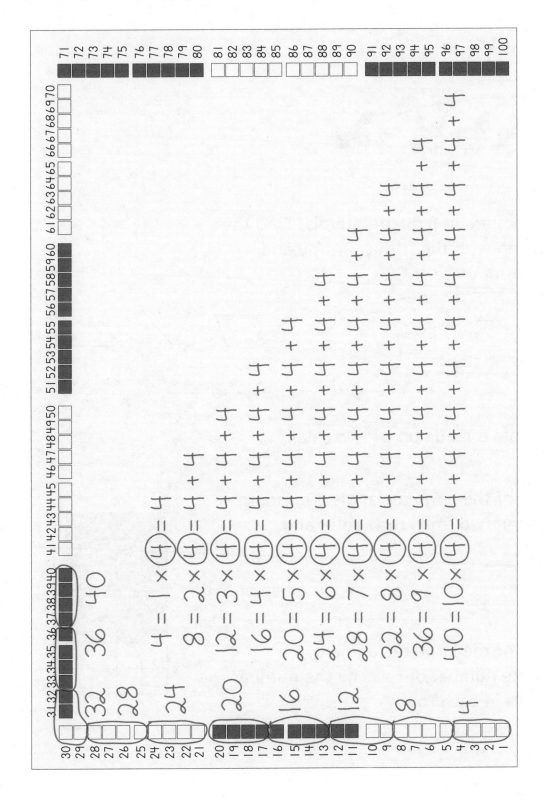

Class Activity

▶Use the 5s Shortcut for 4s

Solve each problem.

1. How many legs are on 6 horses? Find the total by starting with the fifth count-by and counting up from there.

_____ _____

2. How many sides are in 8 quadrilaterals? Find the total by starting with the fifth count-by and counting up from there.

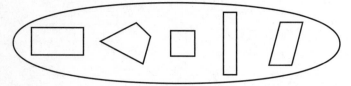 

_____ _____ _____ _____

This large rectangle is made up of two small rectangles.

3. Find the area of the large rectangle by finding the areas of the two small rectangles and adding them.

_____

_____

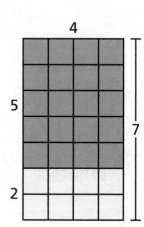

4. Find the area of the large rectangle by multiplying the number of rows by the number of square units in each row.

_____

▶Use Multiplications You Know

You can combine multiplications to find other multiplications.

This Equal-Shares Drawing shows that 7 groups of 4 is the same as 5 groups of 4 plus 2 groups of 4.

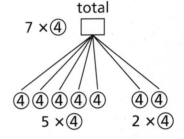

5. Find 5 × ④ and 2 × ④ and add the answers.

_____

6. Find 7 × ④. Did you get the same answer as in exercise 5?

_____

7. Find this product: 5 × 4 = _____

8. Find this product: 4 × 4 = _____

9. Use your answers to exercises 7 and 8 to find this product: 9 × 4 = _____.

▶The Puzzled Penguin

Dear Math Students:

Today I had to find 8 × 4. I didn't know the answer, but I figured it out by combining two multiplications I did know:

$5 \times 2 = 10$
$\underline{3 \times 2 = 6}$
$8 \times 4 = 16$

Is my answer right? If not, please help me understand why it is wrong.

Thank you,
The Puzzled Penguin

10. **On the Back** Make a drawing to show that your answers to exercises 7–9 are correct.

Multiply and Divide with 4

Class Activity

▶ Sprints for 3s

As your teacher reads each multiplication or division, write your answer in the space provided.

× 3	÷ 3
a. _____	a. _____
b. _____	b. _____
c. _____	c. _____
d. _____	d. _____
e. _____	e. _____
f. _____	f. _____
g. _____	g. _____
h. _____	h. _____
i. _____	i. _____
j. _____	j. _____

Use the Strategy Cards

►Play *Solve the Stack*

Read the rules for playing *Solve the Stack*. Then play the game with your group.

Rules for *Solve the Stack*

Number of players: 2–4
What you will need: 1 set of multiplication and division Strategy Cards

1. Shuffle the cards. Place them exercise side up in the center of the table.

2. Players take turns. On each turn, a player finds the answer to the multiplication or division on the top card and then turns the card over to check the answer.

3. If a player's answer is correct, he or she takes the card. If it is incorrect, the card is placed at the bottom of the stack.

4. Play ends when there are no more cards in the stack. The player with the most cards wins.

Play *Solve the Stack*

▶Explore Patterns with 1s

What patterns do you see below?

1.

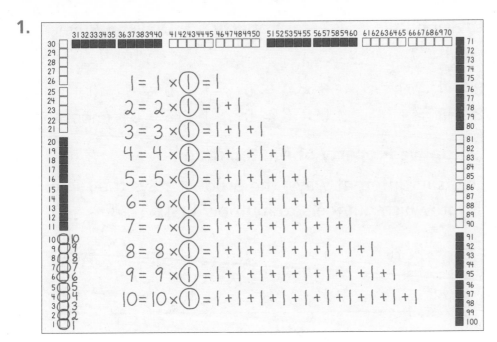

$1 = 1 \times \bigcirc = 1$

$2 = 2 \times \bigcirc = 1 + 1$

$3 = 3 \times \bigcirc = 1 + 1 + 1$

$4 = 4 \times \bigcirc = 1 + 1 + 1 + 1$

$5 = 5 \times \bigcirc = 1 + 1 + 1 + 1 + 1$

$6 = 6 \times \bigcirc = 1 + 1 + 1 + 1 + 1 + 1$

$7 = 7 \times \bigcirc = 1 + 1 + 1 + 1 + 1 + 1 + 1$

$8 = 8 \times \bigcirc = 1 + 1 + 1 + 1 + 1 + 1 + 1 + 1$

$9 = 9 \times \bigcirc = 1 + 1 + 1 + 1 + 1 + 1 + 1 + 1 + 1$

$10 = 10 \times \bigcirc = 1 + 1 + 1 + 1 + 1 + 1 + 1 + 1 + 1 + 1$

▶Explore Patterns with 0s

What patterns do you see below?

2.

$1 \times \bigcirc = 0$

$2 \times \bigcirc = 0 + 0$

$3 \times \bigcirc = 0 + 0 + 0$

$4 \times \bigcirc = 0 + 0 + 0 + 0$

$5 \times \bigcirc = 0 + 0 + 0 + 0 + 0$

$6 \times \bigcirc = 0 + 0 + 0 + 0 + 0 + 0$

$7 \times \bigcirc = 0 + 0 + 0 + 0 + 0 + 0 + 0$

$8 \times \bigcirc = 0 + 0 + 0 + 0 + 0 + 0 + 0 + 0$

$9 \times \bigcirc = 0 + 0 + 0 + 0 + 0 + 0 + 0 + 0 + 0$

$10 \times \bigcirc = 0 + 0 + 0 + 0 + 0 + 0 + 0 + 0 + 0 + 0$

Name _____ **Date** _____

Class Activity

▶Multiplication Properties and Division Rules

Properties and Rules

Property for 1	Division Rule for 1	Zero Property	Division Rule for 0
$1 \times 6 = 6$ $6 \times 1 = 6$	$8 \div 1 = 8$ $8 \div 8 = 1$	$6 \times 0 = 0$ $0 \times 6 = 0$	$0 \div 6 = 0$ $6 \div 0$ is impossible.

Associative Property of Multiplication

When you group factors in different ways, the product stays the same. The parentheses tell you which numbers to multiply first.

$(3 \times 2) \times 5 = \boxed{}$

$6 \times 5 = 30$

$3 \times (2 \times 5) = \boxed{}$

$3 \times 10 = 30$

Find each product.

3. $2 \times (6 \times 1) = \boxed{}$

4. $(4 \times 2) \times 2 = \boxed{}$

5. $7 \times (1 \times 5) = \boxed{}$

6. $(9 \times 8) \times 0 = \boxed{}$

7. $3 \times (2 \times 3) = \boxed{}$

8. $6 \times (0 \times 7) = \boxed{}$

Solve each problem.

Show your work.

9. Shawn gave 1 nickel to each of his sisters. If he gave away 3 nickels, how many sisters does Shawn have? _____

10. Kara has 3 boxes. She put 0 toys in each box. How many toys are in the boxes? _____

11. There are 3 tables in the library. Each table has 2 piles of books on it. If there are 3 books in each pile, how many books are on the tables?

Multiply and Divide with 1 and 0

Class Activity

Name

Date

▶Sprints for 4s

As your teacher reads each multiplication or division, write your answer in the space provided.

× 4	÷ 4
a. _____	a. _____
b. _____	b. _____
c. _____	c. _____
d. _____	d. _____
e. _____	e. _____
f. _____	f. _____
g. _____	g. _____
h. _____	h. _____
i. _____	i. _____
j. _____	j. _____

Play Multiplication and Division Games

▶Check Sheet 5: 1s and 0s

1s Multiplications	1s Divisions	0s Multiplications
1 × 4 = 4	10 / 1 = 10	4 × 0 = 0
5 • 1 = 5	5 ÷ 1 = 5	2 • 0 = 0
7 * 1 = 7	7 / 1 = 7	0 * 8 = 0
1 × 8 = 8	9 ÷ 1 = 9	0 × 5 = 0
1 • 6 = 6	3 / 1 = 3	6 • 0 = 0
10 * 1 = 10	10 ÷ 1 = 10	0 * 7 = 0
1 × 9 = 9	2 / 1 = 2	0 × 2 = 0
3 • 1 = 3	8 ÷ 1 = 8	0 • 9 = 0
1 * 2 = 2	6 / 1 = 6	10 * 0 = 0
1 × 1 = 1	9 / 1 = 9	1 × 0 = 0
8 • 1 = 8	1 ÷ 1 = 1	0 • 6 = 0
1 * 7 = 7	5 / 1 = 5	9 * 0 = 0
1 × 5 = 5	3 ÷ 1 = 3	0 × 4 = 0
6 • 1 = 6	4 / 1 = 4	3 • 0 = 0
1 * 1 = 1	2 ÷ 1 = 2	0 * 3 = 0
1 × 10 = 10	8 / 1 = 8	8 × 0 = 0
9 • 1 = 9	4 ÷ 1 = 4	0 • 10 = 0
4 * 1 = 4	7 ÷ 1 = 7	0 * 1 = 0
2 × 1 = 2	1 / 1 = 1	5 × 0 = 0
1 • 3 = 3	6 ÷ 1 = 6	7 • 0 = 0

▶Check Sheet 6: Mixed 3s, 4s, 0s and 1s

3s, 4s, 0s, 1s Multiplications	3s, 4s, 0s, 1s Multiplications	3s, 4s, 1s Divisions	3s, 4s, 1s Divisions
5 × 3 = 15	0 × 5 = 0	18 / 3 = 6	4 / 1 = 4
6 • 4 = 24	10 • 1 = 10	20 ÷ 4 = 5	21 ÷ 3 = 7
9 * 0 = 0	6 * 3 = 18	1 / 1 = 1	16 / 4 = 4
7 × 1 = 7	2 × 4 = 8	21 ÷ 3 = 7	9 ÷ 1 = 9
3 • 3 = 9	5 • 0 = 0	12 / 4 = 3	15 / 3 = 5
4 * 7 = 28	1 * 2 = 2	5 ÷ 1 = 5	8 ÷ 4 = 2
0 × 10 = 0	10 × 3 = 30	15 / 3 = 5	5 / 1 = 5
1 • 6 = 6	5 • 4 = 20	24 ÷ 4 = 6	30 ÷ 3 = 10
3 * 4 = 12	0 * 8 = 0	7 / 1 = 7	12 / 4 = 3
5 × 4 = 20	9 × 2 = 18	12 / 3 = 4	8 / 1 = 8
0 • 5 = 0	10 • 3 = 30	36 ÷ 4 = 9	27 ÷ 3 = 9
9 * 1 = 9	9 * 4 = 36	6 / 1 = 6	40 / 4 = 10
2 × 3 = 6	1 × 0 = 0	12 ÷ 3 = 4	4 ÷ 1 = 4
3 • 4 = 12	1 • 6 = 6	16 / 4 = 4	9 / 3 = 3
0 * 9 = 0	3 * 6 = 18	7 ÷ 1 = 7	16 ÷ 4 = 4
1 × 5 = 5	7 × 4 = 28	9 / 3 = 3	10 / 1 = 10
2 • 3 = 6	6 • 0 = 0	8 ÷ 4 = 2	9 ÷ 3 = 3
4 * 4 = 16	8 * 1 = 8	2 ÷ 1 = 2	20 ÷ 4 = 5
9 × 0 = 0	3 × 9 = 27	6 / 3 = 2	6 / 1 = 6
1 • 1 = 1	1 • 4 = 4	32 ÷ 4 = 8	24 ÷ 3 = 8

▶Play *Multiplication Three-in-a-Row*

**Read the rules for playing *Multiplication Three-in-a-Row*.
Then play the game with a partner.**

Rules for *Multiplication Three-in-a-Row*

Number of players: 2
What You Will Need: A set of multiplication Strategy Cards, *Three-in-a-Row* Game Grids for each player (see page 295)

1. Each player looks through the cards and writes any nine of the products in the squares of a Game Grid. A player may write the same product more than once.

2. Shuffle the cards and place them exercise side up in the center of the table.

3. Players take turns. On each turn, a player finds the answer to the multiplication on the top card and then turns the card over to check the answer.

4. If the answer is correct, the player looks to see if the product is on the game grid. If it is, the player puts an X through that grid square. If the answer is wrong, or if the product is not on the grid, the player does not mark anything. The player then puts the card problem side up on the bottom of the stack.

5. The first player to mark three squares in a row (horizontally, vertically, or diagonally) wins.

▶Play *Division Race*

Read the rules for playing *Division Race*. Then play the game with a partner.

Rules for *Division Race*

Number of Players: 2
What You Will Need: a set of division Strategy Cards, the *Division Race* game board (see page 296), a different game piece for each player

1. Shuffle the cards and then place them exercise side up on the table.

2. Both players put their game pieces on "START."

3. Players take turns. On each turn, a player finds the answer to the division on the top card and then turns the card over to check the answer.

4. If the answer is correct, the player moves *forward* that number of spaces. If a player's answer is wrong, the player moves *back* a number of spaces equal to the *correct* answer. Players cannot move back beyond the "START" square. The player puts the card on the bottom of the stack.

5. If a player lands on a space with special instructions, he or she should follow those instructions.

6. The first player to reach "END" wins.

Play *Division Race*

Name Date

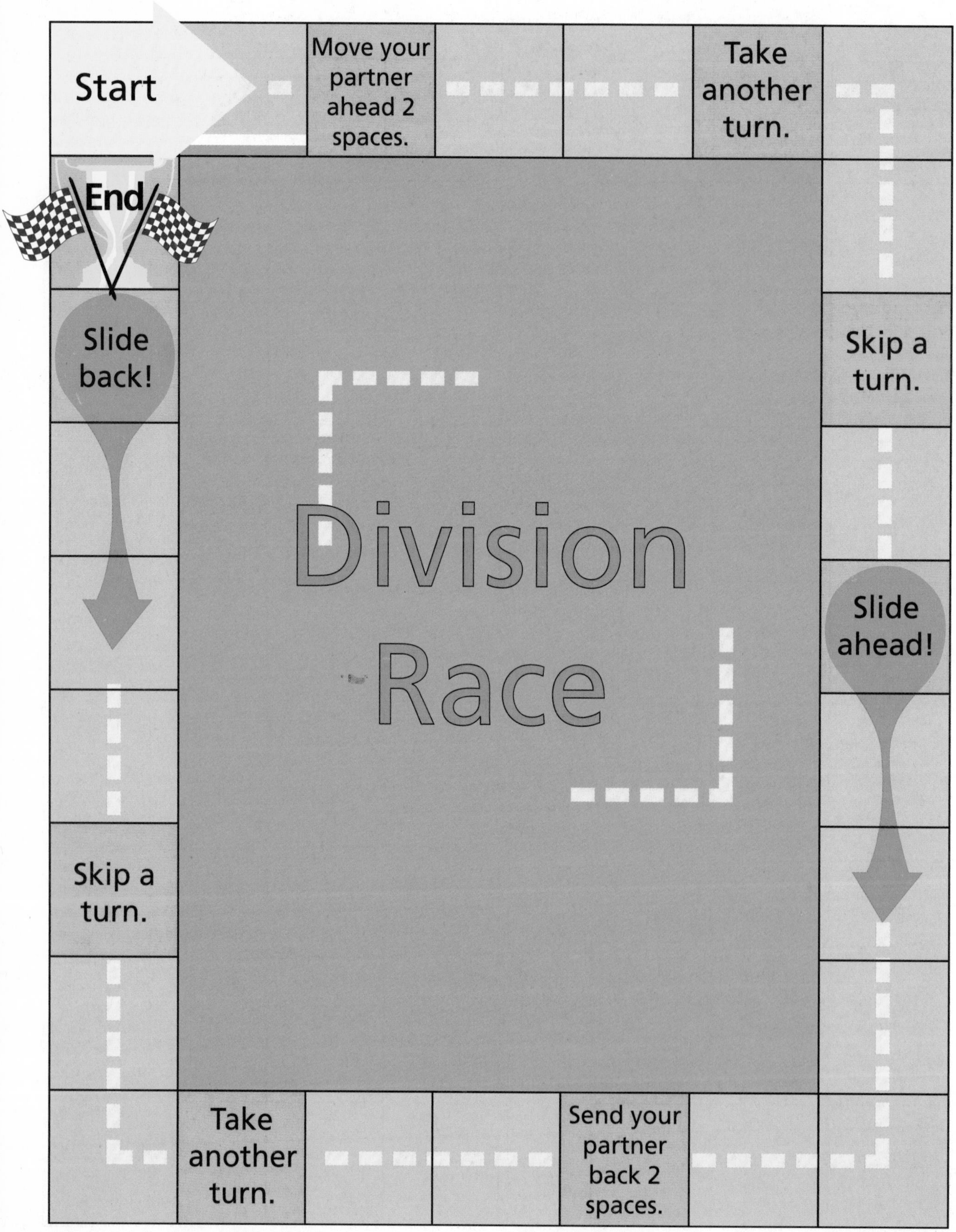
Start
Move your partner ahead 2 spaces.
Take another turn.
End
Slide back!
Skip a turn.
Division Race
Slide ahead!
Skip a turn.
Take another turn.
Send your partner back 2 spaces.

►Check Sheet 7: 0s, 1s, 2s, 3s, 4s, 5s, 9s and 10s

0s, 1s, 2s, 3s, 4s, 5s, 9s, 10s Multiplications	0s, 1s, 2s, 3s, 4s, 5s, 9s, 10s Multiplications	1s, 2s, 3s, 4s, 5s, 9s, 10s Divisions	1s, 2s, 3s, 4s, 5s, 9s, 10s Divisions
$3 \times 0 = 0$	$0 \times 4 = 0$	$9 / 1 = 9$	$40 / 10 = 4$
$7 \cdot 1 = 7$	$5 \cdot 1 = 5$	$4 \div 2 = 2$	$7 \div 1 = 7$
$2 * 2 = 4$	$6 * 7 = 42$	$9 / 3 = 3$	$16 / 2 = 8$
$1 \times 3 = 3$	$2 \times 3 = 6$	$20 \div 4 = 5$	$18 \div 3 = 6$
$4 \cdot 4 = 16$	$5 \cdot 0 = 0$	$15 / 5 = 3$	$16 / 4 = 4$
$6 * 5 = 30$	$1 * 1 = 1$	$45 \div 9 = 5$	$50 \div 5 = 10$
$5 \times 9 = 45$	$10 \times 2 = 20$	$50 / 10 = 5$	$81 / 9 = 9$
$0 \cdot 10 = 0$	$5 \cdot 3 = 15$	$10 \div 1 = 10$	$30 \div 10 = 3$
$0 * 4 = 0$	$4 * 5 = 20$	$8 / 2 = 4$	$10 / 1 = 10$
$1 \times 8 = 8$	$5 \times 6 = 30$	$12 / 3 = 4$	$8 / 2 = 4$
$2 \cdot 5 = 10$	$9 \cdot 7 = 63$	$16 \div 4 = 4$	$27 \div 3 = 9$
$3 * 2 = 6$	$4 * 10 = 40$	$35 / 5 = 7$	$36 / 4 = 9$
$4 \times 3 = 12$	$6 \times 0 = 0$	$27 \div 9 = 3$	$30 \div 5 = 6$
$5 \cdot 4 = 20$	$1 \cdot 6 = 6$	$60 / 10 = 6$	$9 / 9 = 1$
$9 * 6 = 54$	$3 * 2 = 6$	$7 \div 1 = 7$	$80 \div 10 = 8$
$10 \times 7 = 70$	$7 \times 3 = 21$	$8 / 2 = 4$	$10 / 1 = 10$
$0 \cdot 8 = 0$	$4 \cdot 0 = 0$	$18 \div 3 = 6$	$4 \div 2 = 2$
$4 * 9 = 36$	$9 * 5 = 40$	$12 \div 4 = 3$	$21 \div 3 = 7$
$2 \times 0 = 0$	$4 \times 9 = 36$	$40 / 5 = 8$	$8 / 4 = 2$
$1 \cdot 3 = 3$	$10 \cdot 5 = 50$	$36 \div 9 = 4$	$25 \div 5 = 5$

Check Sheet 7: 0s, 1s, 2s, 3s, 4s, 5s, 9s, and 10s

▶Dashes 1–4

Complete each Dash. Check your answers on
page 301.

Dash 1 2s, 5s, 9s, 10s Multiplications	Dash 2 2s, 5s, 9s, 10s Divisions	Dash 3 3s, 4s, 0s, 1s Multiplications	Dash 4 3s, 4s, 1s Divisions
a. $4 \times 5 =$ ___	a. $8 / 2 =$ ___	a. $3 \times 0 =$ ___	a. $12 / 4 =$ ___
b. $10 \cdot 3 =$ ___	b. $50 \div 10 =$ ___	b. $4 \cdot 6 =$ ___	b. $5 \div 1 =$ ___
c. $8 * 9 =$ ___	c. $15 / 5 =$ ___	c. $9 * 1 =$ ___	c. $21 / 3 =$ ___
d. $6 \times 2 =$ ___	d. $63 \div 9 =$ ___	d. $3 \times 3 =$ ___	d. $1 \div 1 =$ ___
e. $5 \cdot 7 =$ ___	e. $90 / 10 =$ ___	e. $8 \cdot 4 =$ ___	e. $16 / 4 =$ ___
f. $10 * 5 =$ ___	f. $90 \div 9 =$ ___	f. $0 * 5 =$ ___	f. $9 \div 3 =$ ___
g. $8 \times 2 =$ ___	g. $35 / 5 =$ ___	g. $1 \times 6 =$ ___	g. $32 / 4 =$ ___
h. $6 \cdot 10 =$ ___	h. $14 \div 2 =$ ___	h. $4 \cdot 3 =$ ___	h. $8 \div 1 =$ ___
i. $9 * 3 =$ ___	i. $27 / 9 =$ ___	i. $7 * 4 =$ ___	i. $24 / 4 =$ ___
j. $2 \times 9 =$ ___	j. $45 / 5 =$ ___	j. $3 \times 7 =$ ___	j. $18 / 3 =$ ___
k. $5 \cdot 8 =$ ___	k. $10 \div 10 =$ ___	k. $0 \cdot 1 =$ ___	k. $10 \div 1 =$ ___
l. $10 * 7 =$ ___	l. $25 / 5 =$ ___	l. $10 * 1 =$ ___	l. $40 / 4 =$ ___
m. $5 \times 5 =$ ___	m. $54 \div 9 =$ ___	m. $4 \times 4 =$ ___	m. $12 \div 3 =$ ___
n. $1 \cdot 5 =$ ___	n. $6 / 2 =$ ___	n. $9 \cdot 3 =$ ___	n. $6 / 3 =$ ___
o. $9 * 6 =$ ___	o. $72 \div 9 =$ ___	o. $8 * 0 =$ ___	o. $4 \div 4 =$ ___
p. $10 \times 10 =$ ___	p. $40 / 5 =$ ___	p. $5 \times 4 =$ ___	p. $7 / 1 =$ ___
q. $4 \cdot 2 =$ ___	q. $80 \div 10 =$ ___	q. $1 \cdot 6 =$ ___	q. $28 \div 4 =$ ___
r. $10 * 8 =$ ___	r. $18 \div 2 =$ ___	r. $3 * 8 =$ ___	r. $24 \div 3 =$ ___
s. $3 \times 9 =$ ___	s. $36 / 9 =$ ___	s. $4 \times 9 =$ ___	s. $20 / 4 =$ ___
t. $9 \cdot 9 =$ ___	t. $30 \div 5 =$ ___	t. $0 \cdot 4 =$ ___	t. $27 \div 3 =$ ___

▶Answers to Dashes 1–4

Use this sheet to check your answers to the Dashes on page 299.

Dash 1 2s, 5s, 9s, 10s Multiplications	Dash 2 2s, 5s, 9s, 10s Divisions	Dash 3 3s, 4s, 0s, 1s Multiplications	Dash 4 3s, 4s, 1s Divisions
a. $4 \times 5 = 20$	a. $8 / 2 = 4$	a. $3 \times 0 = 0$	a. $12 / 4 = 3$
b. $10 \cdot 3 = 30$	b. $50 \div 10 = 5$	b. $4 \cdot 6 = 24$	b. $5 \div 1 = 5$
c. $8 * 9 = 72$	c. $15 / 5 = 3$	c. $9 * 1 = 9$	c. $21 / 3 = 7$
d. $6 \times 2 = 12$	d. $63 \div 9 = 7$	d. $3 \times 3 = 9$	d. $1 \div 1 = 1$
e. $5 \cdot 7 = 35$	e. $90 / 10 = 9$	e. $8 \cdot 4 = 32$	e. $16 / 4 = 4$
f. $10 * 5 = 50$	f. $90 \div 9 = 10$	f. $0 * 5 = 0$	f. $9 \div 3 = 3$
g. $8 \times 2 = 16$	g. $35 / 5 = 7$	g. $1 \times 6 = 6$	g. $32 / 4 = 8$
h. $6 \cdot 10 = 60$	h. $14 \div 2 = 7$	h. $4 \cdot 3 = 12$	h. $8 \div 1 = 8$
i. $9 * 3 = 27$	i. $27 / 9 = 3$	i. $7 * 4 = 28$	i. $24 / 4 = 6$
j. $2 \times 9 = 18$	j. $45 / 5 = 9$	j. $3 \times 7 = 21$	j. $18 / 3 = 6$
k. $5 \cdot 8 = 40$	k. $10 \div 10 = 1$	k. $0 \cdot 1 = 0$	k. $10 \div 1 = 10$
l. $10 * 7 = 70$	l. $25 / 5 = 5$	l. $10 * 1 = 10$	l. $40 / 4 = 10$
m. $5 \times 5 = 25$	m. $54 \div 9 = 6$	m. $4 \times 4 = 16$	m. $12 \div 3 = 4$
n. $1 \cdot 5 = 5$	n. $6 / 2 = 3$	n. $9 \cdot 3 = 27$	n. $6 / 3 = 2$
o. $9 * 6 = 54$	o. $72 \div 9 = 8$	o. $8 * 0 = 0$	o. $4 \div 4 = 1$
p. $10 \times 10 = 100$	p. $40 / 5 = 8$	p. $5 \times 4 = 20$	p. $7 / 1 = 7$
q. $4 \cdot 2 = 8$	q. $80 \div 10 = 8$	q. $1 \cdot 6 = 6$	q. $28 \div 4 = 7$
r. $10 * 8 = 80$	r. $18 \div 2 = 9$	r. $3 * 8 = 24$	r. $24 \div 3 = 8$
s. $3 \times 9 = 27$	s. $36 / 9 = 4$	s. $4 \times 9 = 36$	s. $20 / 4 = 5$
t. $9 \cdot 9 = 81$	t. $30 \div 5 = 6$	t. $0 \cdot 4 = 0$	t. $27 \div 3 = 9$

Answers to Dashes 1–4

► **Solve Word Problems with 2s, 3s, 4s, 5s, 6s, 7s, and 9s**

Solve each problem.

1. Toni counted 36 legs in the lion house at the zoo. How many lions were there?

   _____

2. One wall of an art gallery has a row of 5 paintings and a row of 9 paintings. How many paintings are on the wall?

   _____

3. Josh's muffin pan is an array with 4 rows and 6 columns. How many muffins can Josh make in the pan?

   _____

4. To get ready for the school spelling bee, Tanya studied 3 hours each night for an entire week. How many hours did she study?

   _____

5. The 14 trumpet players in the marching band lined up in 2 equal rows. How many trumpet players were in each row?

   _____

6. The Sunnyside Riding Stable has 9 horses. The owners are going to buy new horseshoes for all the horses. How many horseshoes are needed?

   _____

Name _____ **Date** _____

Going Further

►Use Patterns to Divide 2- and 3-Digit Numbers

Find each quotient.

1. $8 \div 2 = 8$ ones $\div 2 = 4$ ones or _____

   $80 \div 2 = 8$ tens $\div 2 = 4$ tens or _____

   $800 \div 2 = 8$ hundreds $\div 2 = 4$ hundreds or _____

2. $9 \div 3 = 9$ ones $\div 3 =$ _____ ones or _____

   $90 \div 3 = 9$ tens $\div 3 =$ _____ tens or _____

   $900 \div 3 = 9$ hundreds $\div 3 =$ _____ hundreds or _____

3. $8 \div 4 =$ _____

   $80 \div 4 =$ _____

   $800 \div 4 =$ _____

4. $6 \div 2 =$ _____

   $60 \div 2 =$ _____

   $600 \div 2 =$ _____

5. $6 \div 3 =$ _____

   $60 \div 3 =$ _____

   $600 \div 3 =$ _____

6. $4 \div 2 =$ _____

   $40 \div 2 =$ _____

   $400 \div 2 =$ _____

7. $9 \div 3 =$ _____

   $90 \div 3 =$ _____

   $900 \div 3 =$ _____

8. $25 \div 5 =$ _____

   $250 \div 5 =$ _____

   $2,500 \div 5 =$ _____

9. $36 \div 4 =$ _____

   $360 \div 4 =$ _____

   $3,600 \div 4 =$ _____

10. $72 \div 9 =$ _____

    $720 \div 9 =$ _____

    $7,200 \div 9 =$ _____

11. $54 \div 9 =$ _____

    $540 \div 9 =$ _____

    $5,400 \div 9 =$ _____

Practice with 0s, 1s, 2s, 3s, 4s, 5s, 9s, and 10s

Multiply or divide.

1. 8 × 2 = _____

2. 5 • 7 = _____

3. 10 ÷ 1 = _____

4. 81 ÷ 9 = _____

5. 4 × 0 = _____

6. 63 / 9 = _____

7. 6 • 4 = _____

8. 45 / 5 = _____

9. 9 × 3 = _____

10. $\boxed{}$
    3)24

11. 28 ÷ 4 = _____

12. 10 * 8 = _____

Write a multiplication equation to find the total number.

13. _____

14. _____

Write a multiplication equation to represent the area of the rectangle.

15. _____

Name   Date

Complete.

16. $9 + 9 + 9 + 9 + 9 + 9 + 9 + 9 =$ _____ $\times\, 9 =$ _____

Write a related division equation.

17. $8 \times 5 = 40$ _____

Write a related multiplication equation.

18. $18 \div 2 = 9$ _____

Write an equation to solve each problem. Then write the answer.

19. Olivia's CD rack has 4 shelves. It holds 8 CDs on a shelf. How many CDs will fit in the rack altogether?

   _____

20. **Extended Response** Paco set up 7 tables to seat 28 children at his birthday party. The same number of children will sit at each table. How many children will sit at each table? Explain how you found your answer. Make a math drawing to help explain.

   _____

   _____

   _____

▶Visualize Perimeter and Area

Find the perimeter and area of each figure.
Remember to include the correct units in your answers.

1.
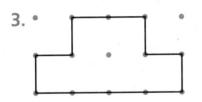

perimeter   area

├─1 cm─┤   ├─ 1 ─┤
sq cm

Perimeter = _____

Area = _____

2.
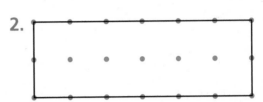

Perimeter = _____

Area = _____

3.
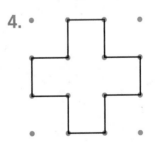

Perimeter = _____

Area = _____

4.

Perimeter = _____

Area = _____

5.
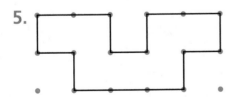

Perimeter = _____

Area = _____

6.
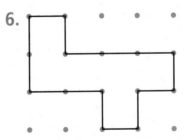

Perimeter = _____

Area = _____

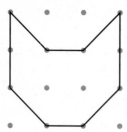

Class Activity

▶Count Whole- and Half-Square Units to Find Area

7. Find the area of this figure and explain what you did.

Area = _____

_____

_____

_____

_____

Find the area of each figure.

8.
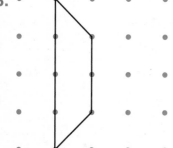

Area = _____

9.
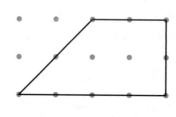

Area = _____

10.
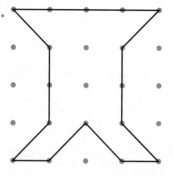

Area = _____

11.
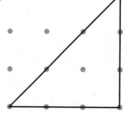

Area = _____

Explore Perimeter and Area

►Solve Area and Perimeter Problems

Read the problem below and complete exercises 12 and 13.

> Debra wants to tile the floor of a rectangular room in her house. The floor is 9 feet long and 8 feet wide. The tiles are squares with sides that are 1 foot long. How many tiles does she need?
>
> 1 ft
> | Tile | 1 ft

12. To find the total number of tiles, do you need to find the perimeter or area of the room? Explain.

_____

_____

_____

13. How many tiles does Debra need? _____

Read the problem below and complete exercises 14 and 15.

> Deshawn wants to build a fence around a rectangular space in his backyard. The space is 5 yards long and 3 yards wide. The fence sections are 1 yard long. How many fence sections does Deshawn need?
>
>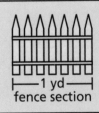
> ├──1 yd──┤
> fence section

14. To find the number of fence sections, do you need to find the perimeter or area of the rectangle? Explain.

_____

_____

_____

15. How many fence sections does Deshawn need? _____

16. **On the Back** Create and solve a word problem that involves finding the area of a figure. Draw a picture to show your answer is correct.

Name _____ **Date** _____

_____

_____

_____

_____

_____

_____

_____

Explore Perimeter and Area

Dear Family,

Your child is currently participating in Geometry activities involving perimeter and area. In this unit, students find the area of a rectangle by counting the number of square units inside the figure. Students also find the perimeter of a rectangle by counting linear units around the outside of the figure.

Students develop and use formulas to find the perimeter and area of a rectangle, as shown below.

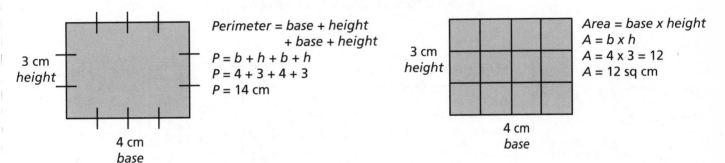

Perimeter = base + height
        + base + height
$P = b + h + b + h$
$P = 4 + 3 + 4 + 3$
$P = 14$ cm

3 cm height

4 cm base

Area = base x height
$A = b \times h$
$A = 4 \times 3 = 12$
$A = 12$ sq cm

3 cm height

4 cm base

Students draw rectangles that have the same perimeter but different areas. They discover that for a given perimeter, the longest, skinniest rectangle has the smallest area and the rectangle with sides closest to the same length or the same length has the greatest area.

Students also draw rectangles that have the same area but different perimeters. They discover that for a given area, the longest, skinniest rectangle has the greatest perimeter and the rectangle with sides closest to the same length or the same length has the least perimeter.

Throughout the unit students apply what they have learned about perimeter and area to real-world problems.

If you have any questions or comments, please call or write to me.

Thank you.

Sincerely,
Your child's teacher

Estimada familia:

Su niño está participando en actividades de geometría relacionadas con el perímetro y el área. En esta unidad los estudiantes hallan el área de un rectángulo contando el número de unidades cuadradas que caben en la figura. Los estudiantes también hallan el perímetro de un rectángulo contando el número de unidades lineales que hay alrededor de la figura.

Los estudiantes desarrollan fórmulas y las usan para hallar el perímetro y el área de un rectángulo, como se muestra a continuación.

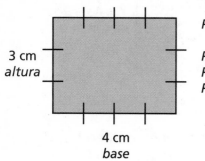

Perímetro = base + altura
              + base + altura
$P = b + h + b + h$
$P = 4 + 3 + 4 + 3 = 14$
$P = 14$ cm

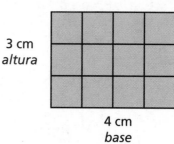

Área = base x altura
$A = b \times h$
$A = 4 \times 3 = 12$
$A = 12$ cm cuadrados

Los estudiantes dibujan rectángulos que tienen el mismo perímetro pero diferentes áreas. Van a notar que, para un determinado perímetro, el rectángulo más largo y delgado tiene el área más pequeña, y el rectángulo con lados que tienen longitudes iguales o casi iguales tiene el área más grande.

Los estudiantes también dibujan rectángulos que tienen la misma área pero diferentes perímetros. Descubren que, para un área determinada, el rectángulo más largo y delgado tiene el perímetro mayor y el rectángulo con lados que tienen longitudes iguales o casi iguales tiene el perímetro menor.

En esta unidad los estudiantes aplican lo que han aprendido acerca del perímetro y el área a problemas de la vida diaria.

Si tiene alguna duda o comentario, por favor comuníquese conmigo.

Atentamente,
El maestro de su niño

Class Activity

Vocabulary

perimeter
area

► **Explore Rectangles with the Same Perimeter**

Complete.

1. On a centimeter dot array, draw all possible rectangles with a **perimeter** of 12 cm and sides whose lengths are whole centimeters. Label the lengths of two adjacent sides of each rectangle.

2. Find and label the **area** of each rectangle. In the table, record the lengths of the sides and the area of each rectangle.

3. Compare the shapes of the rectangles with the least and greatest areas.

Rectangles with Perimeter 12 cm

Lengths of Two Adjacent Sides	Area

4. On a centimeter dot array, draw all possible rectangles with a perimeter of 22 cm and sides whose lengths are whole centimeters. Label the lengths of two adjacent sides of each rectangle.

5. Find and label the area of each rectangle. In the table, record the lengths of the sides and the area of each rectangle.

Rectangles with Perimeter 22 cm

Lengths of Two Adjacent Sides	Area

6. Compare the shapes of the rectangles with the least and greatest areas.

▶Explore Rectangles with the Same Area

Complete.

7. On a centimeter dot array, draw all possible rectangles with an area of 12 sq cm and sides whose lengths are whole centimeters. Label the lengths of two adjacent sides of each rectangle.

8. Find and label the perimeter of each rectangle. In the table, record the lengths of the sides and the perimeter of each rectangle.

Rectangles with Area 12 sq cm

Lengths of Two Adjacent Sides	Perimeter

9. Compare the shapes of the rectangles with the least and greatest perimeter.

_____

_____

10. On a centimeter dot array, draw all possible rectangles with an area of 18 sq cm and with sides whose lengths are whole centimeters. Label the lengths of two adjacent sides of each rectangle.

Rectangles with Area 18 sq cm

11. Find and label the perimeter of each rectangle. In the table, record the lengths of the sides and the perimeter of each rectangle.

Lengths of Two Adjacent Sides	Perimeter

12. Compare the shapes of the rectangles with the least and greatest perimeter.

_____

Relate Area and Perimeter

▶Find the Area of a Rectangle

Find the area of each rectangle. Draw the square units inside rectangles 1 and 2. Label your answer in square units. Write an equation to show how the length of the adjacent sides and area are related.

1.

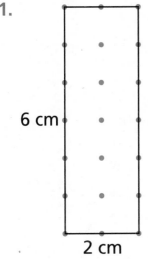

6 cm

2 cm

Area = _____

_____

2.

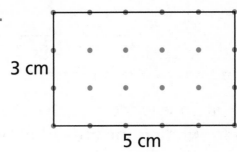

3 cm

5 cm

Area = _____

_____

3.

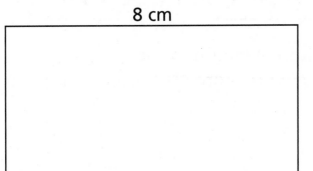

8 cm

4 cm

Area = _____

_____

Class Activity

Name _____ **Date** _____

▶Formula for the Area of a Rectangle

You can call the bottom side of a rectangle the **base**.
You can call one of the adjacent sides the **height**.

height [rectangle]

base

4. Look at your work in exercises 1–3. Complete this
   rule for finding the area of a rectangle using the
   words *height* and *base*.

   The area of a rectangle is _____

5. Fill in the blanks with words to create a shorter
   form of the rule for the area of a rectangle.

   _____ = _____ × _____

A **formula** is an equation with variables that describes a rule.

6. Use the letter *A* for area, *b* for the length of the
   base, and *h* for the height to write a formula for the
   area of a rectangle.

   _____ = _____ × _____

7. A rectangle has a base of 7 feet and a height of
   3 feet. Use the formula from exercise 6 to find the
   area of this rectangle. Remember to include the
   correct unit in your answer.

   _____

Formulas for Area and Perimeter

▶ **Formula for the Perimeter of a Rectangle**

Find the **perimeter** of each rectangle. Remember to include the correct units in your answers.

8.

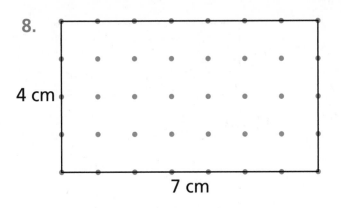

4 cm

7 cm

Perimeter = _____

9.

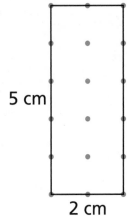

5 cm

2 cm

Perimeter = _____

10.

6 cm

3 cm

Perimeter = _____

11. Write a **formula** for finding the perimeter of a rectangle. Use the letter *P* to represent the perimeter of a rectangle, *b* to represent the length of the base, and *h* to represent the height.

_____

12. A football field (including the end zones) is shaped like a rectangle with a base of 360 feet and a height of 160 feet. Use a formula to find the perimeter of the field.

_____

Class Activity

▶ Formulas for the Perimeter and Area of a Square

Find the perimeter and area of each square. Remember to include the correct units in your answers.

13.

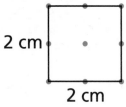

2 cm

2 cm

14.

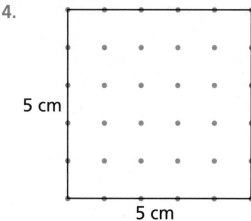

5 cm

5 cm

Perimeter = _____

Area = _____

Perimeter = _____

Area = _____

15.

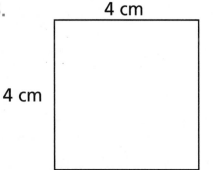

4 cm

4 cm

Perimeter = _____

Area = _____

16. Write a formula for the area of a square and for the perimeter of a square. Let the letter *s* stand for the length of a side of a square.

A = _____

P = _____

17. Use your formulas to find the area and perimeter of a square with sides that are 8 feet long.

_____

Formulas for Area and Perimeter

Find the perimeter and area. Include the correct units in your answers.

1.

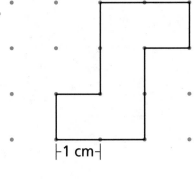

├─1 cm─┤

Perimeter = _____

Area = _____

2.

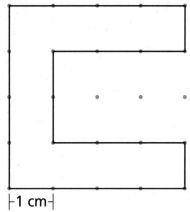

├─1 cm─┤

Perimeter = _____

Area = _____

Find the area.

3.

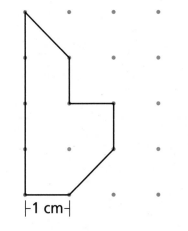

├─1 cm─┤

Area = _____

4.

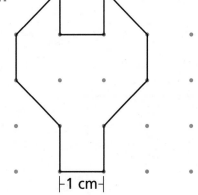

├─1 cm─┤

Area = _____

5. On the dot array, draw all possible rectangles with a perimeter of 14 cm and sides whose lengths are whole centimeters. Label the lengths of the two adjacent sides of each rectangle. Label each rectangle with its area.

6. On the dot array, draw all possible rectangles with an area of 12 sq cm and sides whose lengths are whole centimeters. Label the lengths of the two adjacent sides of each rectangle. Label each rectangle with its perimeter.

7. Use the letter *A* to represent the area of the rectangle, *b* to represent the length of the base, and *h* to represent the height.

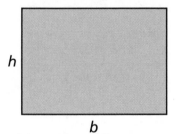

Write a formula for the area of the rectangle.

_____

Use your formula to find the area of a rectangle with a height of 3 feet and a base of 5 feet.

_____

8. Use the letter *P* to represent the perimeter of the rectangle, *b* to represent the length of the base, and *h* to represent the height.

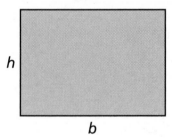

Write a formula for the perimeter of the rectangle.

_____

Use your formula to find the perimeter of a rectangle with a width of 3 feet and a length of 5 feet.

_____

9. Liana wants to put a rope around a rectangular space in her yard where she plans to plant a vegetable garden. The garden will be 8 meters long and 6 meters wide. How much rope does Liana need?

_____

10. **Extended Response** David is sewing together a quilt from quilt squares his grandmother made. He wants the quilt to be a rectangle, with sides of length 5 feet and 7 feet. The quilt squares have sides of length 1 foot.

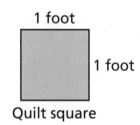

1 foot

1 foot

Quilt square

To find the number of quilt squares he needs, do you need to find the perimeter of the quilt or the area? Explain.

_____

_____

_____

How many quilt squares does David need? Explain how you found your answer.

_____

_____

_____

_____

Class Activity

Name _____   **Date** _____

▶ Explore Patterns with 6s

What patterns do you see below?

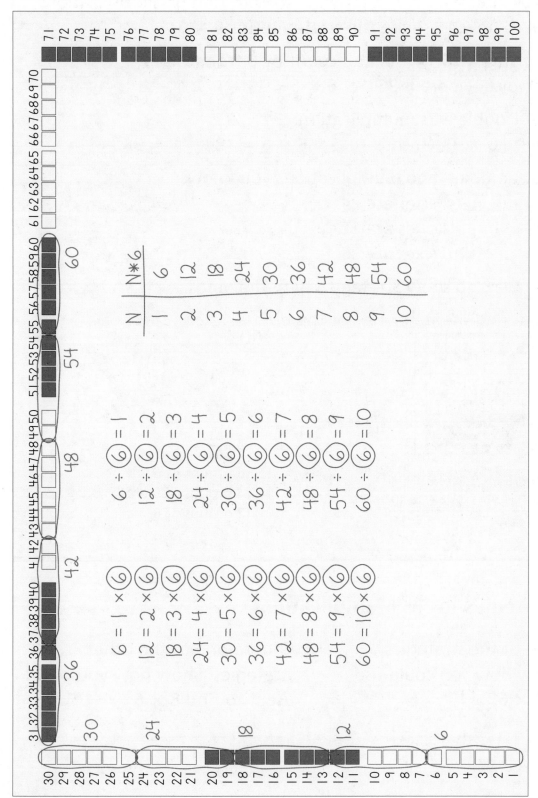

Class Activity

▶ Strategies for Multiplying with 6

You can use 6s multiplications that you know to find 6s multiplications that you don't know. Here are the strategies for 6×6.

- **Strategy 1:** Start with 5×6, and count by 6 from there.
  $5 \times 6 = 30$, plus 6 more is 36. So, $6 \times 6 = 36$.

- **Strategy 2:** Double a 3s multiplication.
  6×6 is twice 6×3, which is 18. So, $6 \times 6 = 18 + 18 = 36$.

- **Strategy 3:** Combine two multiplications you know.

  $4 \times 6 = 24$ 4 sixes are 24.
  $\underline{2 \times 6 = 12}$ $\underline{\text{2 sixes are 12.}}$
  $6 \times 6 = 36$ 6 sixes are 36.

Here are two ways to show Strategy 3 with drawings.

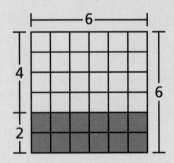

unshaded area: $4 \times 6 = 24$
shaded area: $\underline{2 \times 6 = 12}$
total area: $6 \times 6 = 36$

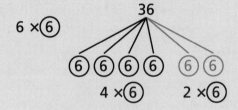

$6 \times \textcircled{6}$

Explanation:
6 groups of 6 is
4 groups of 6 plus
2 groups of 6.

▶ Apply Strategies for 6s Multiplications

1. Choose one of the strategies above. Show how you could use it to find 7×6.

    _____

2. Choose one of the other strategies. Show how you could use it to find 8×6.

    _____

Dear Family,

In this unit, students learn multiplications and divisions for 6s, 7s, and 8s, while continuing to practice the rest of the basic multiplications and divisions covered in Unit 4.

Although students practice all the 6s, 7s, and 8s multiplications, they really have only six new multiplications to learn: 6 × 6, 6 × 7, 6 × 8, 7 × 7, 7 × 8, and 8 × 8. The lessons for these multiplications focus on strategies for finding the products using multiplications they know.

Students are also introduced to comparisons involving multiplication and division. Such comparisons involve one quantity that is a number of times *as many as* or *as much as* another. Here are two examples:

- Teresa has 2 gerbils. Owen has 4 times as many gerbils as Teresa has. How many gerbils does Owen have?

- Eduardo has 12 posters in his room. Manuela has $\frac{1}{3}$ as many posters as Eduardo. How many posters does Manuela have?

This unit also focuses on word problems. Students are presented with a variety of one-step word problems. They use the language and context of each problem to determine which operation—multiplication, division, addition, or subtraction—they must use to solve it. Students solve multi-step problems using a variety of methods.

Please continue to help your child get faster on multiplications and divisions. Use all of the practice materials that your child has brought home. Your support is crucial to your child's learning.

Please call if you have any questions or comments.

Thank you.

Sincerely,
Your child's teacher

Estimada familia:

En esta unidad los estudiantes aprenden las multiplicaciones y divisiones con el 6, el 7 y el 8, mientras siguen practicando las demás multiplicaciones y divisiones que se presentaron en la Unidad 4.

Aunque los estudiantes practican todas las multiplicaciones con el 6, el 7 y el 8, en realidad sólo tienen que aprender seis multiplicaciones nuevas: 6×6, 6×7, 6×8, 7×7, 7×8 y 8×8. Las lecciones de estas multiplicaciones se centran en estrategias para hallar los productos usando multiplicaciones que ya se conocen.

Los estudiantes también empiezan a hacer comparaciones de cantidades que resultan de la multiplicación y la división. Las comparaciones de este tipo tratan de una cantidad que es *tantas veces*. Aquí hay dos ejemplos:

- Teresa tiene 2 gerbos. Owen tiene 4 veces más gerbos que Teresa. ¿Cuántos gerbos tiene Owen?

- Eduardo tiene 12 carteles en su cuarto. Manuela tiene $\frac{1}{3}$ del número de carteles que tiene Eduardo. ¿Cuántos carteles tiene Manuela?

Esta unidad también se centra en problemas verbales. A los estudiantes se les presenta una varidad de problemas verbales de un paso. Aprovechan el lenguaje y el contexto de cada problema para determinar qué operación deben usar para resolverlo: la multiplicación, la división, la suma o la resta. Los estudiantes también resuelven problemas de varios pasos utilizando una variedad de métodos.

Por favor continúe ayudando a su niño a practicar las multiplicaciones y las divisiones. Use todos los materiales de práctica que su niño ha llevado a casa. Su apoyo es importante para el aprendizaje de su niño.

Si tiene alguna duda o pregunta, por favor comuníquese conmigo.

Atentamente,
El maestro de su niño

Multiply and Divide with 6

Study Sheet C

7s

Count-bys	Mixed Up ×	Mixed Up ÷
1 × 7 = 7	6 × 7 = 42	70 ÷ 7 = 10
2 × 7 = 14	8 × 7 = 56	14 ÷ 7 = 2
3 × 7 = 21	5 × 7 = 35	28 ÷ 7 = 4
4 × 7 = 28	9 × 7 = 63	56 ÷ 7 = 8
5 × 7 = 35	4 × 7 = 28	42 ÷ 7 = 6
6 × 7 = 42	10 × 7 = 70	63 ÷ 7 = 9
7 × 7 = 49	3 × 7 = 21	21 ÷ 7 = 3
8 × 7 = 56	1 × 7 = 7	49 ÷ 7 = 7
9 × 7 = 63	7 × 7 = 49	7 ÷ 7 = 1
10 × 7 = 70	2 × 7 = 14	35 ÷ 7 = 5

6s

Count-bys	Mixed Up ×	Mixed Up ÷
1 × 6 = 6	10 × 6 = 60	54 ÷ 6 = 9
2 × 6 = 12	8 × 6 = 48	30 ÷ 6 = 5
3 × 6 = 18	2 × 6 = 12	12 ÷ 6 = 2
4 × 6 = 24	6 × 6 = 36	60 ÷ 6 = 10
5 × 6 = 30	4 × 6 = 24	48 ÷ 6 = 8
6 × 6 = 36	1 × 6 = 6	36 ÷ 6 = 6
7 × 6 = 42	9 × 6 = 54	6 ÷ 6 = 1
8 × 6 = 48	3 × 6 = 18	42 ÷ 6 = 7
9 × 6 = 54	7 × 6 = 42	18 ÷ 6 = 3
10 × 6 = 60	5 × 6 = 30	24 ÷ 6 = 4

Squares

Count-bys	Mixed Up ×	Mixed Up ÷
1 × 1 = 1	3 × 3 = 9	25 ÷ 5 = 5
2 × 2 = 4	9 × 9 = 81	4 ÷ 2 = 2
3 × 3 = 9	4 × 4 = 16	81 ÷ 9 = 9
4 × 4 = 16	6 × 6 = 36	9 ÷ 3 = 3
5 × 5 = 25	2 × 2 = 4	36 ÷ 6 = 6
6 × 6 = 36	7 × 7 = 49	100 ÷ 10 = 10
7 × 7 = 49	10 × 10 = 100	16 ÷ 4 = 4
8 × 8 = 64	1 × 1 = 1	49 ÷ 7 = 7
9 × 9 = 81	5 × 5 = 25	1 ÷ 1 = 1
10 × 10 = 100	8 × 8 = 64	64 ÷ 8 = 8

8s

Count-bys	Mixed Up ×	Mixed Up ÷
1 × 8 = 8	6 × 8 = 48	16 ÷ 8 = 2
2 × 8 = 16	10 × 8 = 80	40 ÷ 8 = 5
3 × 8 = 24	7 × 8 = 56	72 ÷ 8 = 9
4 × 8 = 32	2 × 8 = 16	32 ÷ 8 = 4
5 × 8 = 40	4 × 8 = 32	8 ÷ 8 = 1
6 × 8 = 48	8 × 8 = 64	80 ÷ 8 = 10
7 × 8 = 56	5 × 8 = 40	64 ÷ 8 = 8
8 × 8 = 64	10 × 8 = 80	24 ÷ 8 = 3
9 × 8 = 72	3 × 8 = 24	56 ÷ 8 = 7
10 × 8 = 80	1 × 8 = 8	48 ÷ 8 = 6

Study Sheet C

Class Activity

Name _____ Date _____

▶Missing Number Puzzles

Complete each Missing Number puzzle.

1.

×	5	2	
	30		48
4		8	32
	45		72

2.

×		3	
6	30		42
4			28
	40	24	56

3.

×	4		8
9		81	
	12		24
	20	45	40

▶Area Word Problems

Solve each problem. Label your answers with the correct units.

Show your work.

4. The mattress has a length of 7 feet and a width of 6 feet. What is the area of the mattress?

5. The wading pool at Evans Park is shaped like a square with sides 8 feet long. What is the area of the wading pool?

6. Milo's rug has a length of 5 feet and an area of 40 square feet. What is the width of his rug?

7. Lana wants to enclose a garden plot with a piece of rope that is 36 feet long. Lana wants to have the most space possible for gardening. Draw a picture of what Lana's garden will look like. Label the drawing.

Name _____

Date _____

Going Further

▶Problem-Solving Strategy: Draw a Picture

Draw a picture to help solve each problem.

1. Ana has a ribbon that is 18 inches long. She cut the ribbon into 3 equal pieces. Then she cut each of those pieces in half. How many small pieces of ribbon are there? How long is each piece?

   _____

2. A sign is shaped like a square. Eva draws lines in the sign to make 3 equal rectangles. Each rectangle is 3 inches wide and 9 inches long. What is the area of the square?

   _____

3. Ty puts up a 20-foot-long fence to make a rectangular garden. He divides the rectangle into 4 equal squares all in one row. The side of each square is 2 feet long. What is the area of the garden?

   _____

4. Aaron is stacking cans in a grocery store. The bottom row has 7 cans. Each row above has 1 fewer can. How many cans will be stacked in all?

   _____

5. There are 4 cars in a row. Each car is 13 feet long. There are 6 feet between each car. What is the length from the front of the first car to the back of the last car in the row?

   _____

Solve Area Word Problems

►Check Sheet 8: 6s and 8s

6s Multiplications	6s Divisions	8s Multiplications	8s Divisions
10 × 6 = 60	24 / 6 = 4	2 × 8 = 16	72 / 8 = 9
6 • 4 = 24	48 ÷ 6 = 8	8 • 10 = 80	16 ÷ 8 = 2
6 * 7 = 42	60 / 6 = 10	3 * 8 = 24	40 / 8 = 5
2 × 6 = 12	12 ÷ 6 = 2	9 × 8 = 72	8 ÷ 8 = 1
6 • 5 = 30	42 / 6 = 7	8 • 4 = 32	80 / 8 = 10
6 * 8 = 48	30 ÷ 6 = 5	8 * 7 = 56	48 ÷ 8 = 6
9 × 6 = 54	6 / 6 = 1	5 × 8 = 40	56 / 8 = 7
6 • 1 = 6	18 ÷ 6 = 3	8 • 6 = 48	24 ÷ 8 = 3
6 * 6 = 36	54 / 6 = 9	1 * 8 = 8	64 / 8 = 8
6 × 3 = 18	36 / 6 = 6	8 × 8 = 64	32 / 8 = 4
6 • 6 = 36	48 ÷ 6 = 8	4 • 8 = 32	80 ÷ 8 = 10
5 * 6 = 30	12 / 6 = 2	6 * 8 = 48	56 / 8 = 7
6 × 2 = 12	24 ÷ 6 = 4	8 × 3 = 24	8 ÷ 8 = 1
4 • 6 = 24	60 / 6 = 10	7 • 8 = 56	24 / 8 = 3
6 * 9 = 54	6 ÷ 6 = 1	8 * 2 = 16	64 ÷ 8 = 8
8 × 6 = 48	42 / 6 = 7	8 × 9 = 72	16 / 8 = 2
7 • 6 = 42	18 ÷ 6 = 3	8 • 1 = 8	72 ÷ 8 = 9
6 * 10 = 60	36 ÷ 6 = 6	8 * 8 = 64	32 ÷ 8 = 4
1 × 6 = 6	30 / 6 = 5	10 × 8 = 80	40 / 8 = 5
4 • 6 = 24	54 ÷ 6 = 9	5 • 8 = 40	48 ÷ 8 = 6

Check Sheet 8: 6s and 8s

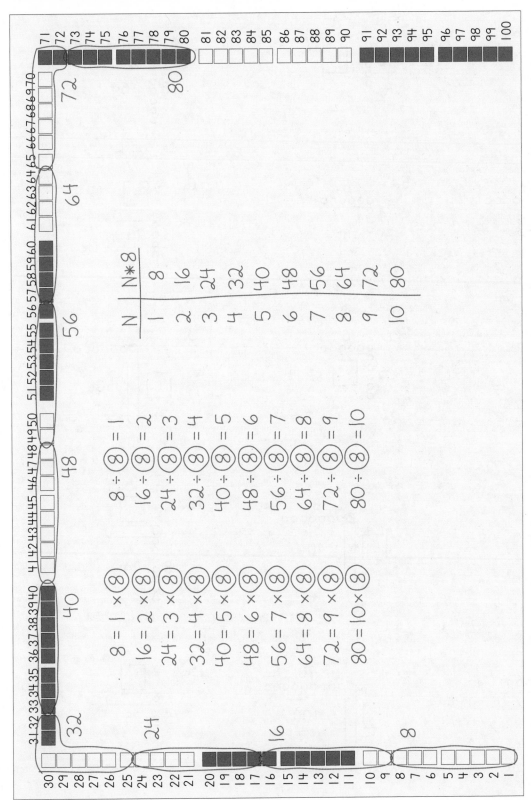

▶Explore Patterns with 8s.

What patterns do you see below?

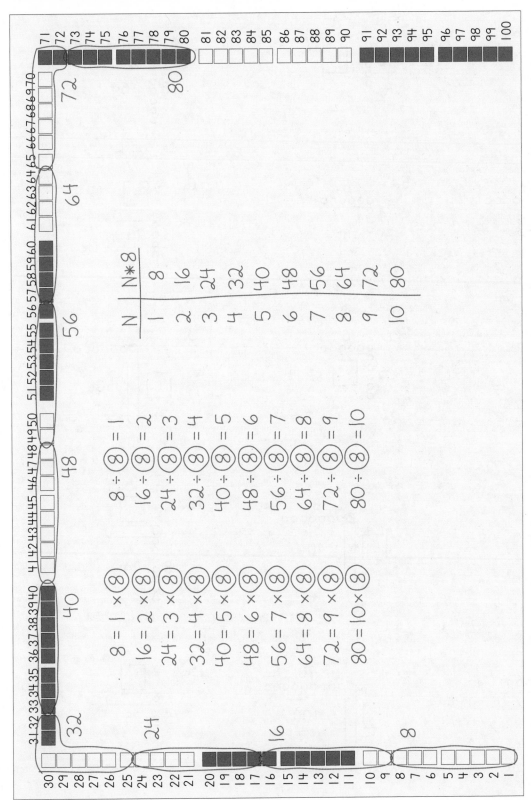

▶Fast-Array Drawings

Find the missing number in each Fast Array-drawing.

1. 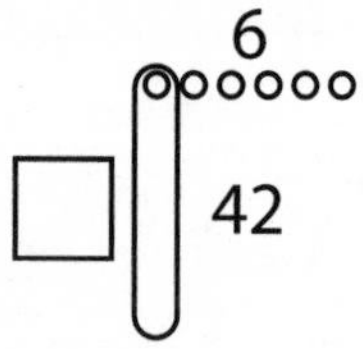
6
$\square$ 42

2. 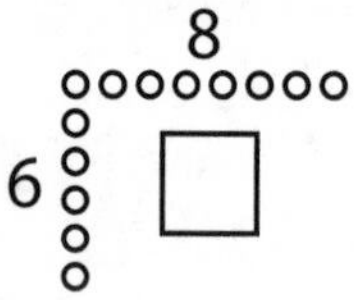
8
6
$\square$

3. 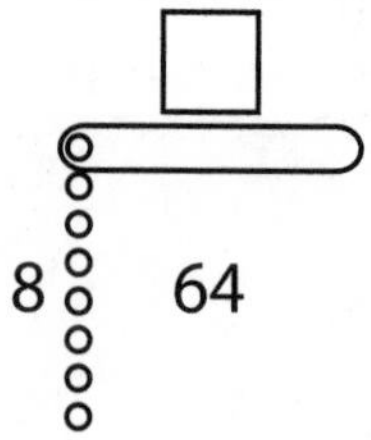
$\square$
8 64

4. 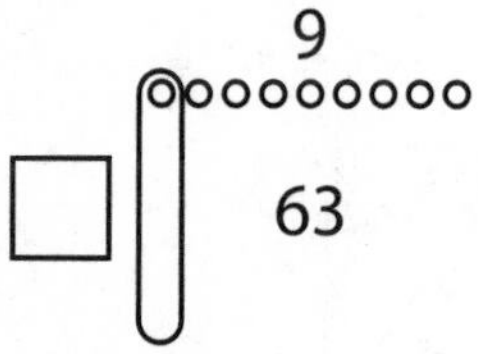
9
$\square$ 63

5. 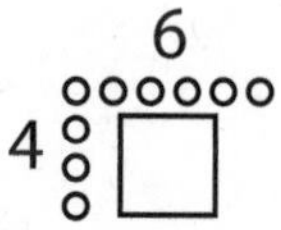
6 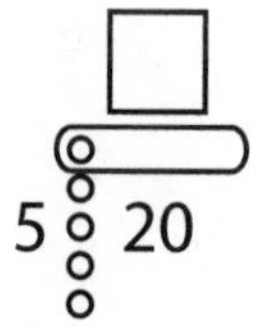
4 $\square$

6.
$\square$
5 20

7. 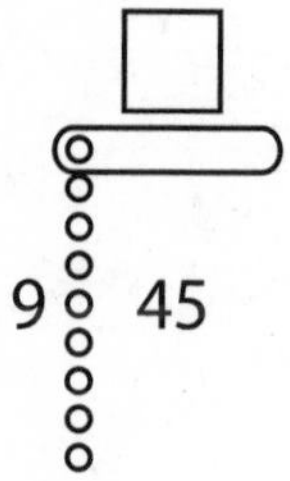
$\square$
9 45

8. 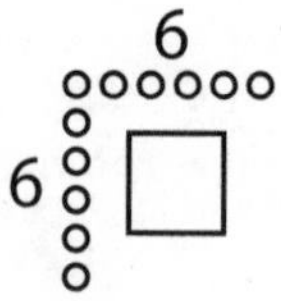
6
6 $\square$

9.
7
$\square$ 56

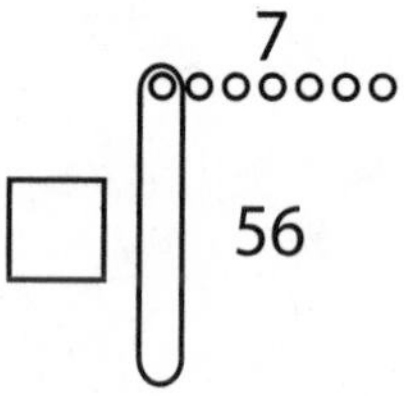

10. 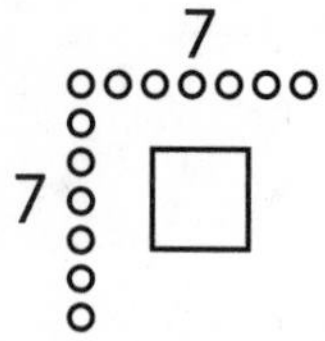
7
7 $\square$

11. 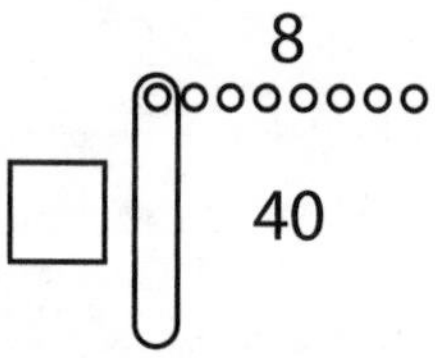
8
$\square$ 40

12. 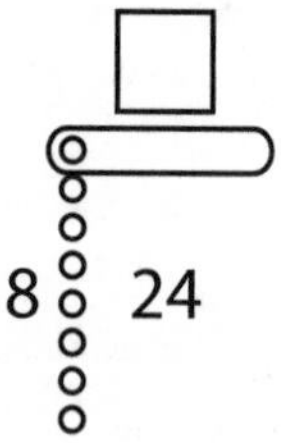
$\square$
8 24

13. 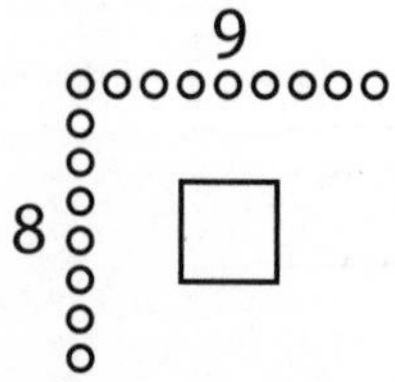
9
8 $\square$

14. 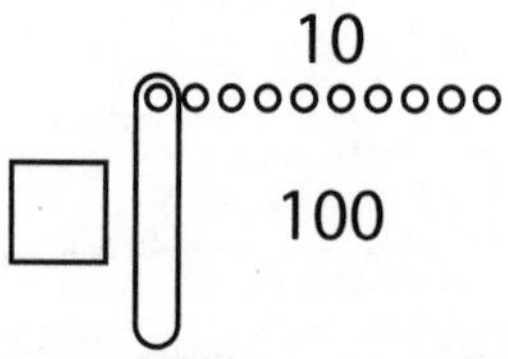
10
$\square$ 100

15. 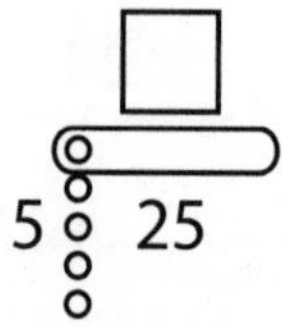
$\square$
5 25

Multiply and Divide with 8

Class Activity

▶ Sprints for 6s

As your teacher reads each multiplication or division, write your answer in the space provided.

× 6	÷ 6
a. _____	a. _____
b. _____	b. _____
c. _____	c. _____
d. _____	d. _____
e. _____	e. _____
f. _____	f. _____
g. _____	g. _____
h. _____	h. _____
i. _____	i. _____
j. _____	j. _____

▶Identify the Type and Choose the Operation

Solve. Then circle what type it is and what operation you use.

1. Students in Mr. Till's class hung their paintings on the wall. They made 6 rows, with 5 paintings in each row. How many paintings did the students hang?

_____

   Circle one: array   repeated groups   area
   Circle one: multiplication   division

2. Write your own problem that is the same type as problem 1. _____

   _____

   _____

3. There are 8 goldfish in each tank at the pet store. If there are 56 goldfish in all, how many tanks are there?

   _____

   Circle one: array   repeated groups   area
   Circle one: multiplication   division

4. Write your own problem that is the same type as problem 3. _____

   _____

   _____

5. Pierre built a rectangular pen for his rabbits. The pen is 4 feet wide and 6 feet long. What is the area of the pen? _____

   Circle one: array   repeated groups   area
   Circle one: multiplication   division

Write Multiplication and Division Word Problems

6. Write your own problem that is the same type as problem 5. _____

_____

_____

_____

Solve the word problem. Then circle what type it is and circle the operation you would use.

7. Paulo arranged 72 baseball cards in 9 rows and a certain number of columns. How many columns did he arrange the cards into? _____

Circle one: array   repeated groups   area
Circle one: multiplication   division

8. Write your own problem that is the same type as Problem 7. _____

_____

_____

_____

9. The store sells bottles of juice in six-packs. Mr. Lee bought 9 six-packs for a picnic. How many bottles did he buy? _____

Circle one: array   repeated groups   area
Circle one: multiplication   division

10. Write your own problem that is the same type as Problem 9. _____

_____

_____

_____

11. **On the Back** Write an area multiplication problem. Draw a Fast Array to solve it.

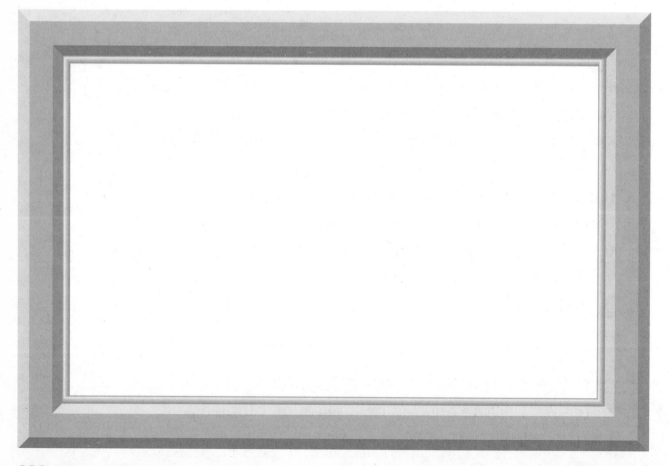

Write Word Problems

▶ Explore Patterns with 7s

What patterns do you see below?

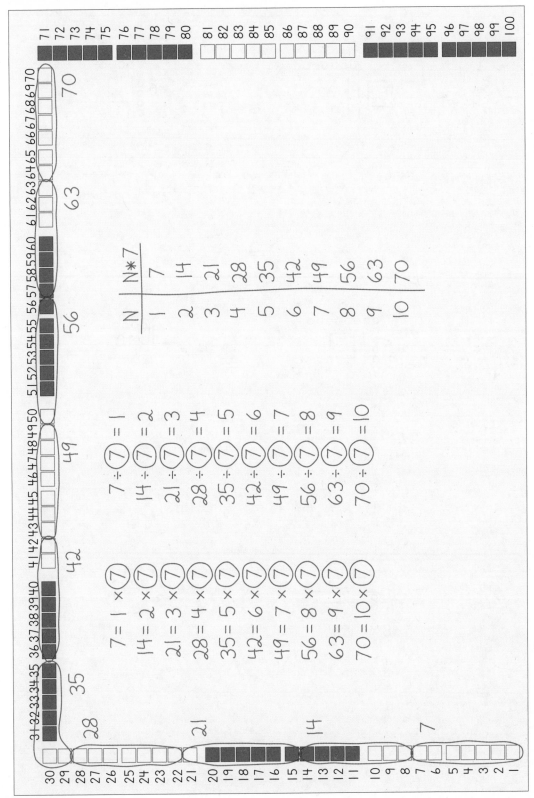

N	N*7
1	7
2	14
3	21
4	28
5	35
6	42
7	49
8	56
9	63
10	70

$7 \div \boxed{7} = 1$
$14 \div \boxed{7} = 2$
$21 \div \boxed{7} = 3$
$28 \div \boxed{7} = 4$
$35 \div \boxed{7} = 5$
$42 \div \boxed{7} = 6$
$49 \div \boxed{7} = 7$
$56 \div \boxed{7} = 8$
$63 \div \boxed{7} = 9$
$70 \div \boxed{7} = 10$

$7 = 1 \times \boxed{7}$
$14 = 2 \times \boxed{7}$
$21 = 3 \times \boxed{7}$
$28 = 4 \times \boxed{7}$
$35 = 5 \times \boxed{7}$
$42 = 6 \times \boxed{7}$
$49 = 7 \times \boxed{7}$
$56 = 8 \times \boxed{7}$
$63 = 9 \times \boxed{7}$
$70 = 10 \times \boxed{7}$

▶More Fast-Array Drawings

Fill in the missing number in each Fast-Array Drawing.

1. 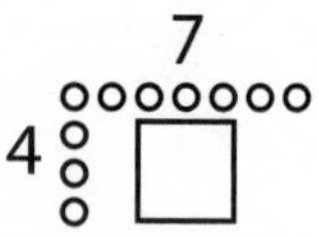   7
 4 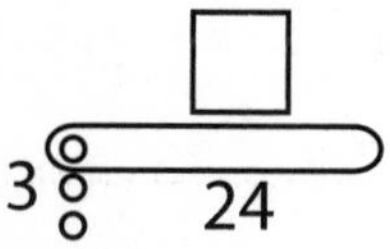 ⬚

2. 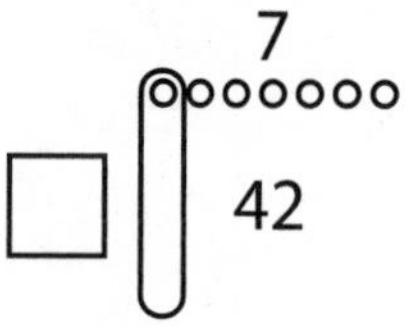   7
 ⬚ 42

3. 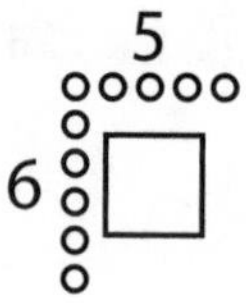   5
 6 ⬚

4. ⬚
 3 24

5. 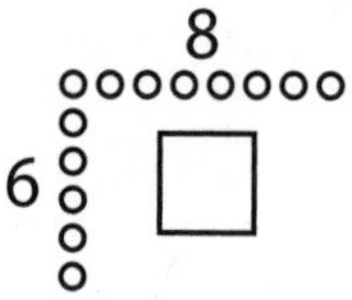   8
 6 ⬚

6. 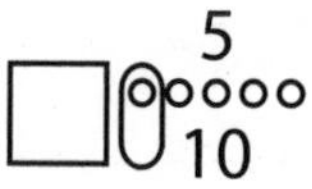 ⬚ 5
    10

7. 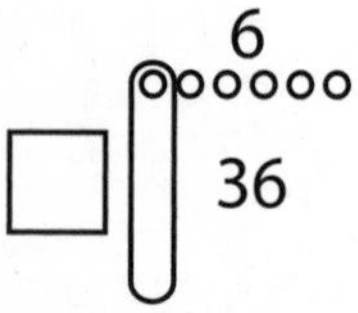 6
 ⬚ 36

8. ⬚
 8 56

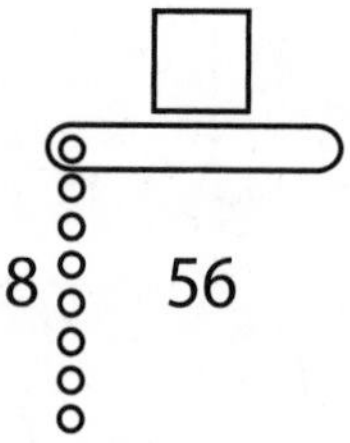

9. 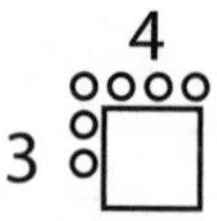   4
 3 ⬚

Multiply and Divide with 7

▶Dashes 5–8

Complete each multiplication and division Dash.
Check your answers on page 343.

Dash 5 2s, 5s, 9s, 10s Multiplications	Dash 6 2s, 5s, 9s, 10s Divisions	Dash 7 0s, 1s, 3s, 4s Multiplications	Dash 8 1s, 3s, 4s Divisions
a. 6 × 2 = ___	a. 18 / 2 = ___	a. 7 × 1 = ___	a. 2 / 1 = ___
b. 9 • 4 = ___	b. 25 ÷ 5 = ___	b. 0 • 6 = ___	b. 28 ÷ 4 = ___
c. 8 * 5 = ___	c. 70 / 10 = ___	c. 4 * 4 = ___	c. 3 / 3 = ___
d. 1 × 10 = ___	d. 54 ÷ 9 = ___	d. 7 × 3 = ___	d. 1 ÷ 1 = ___
e. 2 • 7 = ___	e. 50 / 5 = ___	e. 3 • 1 = ___	e. 40 / 4 = ___
f. 9 * 9 = ___	f. 81 ÷ 9 = ___	f. 4 * 7 = ___	f. 21 ÷ 3 = ___
g. 5 × 6 = ___	g. 8 / 2 = ___	g. 9 × 0 = ___	g. 5 / 1 = ___
h. 10 • 4 = ___	h. 90 ÷ 10 = ___	h. 1 • 1 = ___	h. 16 ÷ 4 = ___
i. 7 * 5 = ___	i. 35 / 5 = ___	i. 3 * 4 = ___	i. 15 / 3 = ___
j. 8 × 2 = ___	j. 27 / 9 = ___	j. 4 × 9 = ___	j. 6 / 1 = ___
k. 10 • 10 = ___	k. 2 ÷ 2 = ___	k. 8 • 1 = ___	k. 12 ÷ 4 = ___
l. 5 * 3 = ___	l. 36 / 9 = ___	l. 3 * 3 = ___	l. 27 / 3 = ___
m. 9 × 7 = ___	m. 45 ÷ 5 = ___	m. 0 × 4 = ___	m. 9 ÷ 1 = ___
n. 9 • 2 = ___	n. 14 / 2 = ___	n. 10 • 3 = ___	n. 8 / 4 = ___
o. 5 * 5 = ___	o. 20 ÷ 10 = ___	o. 6 * 4 = ___	o. 12 ÷ 3 = ___
p. 6 × 9 = ___	p. 9 / 9 = ___	p. 1 × 4 = ___	p. 3 / 1 = ___
q. 5 • 2 = ___	q. 20 ÷ 5 = ___	q. 3 • 6 = ___	q. 36 ÷ 4 = ___
r. 9 * 5 = ___	r. 45 ÷ 9 = ___	r. 4 * 8 = ___	r. 6 ÷ 3 = ___
s. 8 × 10 = ___	s. 5 / 5 = ___	s. 7 × 0 = ___	s. 4 / 1 = ___
t. 5 • 10 = ___	t. 4 ÷ 2 = ___	t. 5 • 3 = ___	t. 4 ÷ 4 = ___

▶Answers to Dashes 5–8

Use this sheet to check your answers to the Dashes on page 341.

Dash 5 2s, 5s, 9s, 10s Multiplications	Dash 6 2s, 5s, 9s, 10s Divisions	Dash 7 0s, 1s, 3s, 4s Multiplications	Dash 8 1s, 3s, 4s Divisions
a. $6 \times 2 = 12$	**a.** $18 / 2 = 9$	**a.** $7 \times 1 = 7$	**a.** $2 / 1 = 2$
b. $9 \cdot 4 = 36$	**b.** $25 \div 5 = 5$	**b.** $0 \cdot 6 = 0$	**b.** $28 \div 4 = 7$
c. $8 * 5 = 40$	**c.** $70 / 10 = 7$	**c.** $4 * 4 = 16$	**c.** $3 / 3 = 1$
d. $1 \times 10 = 10$	**d.** $54 \div 9 = 6$	**d.** $7 \times 3 = 21$	**d.** $1 \div 1 = 1$
e. $2 \cdot 7 = 14$	**e.** $50 / 5 = 10$	**e.** $3 \cdot 1 = 3$	**e.** $40 / 4 = 10$
f. $9 * 9 = 81$	**f.** $81 \div 9 = 9$	**f.** $4 * 7 = 28$	**f.** $21 \div 3 = 7$
g. $5 \times 6 = 30$	**g.** $8 / 2 = 4$	**g.** $9 \times 0 = 0$	**g.** $5 / 1 = 5$
h. $10 \cdot 4 = 40$	**h.** $90 \div 10 = 9$	**h.** $1 \cdot 1 = 1$	**h.** $16 \div 4 = 4$
i. $7 * 5 = 35$	**i.** $35 / 5 = 7$	**i.** $3 * 4 = 12$	**i.** $15 / 3 = 5$
j. $8 \times 2 = 16$	**j.** $27 / 9 = 3$	**j.** $4 \times 9 = 36$	**j.** $6 / 1 = 6$
k. $10 \cdot 10 = 100$	**k.** $2 \div 2 = 1$	**k.** $8 \cdot 1 = 8$	**k.** $12 \div 4 = 3$
l. $5 * 3 = 15$	**l.** $36 / 9 = 4$	**l.** $3 * 3 = 9$	**l.** $27 / 3 = 9$
m. $9 \times 7 = 63$	**m.** $45 \div 5 = 9$	**m.** $0 \times 4 = 0$	**m.** $9 \div 1 = 9$
n. $9 \cdot 2 = 18$	**n.** $14 / 2 = 7$	**n.** $10 \cdot 3 = 30$	**n.** $8 / 4 = 2$
o. $5 * 5 = 25$	**o.** $20 \div 10 = 2$	**o.** $6 * 4 = 24$	**o.** $12 \div 3 = 4$
p. $6 \times 9 = 54$	**p.** $9 / 9 = 1$	**p.** $1 \times 4 = 4$	**p.** $3 / 1 = 3$
q. $5 \cdot 2 = 10$	**q.** $20 \div 5 = 4$	**q.** $3 \cdot 6 = 18$	**q.** $36 \div 4 = 9$
r. $9 * 5 = 45$	**r.** $45 \div 9 = 5$	**r.** $4 * 8 = 32$	**r.** $6 \div 3 = 2$
s. $8 \times 10 = 80$	**s.** $5 / 5 = 1$	**s.** $7 \times 0 = 0$	**s.** $4 / 1 = 4$
t. $5 \cdot 10 = 50$	**t.** $4 \div 2 = 2$	**t.** $5 \cdot 3 = 15$	**t.** $4 \div 4 = 1$

Answers to Dashes 5–8

▶Comparison Statements

Use the sentences and pictures below to complete the comparison statements.

> Martina has 6 tennis balls. Chris has 2 tennis balls.

Martina

Chris

1. Martina has _____ more tennis balls than Chris.

2. Chris has _____ fewer tennis balls than Martina.

3. Martina has _____ times as many tennis balls as Chris.

4. Chris has _____ as many tennis balls as Martina.

Use the sentences and pictures below to complete the comparison statements.

> Bobby has 3 hockey pucks. Wayne has 15 hockey pucks.

Bobby

Wayne

5. Write a comparison statement about the hockey pucks using the word *more.*

_____

6. Write a comparison statement about the hockey pucks using the word *fewer.*

_____

7. Wayne has _____ times as many hockey pucks as Bobby.

8. Bobby has _____ as many hockey pucks as Wayne.

Use the sentences to write and complete the comparison statements. Make a math drawing to show the situation. Then do the exercise.

> Abby has 8 comic books. Pascal has 2 comic books.

9. Write a comparison statement about the comic books using the word *more.*

_____

10. Write a comparison statement about the comic books using the word *fewer.*

_____

11. Abby has _____ as many comic books as Pascal.

12. Pascal has _____ as many comic books as Abby.

> Kai has 3 paintbrushes. Neeta has 18 paintbrushes.

13. Write a comparison statement about the paintbrushes using the word *more.*

_____

14. Write a comparison statement about the paintbrushes using the word *fewer.*

_____

15. Kai has _____ as many paint brushes as Neeta.

16. Neeta has _____ as many paint brushes as Kai.

Comparison Word Problems

▶ Solve Comparison Word Problems

Solve each problem.

17. Teresa has 2 gerbils. Owen has 4 times as many gerbils as Teresa has. How many gerbils does Owen have? _____

18. Eduardo has 12 posters in his room. Manuela has $\frac{1}{3}$ as many posters as Eduardo. How many posters does Manuela have? _____

19. Bart rides his bike 8 blocks to school. Melinda rides 5 times as far as Bart does. How many blocks does Melinda ride? _____

20. Jay ate 14 grapes. Ti ate $\frac{1}{7}$ as many grapes as Jay. How many grapes did Ti eat? _____

21. Lucille has 7 books. Javier has 3 times as many books as Lucille. How many books does Javier have? _____

22. Cho's father is 48 years old. Cho is $\frac{1}{6}$ as old as her father. How old is Cho? _____

Going Further

► Use a Venn Diagram to Show Relationships

A **multiple** is the product of a number and any other number.

For example, 6, 12, 18, and 24 are multiples of 6.

Find the rule that was used for sorting the data. Then label the Venn diagram.

1.

Multiples of ___ and ___

Multiples of _____

Multiples of _____

16 24 9
14
8 18 21
12
22
20 6
4 15 3
10 2

2.

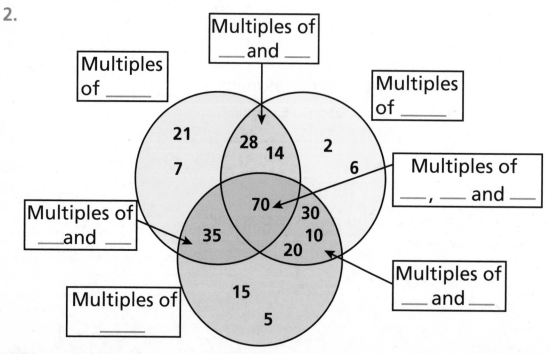

Multiples of ___ and ___

Multiples of _____

Multiples of _____

Multiples of ___, ___ and ___

Multiples of ___ and ___

Multiples of _____

Multiples of ___ and ___

21 28 14 2
7 6
70 30
35 10
20
15
5

Comparison Word Problems

▶**Use Comparison Bars**

**Draw comparison bars to help you solve
each problem.**

> Jadzia's dog Roscoe competes in dog shows. He has won 42 blue ribbons
> and 6 red ribbons.

1. Roscoe has won _____ as many blue ribbons as red ribbons.

2. Roscoe has won _____ as many red ribbons as blue ribbons.

> Daphne is 7 years old. Her grandfather is 56 years old.

3. Daphne is _____ as old as her grandfather.

4. Daphne's grandfather is _____ as old as Daphne.

> Beatrice has 48 dolls. Cathy has 8 dolls.

5. Beatrice has _____ as many dolls as Cathy.

6. Cathy has _____ as many dolls as Beatrice.

Class Activity

Make a drawing to help you solve each problem.

7. Last month Elle earned $8 helping her aunt with chores. This month she earned 4 times as much by doing yard work for her neighbor. How much did Elle earn this month?

_____

8. Minh picked 48 peaches. His little brother Bao picked $\frac{1}{8}$ as many peaches as Minh. How many peaches did Bao pick?

_____

9. Carlos has 49 music CDs. His cousin Luisa has $\frac{1}{7}$ as many music CDs as Carlos. How many CDs does Luisa have?

_____

10. Rose rode the roller coaster 6 times. Leila rode the roller coaster 3 times as many times as Rose. How many times did Leila ride the roller coaster?

_____

▶Use a Bar Graph to Compare

Shannon collects souvenir T-shirts from the places she visits. She made this bar graph to show the colors of the shirts in her collection.

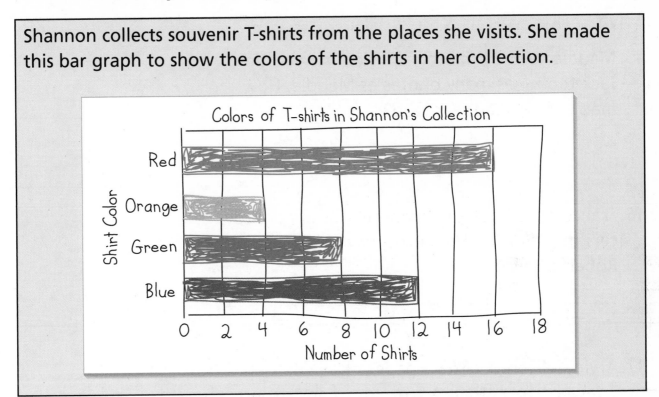

Colors of T-shirts in Shannon's Collection

11. Shannon has _____ as many red shirts as green shirts.

Shannon has _____ as many green shirts as red shirts.

12. Shannon has _____ as many red shirts as orange shirts.

Shannon has _____ as many orange shirts as red shirts.

13. Shannon has _____ as many blue shirts as orange shirts.

Shannon has _____ as many orange shirts as blue shirts.

14. Shannon has _____ as many orange shirts as green shirts.

Shannon has _____ as many green shirts as orange shirts.

Class Activity

▶ Solve Comparison Problems

Solve.

15. Maddie took 21 photographs on her vacation. Jack took $\frac{1}{3}$ as many photos as Maddie. How many photos did Jack take?

_____

16. Franco has 18 toy cars. Roberto has 6 more toy cars than Franco. How many toy cars does Roberto have?

_____

17. Arvin delivered 42 newspapers. Kelly delivered 7 fewer papers than Arvin. How many papers did Kelly deliver?

_____

18. Jasmine's dog weighs 8 pounds. Shaunda's dog weighs 5 times as much as Jasmine's dog. How much does Shaunda's dog weigh?

_____

19. Charles is $\frac{1}{4}$ as old as his father. His father is 36 years old. How old is Charles?

_____

More Comparison Word Problems

▶Sprints for 8s

As your teacher reads each multiplication or division, write your answer in the space provided.

× 8	÷ 8
a. _____	a. _____
b. _____	b. _____
c. _____	c. _____
d. _____	d. _____
e. _____	e. _____
f. _____	f. _____
g. _____	g. _____
h. _____	h. _____
i. _____	i. _____
j. _____	j. _____

Square Numbers

▶Check Sheet 9: 7s and Squares

7s Multiplications	7s Divisions	Squares Multiplications	Squares Divisions
4 × 7 = 28	14 / 7 = 2	8 × 8 = 64	81 / 9 = 9
7 • 2 = 14	28 ÷ 7 = 4	10 • 10 = 100	4 ÷ 2 = 2
7 * 8 = 56	70 / 7 = 10	3 * 3 = 9	25 / 5 = 5
7 × 7 = 49	56 ÷ 7 = 8	9 × 9 = 81	1 ÷ 1 = 1
7 • 1 = 7	42 / 7 = 6	4 • 4 = 16	100 / 10 = 10
7 * 10 = 70	63 ÷ 7 = 9	7 * 7 = 49	36 ÷ 6 = 6
3 × 7 = 21	7 / 7 = 1	5 × 5 = 25	49 / 7 = 7
7 • 6 = 42	49 ÷ 7 = 7	6 • 6 = 36	9 ÷ 3 = 3
5 * 7 = 35	21 / 7 = 3	1 * 1 = 1	64 / 8 = 8
7 × 9 = 63	35 / 7 = 5	5 * 5 = 25	16 / 4 = 4
7 • 4 = 28	7 ÷ 7 = 1	1 • 1 = 1	100 ÷ 10 = 10
9 * 7 = 63	63 / 7 = 9	3 • 3 = 9	49 / 7 = 7
2 × 7 = 14	14 ÷ 7 = 2	10 × 10 = 100	1 ÷ 1 = 1
7 • 5 = 35	70 / 7 = 10	4 × 4 = 16	9 / 3 = 3
8 * 7 = 56	21 ÷ 7 = 3	9 * 9 = 81	64 ÷ 8 = 8
7 × 3 = 21	49 / 7 = 7	2 × 2 = 4	4 / 2 = 2
6 • 7 = 42	28 ÷ 7 = 4	6 * 6 = 36	81 ÷ 9 = 9
10 * 7 = 70	56 ÷ 7 = 8	7 × 7 = 49	16 ÷ 4 = 4
1 × 7 = 7	35 / 7 = 5	5 • 5 = 25	25 / 5 = 5
7 • 7 = 49	42 ÷ 7 = 6	8 • 8 = 64	36 ÷ 6 = 6

Check Sheet 9: 7s and Squares

Class Activity

▶Explore Square Numbers

Write an equation to show the area of each large square.

1. 1 × 1 = 1   2. _____   3. _____   4. _____

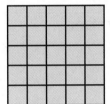

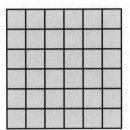

5. _____   6. _____

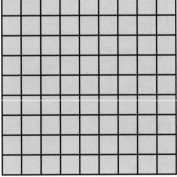   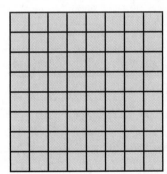

7. _____   8. _____

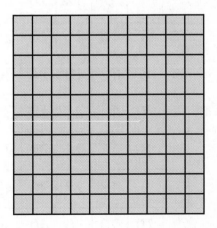

9. _____   10. _____

Class Activity

Vocabulary

square numbers

▶Look for Patterns

11. List the products in exercises 1–10 in order. Discuss the patterns you see with your class.

_____

The numbers you listed in exercise 11 are called **square numbers** because they are the areas of squares with whole-number lengths of sides. A square number is the product of a whole number and itself. So, if n is a whole number, $n \times n$ is a square number.

▶Patterns on the Multiplication Table

12. In the table below, circle the products that are square numbers. Discuss the patterns you see with your class.

X	1	2	3	4	5	6	7	8	9	10
1	1	2	3	4	5	6	7	8	9	10
2	2	4	6	8	10	12	14	16	18	20
3	3	6	9	12	15	18	21	24	27	30
4	4	8	12	16	20	24	28	32	36	40
5	5	10	15	20	25	30	35	40	45	50
6	6	12	18	24	30	36	42	48	54	60
7	7	14	21	28	35	42	49	56	63	70
8	8	16	24	32	40	48	56	64	72	80
9	9	18	27	36	45	54	63	72	81	90
10	10	20	30	40	50	60	70	80	90	100

Square Numbers

▶Dashes 9–12

Complete each Dash. Check your answers on page 361.

Dash 9 2s, 3s, 4s, 5s, 9s Multiplications	Dash 10 2s, 3s, 4s, 5s, 9s Divisions	Dash 11 6s, 7s, 8s Multiplications	Dash 12 6s, 7s, 8s Divisions
a. $6 \times 3 =$ ___	**a.** $16 / 4 =$ ___	**a.** $7 \times 7 =$ ___	**a.** $21 / 7 =$ ___
b. $4 \cdot 7 =$ ___	**b.** $54 \div 9 =$ ___	**b.** $6 \cdot 3 =$ ___	**b.** $16 \div 8 =$ ___
c. $8 * 2 =$ ___	**c.** $4 / 2 =$ ___	**c.** $8 * 6 =$ ___	**c.** $54 / 6 =$ ___
d. $5 \times 3 =$ ___	**d.** $28 \div 4 =$ ___	**d.** $6 \times 6 =$ ___	**d.** $48 \div 8 =$ ___
e. $4 \cdot 4 =$ ___	**e.** $25 / 5 =$ ___	**e.** $7 \cdot 6 =$ ___	**e.** $64 / 8 =$ ___
f. $3 * 9 =$ ___	**f.** $21 \div 3 =$ ___	**f.** $4 * 7 =$ ___	**f.** $42 \div 6 =$ ___
g. $9 \times 9 =$ ___	**g.** $40 / 4 =$ ___	**g.** $9 \times 7 =$ ___	**g.** $56 / 7 =$ ___
h. $8 \cdot 9 =$ ___	**h.** $81 \div 9 =$ ___	**h.** $8 \cdot 6 =$ ___	**h.** $72 \div 8 =$ ___
i. $6 * 4 =$ ___	**i.** $35 / 5 =$ ___	**i.** $6 * 4 =$ ___	**i.** $18 / 6 =$ ___
j. $3 \times 3 =$ ___	**j.** $12 / 3 =$ ___	**j.** $8 \times 8 =$ ___	**j.** $28 / 7 =$ ___
k. $2 \cdot 7 =$ ___	**k.** $2 \div 2 =$ ___	**k.** $7 \cdot 3 =$ ___	**k.** $56 \div 8 =$ ___
l. $8 * 5 =$ ___	**l.** $63 / 9 =$ ___	**l.** $8 * 7 =$ ___	**l.** $30 / 6 =$ ___
m. $4 \times 9 =$ ___	**m.** $36 \div 4 =$ ___	**m.** $6 \times 7 =$ ___	**m.** $63 \div 7 =$ ___
n. $9 \cdot 5 =$ ___	**n.** $18 / 2 =$ ___	**n.** $3 \cdot 6 =$ ___	**n.** $32 / 8 =$ ___
o. $7 * 3 =$ ___	**o.** $9 \div 3 =$ ___	**o.** $2 * 7 =$ ___	**o.** $48 \div 6 =$ ___
p. $2 \times 2 =$ ___	**p.** $36 / 9 =$ ___	**p.** $9 \times 8 =$ ___	**p.** $49 / 7 =$ ___
q. $8 \cdot 4 =$ ___	**q.** $40 \div 5 =$ ___	**q.** $5 \cdot 6 =$ ___	**q.** $36 \div 6 =$ ___
r. $5 * 1 =$ ___	**r.** $12 \div 4 =$ ___	**r.** $7 * 8 =$ ___	**r.** $24 \div 8 =$ ___
s. $5 \times 5 =$ ___	**s.** $9 / 9 =$ ___	**s.** $3 \times 7 =$ ___	**s.** $42 / 7 =$ ___
t. $6 \cdot 9 =$ ___	**t.** $14 \div 2 =$ ___	**t.** $9 \cdot 6 =$ ___	**t.** $24 \div 6 =$ ___

Dashes 9–12

►Answers to Dashes 9–12

Use this sheet to check your answers to the dashes on page 359.

Dash 9 2s, 3s, 4s, 5s, 9s Multiplications	Dash 10 2s, 3s, 4s, 5s, 9s Divisions	Dash 11 6s, 7s, 8s Multiplications	Dash 12 6s, 7s, 8s Divisions
a. $6 \times 3 = 18$	a. $16 / 4 = 4$	a. $7 \times 7 = 49$	a. $21 / 7 = 3$
b. $4 \cdot 7 = 28$	b. $54 \div 9 = 6$	b. $6 \cdot 3 = 18$	b. $16 \div 8 = 2$
c. $8 * 2 = 16$	c. $4 / 2 = 2$	c. $8 * 6 = 48$	c. $54 / 6 = 9$
d. $5 \times 3 = 15$	d. $28 \div 4 = 7$	d. $6 \times 6 = 36$	d. $48 \div 8 = 6$
e. $4 \cdot 4 = 16$	e. $25 / 5 = 5$	e. $7 \cdot 6 = 42$	e. $64 / 8 = 8$
f. $3 * 9 = 27$	f. $21 \div 3 = 7$	f. $4 * 7 = 28$	f. $42 \div 6 = 7$
g. $9 \times 9 = 81$	g. $40 / 4 = 10$	g. $9 \times 7 = 63$	g. $56 / 7 = 8$
h. $8 \cdot 9 = 72$	h. $81 \div 9 = 9$	h. $6 \cdot 9 = 54$	h. $72 \div 8 = 9$
i. $6 * 4 = 24$	i. $35 / 5 = 7$	i. $6 * 4 = 24$	i. $18 / 6 = 3$
j. $3 \times 3 = 9$	j. $12 / 3 = 4$	j. $8 \times 8 = 64$	j. $28 / 7 = 4$
k. $2 \cdot 7 = 14$	k. $2 \div 2 = 1$	k. $7 \cdot 3 = 21$	k. $56 \div 8 = 7$
l. $8 * 5 = 40$	l. $63 / 9 = 7$	l. $8 * 7 = 56$	l. $30 / 6 = 5$
m. $4 \times 9 = 36$	m. $36 \div 4 = 9$	m. $6 \times 7 = 42$	m. $63 \div 7 = 9$
n. $9 \cdot 5 = 45$	n. $18 / 2 = 9$	n. $3 \cdot 6 = 18$	n. $32 / 8 = 4$
o. $7 * 3 = 21$	o. $9 \div 3 = 3$	o. $2 * 7 = 14$	o. $48 \div 6 = 8$
p. $2 \times 2 = 4$	p. $36 / 9 = 4$	p. $9 \times 8 = 72$	p. $49 / 7 = 7$
q. $8 \cdot 4 = 32$	q. $40 \div 5 = 8$	q. $5 \cdot 6 = 30$	q. $36 \div 6 = 6$
r. $5 * 1 = 5$	r. $12 \div 4 = 3$	r. $7 * 8 = 56$	r. $24 \div 8 = 3$
s. $5 \times 5 = 25$	s. $9 / 9 = 1$	s. $3 \times 7 = 21$	s. $42 / 7 = 6$
t. $6 \cdot 9 = 54$	t. $14 \div 2 = 7$	t. $9 \cdot 6 = 54$	t. $24 \div 6 = 4$

Answers to Dashes 9–12

▶**Check Sheet 10: 6s, 7s, and 8s**

6s, 7s, and 8s Multiplications	6s, 7s, and 8s Multiplications	6s, 7s, and 8s Divisions	6s, 7s, and 8s Divisions
$1 \times 6 = 6$	$0 \times 8 = 0$	$24 / 6 = 4$	$54 / 6 = 9$
$6 \cdot 7 = 42$	$6 \cdot 2 = 12$	$21 \div 7 = 3$	$24 \div 8 = 3$
$3 * 8 = 24$	$4 * 7 = 28$	$16 / 8 = 2$	$14 / 7 = 2$
$6 \times 2 = 12$	$8 \times 3 = 24$	$24 \div 8 = 3$	$32 \div 8 = 4$
$7 \cdot 5 = 35$	$5 \cdot 6 = 30$	$14 / 7 = 2$	$18 / 6 = 3$
$8 * 4 = 32$	$7 * 2 = 14$	$30 \div 6 = 5$	$56 \div 7 = 8$
$6 \times 6 = 36$	$3 \times 8 = 24$	$35 / 7 = 5$	$40 / 8 = 5$
$8 \cdot 7 = 56$	$6 \cdot 4 = 24$	$24 \div 8 = 3$	$35 \div 7 = 5$
$9 * 8 = 72$	$0 * 7 = 0$	$18 / 6 = 3$	$12 / 6 = 2$
$6 \times 10 = 60$	$8 \times 1 = 8$	$12 / 6 = 2$	$21 / 7 = 3$
$7 \cdot 1 = 7$	$8 \cdot 6 = 48$	$42 \div 7 = 6$	$16 \div 8 = 2$
$8 * 3 = 24$	$7 * 9 = 63$	$56 / 8 = 7$	$42 / 6 = 7$
$5 \times 6 = 30$	$10 \times 8 = 80$	$49 \div 7 = 7$	$80 \div 8 = 10$
$4 \cdot 7 = 28$	$6 \cdot 10 = 60$	$16 / 8 = 2$	$36 / 6 = 6$
$2 * 8 = 16$	$3 * 7 = 21$	$60 \div 6 = 10$	$7 \div 7 = 1$
$7 \times 7 = 49$	$8 \times 4 = 32$	$54 / 6 = 9$	$64 / 8 = 8$
$7 \cdot 6 = 42$	$6 \cdot 5 = 30$	$8 \div 8 = 1$	$24 \div 6 = 4$
$8 * 8 = 64$	$7 * 4 = 28$	$28 \div 7 = 4$	$21 \div 7 = 3$
$9 \times 6 = 54$	$8 \times 8 = 64$	$72 / 8 = 9$	$49 / 7 = 7$
$10 \cdot 7 = 70$	$6 \cdot 9 = 54$	$56 \div 7 = 8$	$24 \div 8 = 3$

Name _____ **Date** _____

►Check Sheet 11: 0s–10s

0s–10s Multiplications	0s–10s Multiplications	0s–10s Divisions	0s–10s Divisions
9 × 0 = 0	9 × 4 = 36	9 / 1 = 9	90 / 10 = 9
1 • 1 = 1	5 • 9 = 45	12 ÷ 3 = 4	64 ÷ 8 = 8
2 * 3 = 6	6 * 10 = 60	14 / 2 = 7	15 / 5 = 3
1 × 3 = 3	7 × 3 = 21	20 ÷ 4 = 5	12 ÷ 6 = 2
5 • 4 = 20	5 • 3 = 15	10 / 5 = 2	14 / 7 = 2
7 * 5 = 35	4 * 1 = 4	48 ÷ 8 = 6	45 ÷ 9 = 5
6 × 9 = 54	7 × 5 = 35	35 / 7 = 5	8 / 1 = 8
0 • 7 = 0	6 • 3 = 18	60 ÷ 6 = 10	30 ÷ 3 = 10
1 * 8 = 8	8 * 7 = 56	81 / 9 = 9	16 / 4 = 4
9 × 8 = 72	5 × 8 = 40	20 / 10 = 2	8 / 2 = 4
2 • 10 = 20	9 • 9 = 81	16 ÷ 2 = 8	80 ÷ 10 = 8
0 * 7 = 0	9 * 10 = 90	30 / 5 = 6	36 / 4 = 9
4 × 1 = 4	0 × 0 = 0	49 ÷ 7 = 7	25 ÷ 5 = 5
2 • 4 = 8	1 • 0 = 0	60 / 6 = 10	42 / 7 = 6
10 * 3 = 30	1 * 6 = 6	30 ÷ 3 = 10	36 ÷ 6 = 6
8 × 4 = 32	7 × 2 = 14	8 / 1 = 8	90 / 9 = 10
5 • 8 = 40	6 • 3 = 18	16 ÷ 4 = 4	24 ÷ 8 = 3
4 * 6 = 24	4 * 5 = 20	16 ÷ 8 = 2	6 ÷ 2 = 3
7 × 0 = 0	6 × 6 = 36	40 / 10 = 4	9 / 3 = 3
1 • 8 = 8	10 • 7 = 70	36 ÷ 9 = 4	1 ÷ 1 = 1

Class Activity

▶Play *High Card Wins*

Read the rules for playing *High Card Wins*. Then play the game with your partner.

Rules for *High Card Wins*

Number of players: 2
What you will need: 1 set of multiplication Strategy Cards *or* 1 set of division Strategy Cards

1. Shuffle the cards. Then deal all the cards evenly between the two players.

2. Players put their stacks in front of them, problem side up.

3. Each player takes the top card from his or her stack and puts it problem side up in the center of the table.

4. Each player says the answer (product or quotient) and then turns the card over to check. Then do one of the following:
   - If one player says the wrong answer, the other player takes both cards and puts them at the bottom of his or her pile.
   - If both players say the wrong answer, both players take back their cards and put them at the bottom of their piles.
   - If both players say the correct answer, the player with the higher product takes both cards and puts them at the bottom of his or her pile. If the answers are the same, the players set the cards aside and play another round. The winner of the next round takes all the cards.

5. When time is up, the player with the most cards wins.

Play *High Card Wins*

Going Further

►Multiply and Divide with 11 and 12

What patterns do you see?

× 11	÷ 11
1 × 11 = 11	11 ÷ 11 = 1
2 × 11 = 22	22 ÷ 11 = 2
3 × 11 = 33	33 ÷ 11 = 3
4 × 11 = 44	44 ÷ 11 = 4
5 × 11 = 55	55 ÷ 11 = 5
6 × 11 = 66	66 ÷ 11 = 6
7 × 11 = 77	77 ÷ 11 = 7
8 × 11 = 88	88 ÷ 11 = 8
9 × 11 = 99	99 ÷ 11 = 9
10 × 11 = 110	110 ÷ 11 = 10

× 12	÷ 12
1 × 12 = 12	12 ÷ 12 = 1
2 × 12 = 24	24 ÷ 12 = 2
3 × 12 = 36	36 ÷ 12 = 3
4 × 12 = 48	48 ÷ 12 = 4
5 × 12 = 60	60 ÷ 12 = 5
6 × 12 = 72	72 ÷ 12 = 6
7 × 12 = 84	84 ÷ 12 = 7
8 × 12 = 96	96 ÷ 12 = 8
9 × 12 = 108	108 ÷ 12 = 9
10 × 12 = 120	120 ÷ 12 = 10

►11s and 12s Multiplication Table

Complete the multiplication table.

You can use multiplications you know to help.

$8 \times 12 = 8 \times (5 + 7)$

$= (8 \times 5) + (8 \times 7)$

$= 40 + 56$

$= 96$

or

$8 \times 12 = 8 \times (10 + 2)$

$= (8 \times 10) + (8 \times 2)$

$= 80 + 16$

$= 96$

X	1	2	3	4	5	6	7	8	9	10	11	12
1	1	2	3	4	5	6	7	8	9	10		
2	2	4	6	8	10	12	14	16	18	20		
3	3	6	9	12	15	18	21	24	27	30		
4	4	8	12	16	20	24	28	32	36	40		
5	5	10	15	20	25	30	35	40	45	50		
6	6	12	18	24	30	36	42	48	54	60		
7	7	14	21	28	35	42	49	56	63	70		
8	8	16	24	32	40	48	56	64	72	80		
9	9	18	27	36	45	54	63	72	81	90		
10	10	20	30	40	50	60	70	80	90	100		
11												
12												

Practice with 6s, 7s, and 8s

▶ Sprints for 7s

As your teacher reads each multiplication or division, write your answer in the space provided.

× 7	÷ 7
a. _____	a. _____
b. _____	b. _____
c. _____	c. _____
d. _____	d. _____
e. _____	e. _____
f. _____	f. _____
g. _____	g. _____
h. _____	h. _____
i. _____	i. _____
j. _____	j. _____

▶Choose the Operation

Solve.

1. Ernie helped his mother work in the yard for 3 days. He earned $6 each day. How much did he earn in all?

   _____

2. Ernie helped his mother work in the yard for 3 days. He earned $6 the first day, $5 the second day, and $7 the third day. How much did he earn in all?

   _____

3. Troy had $18. He gave $6 to each of his brothers and had no money left. How many brothers does Troy have?

   _____

4. Troy gave $18 to his brothers. He gave $4 to Raj, $7 to Darnell, and the rest to Jai. How much money did Jai get?

   _____

5. Jinja has 4 cousins. Grant has 7 more cousins than Jinja. How many cousins does Grant have?

   _____

6. Jinja has 4 cousins. Grant has 7 times as many cousins as Jinja. How many cousins does Grant have?

   _____

7. Camille has 15 fewer books than Jane has. Camille has 12 books. How many does Jane have?

   _____

8. Camille has half as many books as Jane has. Camille has 15 books. How many books does Jane have?

   _____

▶Write an Equation

Write an equation to solve each problem.

Show your work.

9. Luke had a $5 bill. He spent $3.73 on a sandwich. How much change did he get?

_____

10. Ramona is putting tiles on the kitchen floor. She will lay 8 rows of tiles, with 7 tiles in each row. How many tiles will Ramona use?

_____

11. Josh earned As on 6 tests last year. Jenna earned As on 6 times as many tests. How many As did Jenna earn?

_____

12. Sophie bought a stuffed animal for $2.76 and a board game for $6.99. How much money did Sophie spend?

_____

13. The Duarte family has 15 pets. Each of the 3 Duarte children care for the same number of pets. How many pets does each child care for?

_____

14. Ahmed spent $9 on CD. Zal paid $6 more for the same CD at a different store. How much did Zal spend on the CD?

_____

► Write the Question

Write a question for the given information and solve.

15. Anna read 383 pages this month. Chris read 416 pages.

Question: _____

Solution: _____

16. Marisol had 128 beads in her jewelry box. She gave away 56 of them.

Question: _____

Solution: _____

17. Louis put 72 marbles in 8 bags. He put the same number of marbles in each bag.

Question: _____

Solution: _____

18. Geoff planted 4 pots of seeds. He planted 6 seeds in each pot.

Question: _____

Solution: _____

19. Last week, Marly read for 2 hours. Jamal read for 7 times as many hours as Marly did.

Question: _____

Solution: _____

▶Write the Problem

Write a problem that can be solved using the given equation.

20. $9 \times 6 = \square$ **Solution:** _____

_____

_____

_____

21. $324 - 176 = \square$ **Solution:** _____

_____

_____

_____

22. $56 \div 7 = \square$ **Solution:** _____

_____

_____

_____

23. $459 + 635 = \square$ **Solution:** _____

_____

_____

_____

24. On the Back Choose an operation. Write a word problem that involves that operation. Write an equation to solve your word problem.

Solve Mixed Word Problems

▶Use Order of Operations

> This exercise involves subtraction and multiplication:
>
> 10 − 3 × 2

1. What do you get if you subtract first and then multiply? _____

2. What do you get if you multiply first and then subtract? _____

To make sure everyone has the same answer to problems like this one, people have decided that multiplication and division will be done *before* addition and subtraction. The answer you found in question 2 is correct.

If you want to tell people to add or subtract first, you must use parentheses. Parentheses mean "Do this first." For example, if you want people to subtract first in the exercise above, write it like this:

(10 − 3) × 2

Find the answer.

3. 5 + 4 × 2 = _____

4. (9 − 3) × 6 = _____

5. 8 ÷ 2 + 2 = _____

6. 6 × (8 − 1) = _____

Rewrite each statement, using symbols and numbers instead of words.

7. Add 4 and 3, and multiply the total by 8. _____

8. Multiply 3 by 8, and add 4 to the total. _____

Class Activity

▶Multi-Step Problems

Solve each problem.

Show your work.

9. A roller coaster has 7 cars. Each car has 4 seats. If there were 3 empty seats, how many people were on the roller coaster?

_____

10. Each week, Marta earns $10 babysitting. She always spends $3 and saves the rest. How much does she save in 8 weeks?

_____

11. Abu bought 6 packs of stickers. Each pack had 8 stickers. Then Abu's friend gave him 10 more stickers. How many stickers does Abu have now?

_____

12. Zoe made some snacks. She put 4 apple slices and 2 melon slices on each plate. She prepared 5 plates. How many slices of fruit did Zoe use in all?

_____

13. Kyle ordered 8 pizzas for his party. Each pizza was cut into 8 slices. 48 of the slices were plain cheese, and the rest had mushrooms. How many slices of pizza had mushrooms?

_____

14. Nadia counted 77 birds on the pond. 53 were ducks, and the rest were geese. Then the geese flew away in 4 equal flocks. How many geese were in each flock?

_____

Name _____ **Date** _____

Class Activity

▶More Multi-Step Problems

Solve each problem. Draw a picture if you need to. | *Show your work.*

15. Lakesha has filled two pages of her stamp book. Both pages have 5 rows of stamps. On one page, there are 5 stamps in each row. On the opposite page, there are 3 stamps in each row. How many stamps are on the two pages?

   _____

16. Kagami baked 86 blueberry muffins. Her sisters ate 5 of them. Kagami divided the remaining muffins equally among 9 plates. How many muffins did she put on each plate?

   _____

17. Lucia had 42 plums. Jorge had 12 more plums than Lucia. Jorge divided his plums equally among 6 people. How many plums did each person get?

   _____

18. Dana arranged her books on 5 shelves, with 8 books on each shelf. Hassan arranged his books on 4 shelves, with 9 books on each shelf. Who has more books? How many more?

   _____

19. Juana has 21 shirts. Leslie had one third as many shirts as Juana, but then she bought 4 more. How many shirts does Leslie have now?

   _____

Name _____ **Date** _____

Going Further

▶ Multiply 2- and 3-Digit Numbers by 1-Digit Numbers

There are 26 cars in the water ride at Smiley Park. Each car can fit 7 people. How many people in all can fit in the cars of the water ride?

$26 \times 7 = \square$

The Expanded Notation Method

$$
\begin{array}{r}
7 = \quad + 7 \\
\times\ 26 = 20 + 6 \\
\hline
20 \times 7 = \quad 140 \\
6 \times 7 = \quad + 42 \\
\hline
182
\end{array}
$$

You can multiply by the ones first.

$$
\begin{array}{r}
346 = 300 + 40 + 6 \\
\times\ 2 = \qquad\qquad 2 \\
\hline
2 \times 300 = \quad 600 \\
2 \times\ 40 = \quad\ 80 \\
2 \times\ \ 6 = \quad + 12 \\
\hline
692
\end{array}
$$

The Rectangle Sections Method

$$
\begin{array}{r}
7 \\
7 \\
\times\ 20 \\
\hline
140 \\
\end{array}
\qquad
\begin{array}{r}
140 \\
+\ 42 \\
\hline
182
\end{array}
$$

$$
\begin{array}{r}
7 \\
\times\ 6 \\
\hline
42
\end{array}
$$

$$
300 + 40 + 6
$$

300	40	6
2 × 2	× 2	× 2
600	80	12

$$
\begin{array}{r}
600 \\
80 \\
+\ 12 \\
\hline
692
\end{array}
$$

Multiply.

1. $\begin{array}{r} 14 \\ \times\ 4 \\ \hline \end{array}$

2. $\begin{array}{r} 78 \\ \times\ 8 \\ \hline \end{array}$

3. $\begin{array}{r} 86 \\ \times\ 6 \\ \hline \end{array}$

4. $\begin{array}{r} 325 \\ \times\ \ 3 \\ \hline \end{array}$

5. $\begin{array}{r} 497 \\ \times\ \ 2 \\ \hline \end{array}$

6. $\begin{array}{r} 637 \\ \times\ \ 5 \\ \hline \end{array}$

Solve Multi-Step Word Problems

Name _____   Date _____

▶Dashes 13–16

Complete each Dash. Check your answers on page 381.

Dash 13 2s, 3s, 4s, 5s, 9s Multiplications	Dash 14 2s, 3s, 4s, 5s, 9s Divisions	Dash 15 6s, 7s, 8s Multiplications	Dash 16 6s, 7s, 8s Divisions
a. $7 \times 4 =$ ___	a. $9 / 3 =$ ___	a. $8 \times 8 =$ ___	a. $72 / 8 =$ ___
b. $5 \cdot 5 =$ ___	b. $45 \div 9 =$ ___	b. $9 \cdot 6 =$ ___	b. $49 \div 7 =$ ___
c. $2 * 9 =$ ___	c. $81 / 9 =$ ___	c. $7 * 6 =$ ___	c. $35 / 7 =$ ___
d. $3 \times 8 =$ ___	d. $36 \div 4 =$ ___	d. $5 \times 7 =$ ___	d. $64 \div 8 =$ ___
e. $4 \cdot 4 =$ ___	e. $20 / 5 =$ ___	e. $3 \cdot 8 =$ ___	e. $14 / 7 =$ ___
f. $5 * 9 =$ ___	f. $16 \div 4 =$ ___	f. $8 * 6 =$ ___	f. $18 \div 6 =$ ___
g. $6 \times 3 =$ ___	g. $12 / 2 =$ ___	g. $6 \times 3 =$ ___	g. $64 / 8 =$ ___
h. $7 \cdot 2 =$ ___	h. $54 \div 9 =$ ___	h. $7 \cdot 7 =$ ___	h. $48 \div 6 =$ ___
i. $9 * 9 =$ ___	i. $15 / 3 =$ ___	i. $4 * 8 =$ ___	i. $8 / 8 =$ ___
j. $6 \times 4 =$ ___	j. $27 / 3 =$ ___	j. $6 \times 6 =$ ___	j. $56 / 7 =$ ___
k. $2 \cdot 2 =$ ___	k. $18 \div 2 =$ ___	k. $4 \cdot 6 =$ ___	k. $32 \div 8 =$ ___
l. $5 * 3 =$ ___	l. $28 / 4 =$ ___	l. $7 * 9 =$ ___	l. $63 / 7 =$ ___
m. $4 \times 8 =$ ___	m. $40 \div 5 =$ ___	m. $5 \times 6 =$ ___	m. $30 \div 6 =$ ___
n. $3 \cdot 3 =$ ___	n. $45 / 5 =$ ___	n. $4 \cdot 7 =$ ___	n. $56 / 8 =$ ___
o. $7 * 5 =$ ___	o. $4 \div 2 =$ ___	o. $8 * 2 =$ ___	o. $72 \div 8 =$ ___
p. $8 \times 5 =$ ___	p. $9 / 3 =$ ___	p. $1 \times 6 =$ ___	p. $36 / 6 =$ ___
q. $4 \cdot 3 =$ ___	q. $32 \div 4 =$ ___	q. $2 \cdot 7 =$ ___	q. $40 \div 8 =$ ___
r. $2 * 8 =$ ___	r. $63 \div 9 =$ ___	r. $8 * 5 =$ ___	r. $21 \div 7 =$ ___
s. $9 \times 4 =$ ___	s. $15 / 3 =$ ___	s. $8 \times 1 =$ ___	s. $42 / 6 =$ ___
t. $6 \cdot 9 =$ ___	t. $24 \div 4 =$ ___	t. $9 \cdot 8 =$ ___	t. $7 \div 7 =$ ___

Dashes 13–16

▶ Answers to Dashes 13–16

Use this sheet to check your answers to the dashes on page 379.

Dash 13 2s, 3s, 4s, 5s, 9s Multiplications	Dash 14 2s, 3s, 4s, 5s, 9s Divisions	Dash 15 6s, 7s, 8s Multiplications	Dash 16 6s, 7s, 8s Divisions
a. $7 \times 4 = 28$	a. $9 / 3 = 3$	a. $8 \times 8 = 64$	a. $72 / 8 = 9$
b. $5 \cdot 5 = 25$	b. $45 \div 9 = 5$	b. $9 \cdot 6 = 54$	b. $49 \div 7 = 7$
c. $2 * 9 = 18$	c. $81 / 9 = 9$	c. $7 * 6 = 42$	c. $35 / 7 = 5$
d. $3 \times 8 = 24$	d. $36 \div 4 = 9$	d. $5 \times 7 = 35$	d. $64 \div 8 = 8$
e. $4 \cdot 4 = 16$	e. $20 / 5 = 4$	e. $3 \cdot 8 = 24$	e. $14 / 7 = 2$
f. $5 * 9 = 45$	f. $16 \div 4 = 4$	f. $8 * 6 = 48$	f. $18 \div 6 = 3$
g. $6 \times 3 = 18$	g. $12 / 2 = 6$	g. $6 \times 3 = 18$	g. $64 / 8 = 8$
h. $7 \cdot 2 = 14$	h. $54 \div 9 = 6$	h. $7 \cdot 7 = 49$	h. $48 \div 6 = 8$
i. $9 * 9 = 81$	i. $15 / 3 = 5$	i. $4 * 8 = 32$	i. $8 / 8 = 1$
j. $6 \times 4 = 24$	j. $27 / 3 = 9$	j. $6 \times 6 = 36$	j. $56 / 7 = 8$
k. $2 \cdot 2 = 4$	k. $18 \div 2 = 9$	k. $4 \cdot 6 = 24$	k. $32 \div 8 = 4$
l. $5 * 3 = 15$	l. $28 / 4 = 7$	l. $7 * 9 = 63$	l. $63 / 7 = 9$
m. $4 \times 8 = 32$	m. $40 \div 5 = 8$	m. $5 \times 6 = 30$	m. $30 \div 6 = 5$
n. $3 \cdot 3 = 9$	n. $45 / 5 = 9$	n. $4 \cdot 7 = 28$	n. $56 / 8 = 7$
o. $7 * 5 = 35$	o. $4 \div 2 = 2$	o. $8 * 2 = 16$	o. $72 \div 8 = 9$
p. $8 \times 5 = 40$	p. $9 / 3 = 3$	p. $1 \times 6 = 6$	p. $36 / 6 = 6$
q. $4 \cdot 3 = 12$	q. $32 \div 4 = 8$	q. $2 \cdot 7 = 14$	q. $40 \div 8 = 5$
r. $2 * 8 = 16$	r. $63 \div 9 = 7$	r. $8 * 5 = 40$	r. $21 \div 7 = 3$
s. $9 \times 4 = 36$	s. $15 / 3 = 5$	s. $8 \times 1 = 8$	s. $42 / 6 = 7$
t. $6 \cdot 9 = 54$	t. $24 \div 4 = 6$	t. $9 \cdot 8 = 72$	t. $7 \div 7 = 1$

Answers to Dashes 13–16

Class Activity

Name _____   **Date** _____

▶Complex Multi-Step Word Problems

Solve.

1. A farm had 413 chickens. Then 9 of the hens laid 6 eggs each. All of the eggs have hatched except 3. How many chickens does the farm have now?

   _____

2. There are 8 houses on Jeremiah's street. Each house has 1 willow tree, 6 apple trees, and 2 olive trees. How many trees are on Jeremiah's street in all?

   _____

3. Tim has 6 marbles. Adrian has twice as many marbles as Tim. Ryan has 3 fewer marbles than Adrian. Leslie has 5 times as many marbles as Ryan. How many marbles does Leslie have?

   _____

4. Allen has 548 baseball cards. Drew has 362 more cards than Allen. Lacy has 76 fewer baseball cards than Drew. How many more baseball cards does Lacy have than Allen?

   _____

5. Angela had $4.00. She bought 3 gumballs for 9¢ each and 2 apples for 63¢ each. How much money does Angela have now?

   _____

6. Jasmine has $40. Ahmad has half as much money. Ahmad wants to buy an action figure for $5.76 and a backpack for $14.89. Does Ahmad have enough money?

   _____

Name _____   **Date** _____

▶More Complex Word Problems

Solve. Show your work on another sheet of paper.

7. Mr. Marconi made 9 pizzas. He divided the pizzas into 3 equal groups. One group was pizzas with mushrooms, one group had peppers, and one group was plain cheese. He cut each pizza into 8 slices. How many slices had either mushrooms or peppers?

_____

8. Kelsey wants to see all 700 paintings in the art museum. Last week she saw 473 of them. Today she visited 9 more rooms in the museum. There are 8 paintings in each room. How many paintings does Kelsey still have to see?

_____

9. The Nelson Notebook Company makes 3 kinds of wire spirals for their notebooks.

Each type of spiral comes in 3 colors. The table gives information about all 9 spirals the company makes.

Which spiral colors are tight, which are medium, and which are loose? How do you know?

Tight   Medium   Loose

Color	Length of Wire Before Spiral	Length of Spiral
Blue	18 in.	9 in.
Red	20 in.	10 in.
Black	21 in.	7 in.
Green	24 in.	6 in.
White	26 in.	13 in.
Orange	27 in.	9 in.
Silver	28 in.	7 in.
Purple	33 in.	11 in.
Gold	40 in.	10 in.

_____

_____

_____

_____

Solve Complex Multi-Step Word Problems

▶Dashes 17–20

Complete each Dash. Check your answers on page 387.

Dash 17 All Factors Multiplications	Dash 18 All Factors Divisions	Dash 19 All Factors Multiplications	Dash 20 All Factors Divisions
a. 5×4 = ___	a. $100 / 10$ = ___	a. 4×5 = ___	a. $81 / 9$ = ___
b. $8 \cdot 10$ = ___	b. $36 \div 4$ = ___	b. $8 \cdot 8$ = ___	b. $21 \div 7$ = ___
c. $6 * 6$ = ___	c. $56 / 7$ = ___	c. $6 * 1$ = ___	c. $30 / 6$ = ___
d. 9×2 = ___	d. $14 \div 2$ = ___	d. 6×7 = ___	d. $42 \div 6$ = ___
e. $7 \cdot 7$ = ___	e. $32 / 8$ = ___	e. $9 \cdot 3$ = ___	e. $15 / 3$ = ___
f. $3 * 8$ = ___	f. $36 \div 6$ = ___	f. $7 * 8$ = ___	f. $72 \div 8$ = ___
g. 8×9 = ___	g. $40 / 5$ = ___	g. 10×7 = ___	g. $28 / 4$ = ___
h. $4 \cdot 1$ = ___	h. $64 \div 8$ = ___	h. $6 \cdot 0$ = ___	h. $48 \div 8$ = ___
i. $2 * 2$ = ___	i. $5 / 1$ = ___	i. $4 * 4$ = ___	i. $49 / 7$ = ___
j. 8×7 = ___	j. $21 / 3$ = ___	j. 7×5 = ___	j. $18 / 2$ = ___
k. $5 \cdot 5$ = ___	k. $48 \div 6$ = ___	k. $6 \cdot 4$ = ___	k. $63 \div 9$ = ___
l. $7 * 6$ = ___	l. $42 / 7$ = ___	l. $9 * 7$ = ___	l. $54 / 9$ = ___
m. 4×8 = ___	m. $5 \div 5$ = ___	m. 2×6 = ___	m. $20 \div 10$ = ___
n. $9 \cdot 4$ = ___	n. $72 / 9$ = ___	n. $4 \cdot 7$ = ___	n. $24 / 4$ = ___
o. $9 * 9$ = ___	o. $54 \div 6$ = ___	o. $9 * 6$ = ___	o. $56 \div 8$ = ___
p. 10×3 = ___	p. $18 / 6$ = ___	p. 6×3 = ___	p. $60 / 6$ = ___
q. $6 \cdot 8$ = ___	q. $60 \div 6$ = ___	q. $3 \cdot 3$ = ___	q. $36 \div 9$ = ___
r. $5 * 9$ = ___	r. $63 \div 7$ = ___	r. $10 * 10$ = ___	r. $20 \div 4$ = ___
s. 6×9 = ___	s. $16 / 4$ = ___	s. 8×2 = ___	s. $45 / 5$ = ___
t. $0 \cdot 1$ = ___	t. $24 \div 6$ = ___	t. $5 \cdot 9$ = ___	t. $28 \div 7$ = ___

Dashes 17–20

▶Answers to Dashes 17–20

Use this sheet to check your answers to the dashes on page 385.

Dash 17 All Factors Multiplications	Dash 18 All Factors Divisions	Dash 19 All Factors Multiplications	Dash 20 All Factors Divisions
a. $5 \times 4 = 20$	a. $100 / 10 = 10$	a. $4 \times 5 = 20$	a. $81 / 9 = 9$
b. $8 \cdot 10 = 80$	b. $36 \div 4 = 9$	b. $8 \cdot 8 = 64$	b. $21 \div 7 = 3$
c. $6 * 6 = 36$	c. $56 / 7 = 8$	c. $6 * 1 = 6$	c. $30 / 6 = 5$
d. $9 \times 2 = 18$	d. $14 \div 2 = 7$	d. $6 \times 7 = 42$	d. $42 \div 6 = 7$
e. $7 \cdot 7 = 49$	e. $32 / 8 = 4$	e. $9 \cdot 3 = 27$	e. $15 / 3 = 5$
f. $3 * 8 = 24$	f. $36 \div 6 = 6$	f. $7 * 8 = 56$	f. $72 \div 8 = 9$
g. $8 \times 9 = 72$	g. $40 / 5 = 8$	g. $10 \times 7 = 70$	g. $28 / 4 = 7$
h. $4 \cdot 1 = 4$	h. $64 \div 8 = 8$	h. $6 \cdot 0 = 0$	h. $48 \div 8 = 6$
i. $2 * 2 = 4$	i. $5 / 1 = 5$	i. $4 * 4 = 16$	i. $49 / 7 = 7$
j. $8 \times 7 = 56$	j. $21 / 3 = 7$	j. $7 \times 5 = 35$	j. $18 / 2 = 9$
k. $5 \cdot 5 = 25$	k. $48 \div 6 = 8$	k. $6 \cdot 4 = 24$	k. $63 \div 9 = 7$
l. $7 * 6 = 42$	l. $42 / 7 = 6$	l. $9 * 7 = 63$	l. $54 / 9 = 6$
m. $4 \times 8 = 32$	m. $5 \div 5 = 1$	m. $2 \times 6 = 12$	m. $20 \div 10 = 2$
n. $9 \cdot 4 = 36$	n. $72 / 9 = 8$	n. $4 \cdot 7 = 28$	n. $24 / 4 = 6$
o. $9 * 9 = 81$	o. $54 \div 6 = 9$	o. $9 * 6 = 54$	o. $56 \div 8 = 7$
p. $10 \times 3 = 30$	p. $18 / 6 = 3$	p. $6 \times 3 = 18$	p. $60 / 6 = 10$
q. $6 \cdot 8 = 48$	q. $60 \div 6 = 10$	q. $3 \cdot 3 = 9$	q. $36 \div 9 = 4$
r. $5 * 9 = 45$	r. $63 \div 7 = 9$	r. $10 * 10 = 100$	r. $20 \div 4 = 5$
s. $6 \times 9 = 54$	s. $16 / 4 = 4$	s. $8 \times 2 = 16$	s. $45 / 5 = 9$
t. $0 \cdot 1 = 0$	t. $24 \div 6 = 4$	t. $5 \cdot 9 = 45$	t. $28 \div 7 = 4$

Answers to Dashes 17–20

Class Activity

▶Solve Multi-Step Word Problems

Solve.

1. Raul spent 8 minutes doing his homework. His older sister spent 5 minutes less than 7 times as many minutes doing her homework. How many minutes did Raul's sister spend on her homework?

2. At Sonya's cello recital, there were 8 rows of chairs, with 6 chairs in each row. There was a person in each chair, and there were 17 more people standing. How many people were in the audience altogether?

3. Tova's art teacher asked her to cut out construction paper squares with an area of 36 square centimeters each. What should the side lengths of the squares be?

4. Mukesh was making 7 salads. He opened a can of olives and put 6 olives on each salad. Then he ate the rest of the olives in the can. If there were 51 olives to start with, how many olives did Mukesh eat?

5. Peter wallpapered a wall that was 8 feet wide and 9 feet high. He had 28 square feet of wallpaper left over. How many square feet of wallpaper did he start with?

Class Activity

▶What's My Rule?

A **function table** is a table of ordered pairs. For every input number, there is only one output number. The rule describes what to do to the input number to get the output number.

Write the rule and then complete the function table.

6.

Rule _____

Input	Output
7	42
8	_____
_____	54
6	36

7.

Rule _____

Input	Output
81	9
45	5
72	_____
_____	7

8.

Rule _____

Input	Output
4	28
8	56
6	_____
7	_____

9.

Rule _____

Input	Output
32	8
8	2
_____	3
24	_____

10.

Rule _____

Input	Output
21	7
27	9
_____	6
15	_____

11.

Rule _____

Input	Output
5	25
_____	40
9	_____
3	15

Play Multiplication and Division Games

▶Play *Division Three-in-a-Row*

Rules for *Division Three-in-a-Row*

Number of players: 2
What You Will Need: Division Strategy Cards, one
Three-in-a-Row Game Grid for each player

1. Each player writes any nine quotients in the squares of a game grid. A player may write the same quotient more than once.

2. Shuffle the cards. Place them division side up in the center of the table.

3. Players take turns. On each turn, a player completes the division on the top card and then turns the card over to check the answer.

4. For a correct answer, if the quotient is on the game grid, the player puts an X through that grid square. If the answer is wrong, or if the quotient is not on the grid, the player doesn't mark anything. The player puts the card division side up on the bottom of the stack.

5. The first player to mark three squares in a row (horizontally, vertically, or diagonally) wins.

Play *Division Three-in-a-Row*

Basic Multiplications

1. $8 \times 9 =$ ___   2. $1 * 10 =$ ___   3. $3 \cdot 5 =$ ___   4. $2 * 8 =$ ___

5. $5 * 3 =$ ___   6. $0 \times 7 =$ ___   7. $8 \times 8 =$ ___   8. $2 * 7 =$ ___

9. $4 \cdot 10 =$ ___   10. $7 \cdot 2 =$ ___   11. $3 \cdot 8 =$ ___   12. $7 * 10 =$ ___

13. $4 \cdot 4 =$ ___   14. $1 * 3 =$ ___   15. $0 \times 0 =$ ___   16. $4 * 9 =$ ___

17. $10 \cdot 6 =$ ___   18. $1 \times 5 =$ ___   19. $7 \cdot 5 =$ ___   20. $2 \cdot 6 =$ ___

21. $5 \times 8 =$ ___   22. $4 * 5 =$ ___   23. $6 \cdot 8 =$ ___   24. $0 \times 3 =$ ___

25. $9 * 9 =$ ___   26. $9 * 2 =$ ___   27. $0 \times 10 =$ ___   28. $0 \times 2 =$ ___

29. $7 * 8 =$ ___   30. $8 \cdot 7 =$ ___   31. $1 \cdot 7 =$ ___   32. $1 \times 9 =$ ___

33. $2 * 9 =$ ___   34. $6 \cdot 10 =$ ___   35. $5 \times 9 =$ ___   36. $5 \times 5 =$ ___

37. $2 * 3 =$ ___   38. $3 \cdot 2 =$ ___   39. $3 \times 4 =$ ___   40. $0 * 4 =$ ___

41. $9 \times 10 =$ ___   42. $3 \times 6 =$ ___   43. $0 \times 6 =$ ___   44. $9 \times 6 =$ ___

45. $6 \times 7 =$ ___   46. $10 \times 10 =$ ___   47. $8 \times 3 =$ ___   48. $6 \times 2 =$ ___

49. $10 \times 5 =$ ___   50. $6 \times 4 =$ ___

Basic Multiplications

51. $1 * 0 =$ ___   52. $8 \cdot 2 =$ ___   53. $10 * 7 =$ ___   54. $1 * 2 =$ ___

55. $5 * 2 =$ ___   56. $9 \cdot 7 =$ ___   57. $8 \times 5 =$ ___   58. $6 \cdot 6 =$ ___

59. $7 \cdot 9 =$ ___   60. $1 * 1 =$ ___   61. $7 * 3 =$ ___   62. $0 * 9 =$ ___

63. $4 * 2 =$ ___   64. $10 \times 8 =$ ___   65. $2 \cdot 4 =$ ___   66. $4 \cdot 8 =$ ___

67. $2 * 2 =$ ___   68. $1 * 4 =$ ___   69. $1 \times 6 =$ ___   70. $0 \cdot 1 =$ ___

71. $5 \cdot 10 =$ ___   72. $3 \cdot 10 =$ ___   73. $0 \cdot 8 =$ ___   74. $7 * 4 =$ ___

75. $9 * 3 =$ ___   76. $4 \times 3 =$ ___   77. $6 \times 9 =$ ___   78. $7 * 6 =$ ___

79. $3 \cdot 7 =$ ___   80. $2 \cdot 10 =$ ___   81. $8 * 4 =$ ___   82. $9 * 8 =$ ___

83. $6 \cdot 3 =$ ___   84. $5 \times 6 =$ ___   85. $3 * 9 =$ ___   86. $9 \cdot 5 =$ ___

87. $1 \times 8 =$ ___   88. $8 \times 10 =$ ___   89. $2 \times 5 =$ ___   90. $5 \times 4 =$ ___

91. $0 \times 5 =$ ___   92. $10 \times 9 =$ ___   93. $4 \times 7 =$ ___   94. $7 \times 7 =$ ___

95. $6 \times 5 =$ ___   96. $9 \times 4 =$ ___   97. $4 \times 6 =$ ___   98. $5 \times 7 =$ ___

99. $8 \times 6 =$ ___   100. $3 \times 3 =$ ___

Basic Divisions

1. $6 / 3 =$ ___   2. $40 / 8 =$ ___   3. $10 \div 1 =$ ___   4. $40 \div 10 =$ ___

5. $32 / 8 =$ ___   6. $2 \div 2 =$ ___   7. $80 \div 10 =$ ___   8. $4 \div 1 =$ ___

9. $16 \div 2 =$ ___   10. $30 / 6 =$ ___   11. $90 / 10 =$ ___   12. $24 \div 6 =$ ___

13. $4 / 2 =$ ___   14. $8 / 4 =$ ___   15. $9 / 9 =$ ___   16. $6 \div 1 =$ ___

17. $24 \div 3 =$ ___   18. $81 / 9 =$ ___   19. $15 \div 5 =$ ___   20. $7 \div 7 =$ ___

21. $12 \div 6 =$ ___   22. $20 / 10 =$ ___   23. $35 \div 7 =$ ___   24. $72 / 9 =$ ___

25. $7 \overline{)28}$ 26. $9 \overline{)27}$ 27. $3 \overline{)3}$ 28. $7 \overline{)49}$

29. $3 \overline{)27}$ 30. $3 \overline{)15}$ 31. $4 \overline{)28}$ 32. $8 \overline{)16}$

33. $1 \overline{)2}$ 34. $5 \overline{)45}$ 35. $5 \overline{)10}$ 36. $8 \overline{)72}$

37. $10 \overline{)70}$ 38. $5 \overline{)5}$ 39. $7 \overline{)70}$ 40. $6 \overline{)18}$

41. $\dfrac{56}{7} =$ ___   42. $\dfrac{48}{8} =$ ___   43. $\dfrac{21}{7} =$ ___   44. $\dfrac{36}{4} =$ ___

45. $\dfrac{3}{1} =$ ___   46. $\dfrac{42}{6} =$ ___   47. $\dfrac{18}{3} =$ ___   48. $\dfrac{30}{3} =$ ___

49. $\dfrac{45}{9} =$ ___   50. $\dfrac{16}{4} =$ ___

Basic Divisions

51. $6 \div 6 =$ ___   52. $42 / 7 =$ ___   53. $20 \div 5 =$ ___   54. $90 / 9 =$ ___

55. $36 / 9 =$ ___   56. $35 \div 5 =$ ___   57. $1 / 1 =$ ___   58. $50 \div 10 =$ ___

59. $54 / 9 =$ ___   60. $12 \div 2 =$ ___   61. $10 \div 2 =$ ___   62. $24 / 8 =$ ___

63. $14 \div 7 =$ ___   64. $12 \div 3 =$ ___   65. $63 / 7 =$ ___   66. $4 \div 4 =$ ___

67. $6 / 2 =$ ___   68. $25 \div 5 =$ ___   69. $5 \div 1 =$ ___   70. $7 \div 1 =$ ___

71. $60 / 10 =$ ___   72. $18 \div 2 =$ ___   73. $60 / 6 =$ ___   74. $9 / 3 =$ ___

75. $5\overline{)50}$ 76. $10\overline{)10}$ 77. $4\overline{)12}$ 78. $8\overline{)80}$

79. $5\overline{)30}$ 80. $8\overline{)56}$ 81. $6\overline{)54}$ 82. $9\overline{)63}$

83. $4\overline{)24}$ 84. $8\overline{)8}$ 85. $8\overline{)64}$ 86. $1\overline{)7}$

87. $2\overline{)8}$ 88. $10\overline{)30}$ 89. $4\overline{)40}$ 90. $6\overline{)48}$

91. $\frac{32}{4} =$ ___   92. $\frac{9}{1} =$ ___   93. $\frac{36}{6} =$ ___   94. $\frac{100}{10} =$ ___

95. $\frac{14}{2} =$ ___   96. $\frac{21}{3} =$ ___   97. $\frac{40}{5} =$ ___   98. $\frac{20}{4} =$ ___

99. $\frac{20}{2} =$ ___   100. $\frac{18}{9} =$ ___

Basic Divisions Test

Multiply or divide.

1. $7 \times 8 = \boxed{}$

2. $6 \cdot 9 = \boxed{}$

3. $55 \div 1 = \boxed{}$

4. $72 \div 9 = \boxed{}$

5. $30 \times 0 = \boxed{}$

6. $49 / 7 = \boxed{}$

7. $4 \cdot 3 = \boxed{}$

8. $2 * 10 = \boxed{}$

9. $3 \times 9 = \boxed{}$

10. $6\overline{)24}$

11. $7\overline{)28}$

12. $9\overline{)45}$

Solve.

Show your work.

13. Lucinda collected 4 eggs from the chicken house. Mark collected 32 eggs. How many times as many eggs did Mark collect than Lucinda?

_____

14. Carrie found 7 seashells at the beach. Her brother found 4 times as many. How many seashells did her brother find?

_____

15. The supermarket sells small boxes of cereal in packages of 8. Mrs. Smith bought 6 packages. How many boxes of cereal did she buy?

_____

16. The area of Keshawn's garden is 36 square feet. Its width is 4 feet. What is the length of his garden?

_____

Write an equation to solve the problem.

17. A class has 35 goldfish and 5 fish bowls. How many fish will be in each bowl if the same number of fish are in each bowl?

_____

Solve.

18. Mr. Howell arranged 56 books on 8 shelves with the same number on each shelf. How many books were on each shelf?

_____

19. Mr. Alberto has 48 students to divide into teams of 8. Mr. Yates has 81 students to divide into teams of 9. How many more teams does Mr. Yates have than Mr. Alberto?

_____

20. **Extended Response** Marcie has 7 bean bag dolls. Lucy has 3 times as many dolls as Marcie. Janice has twice as many dolls as Marcie and Lucy combined. How many more dolls does Janice have than Marcie? Explain the steps you used to solve the problem.

_____

_____

_____

_____

_____

_____

Class Activity

Name _____ Date _____

▶ Make an Analog Clock

Attach the clock hands to the clock face using a prong fastener.

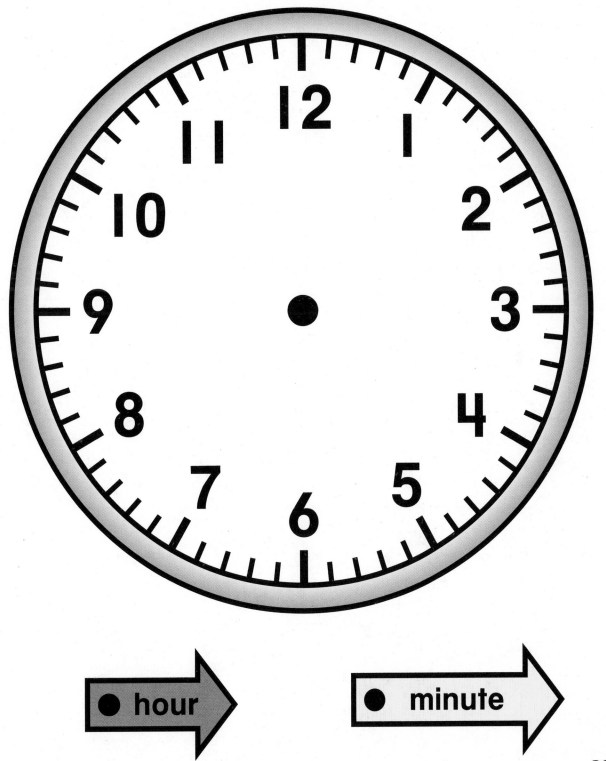

Paper Clock

▶Time to 15 Minutes

Write the time on the digital clock. Then write how to say the time.

1.

┌─────────┐
│   :   │
└─────────┘

_____

2.

┌─────────┐
│   :   │
└─────────┘

_____

3.

┌─────────┐
│   :   │
└─────────┘

_____

4.

┌─────────┐
│   :   │
└─────────┘

_____

Write the time on the digital clock. Write two ways to say the time.

5.

┌─────────┐
│   :   │
└─────────┘

_____
_____

6.

┌─────────┐
│   :   │
└─────────┘

_____
_____

7.

┌─────────┐
│   :   │
└─────────┘

_____
_____

8.

┌─────────┐
│   :   │
└─────────┘

_____
_____

9.

┌─────────┐
│   :   │
└─────────┘

_____

10.

┌─────────┐
│   :   │
└─────────┘

_____

11.

┌─────────┐
│   :   │
└─────────┘

_____

12.

┌─────────┐
│   :   │
└─────────┘

_____

Class Activity

Name _____

Date _____

▶Show Time to 15 Minutes

Draw the hands on the analog clock. Write the time on the digital clock.

13. nine fifteen

14. half past seven

15. three o'clock

16. seven thirty

17. one forty-five

18. fifteen minutes after two

▶Times of Daily Activities

19. Complete the table.

Time	Light or Dark	Part of the Day	Activity
3:15 A.M.			
8:00 A.M.			
2:30 P.M.			
6:15 P.M.			
8:45 P.M.			

▶Time to 5 Minutes

Write the time on the digital clock. Then write how to say the time.

20.

[:]

_____

21.

[:]

_____

22.

[:]

_____

23.

[:]

_____

Write the time on the digital clock.

24. ten minutes after eight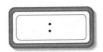

[:]

25. seven twenty-five

[:]

26. eleven fifty

[:]

▶Time to 1 Minute

Write the time on the digital clock. Then write how to say the time.

27.

[:]

_____

28.

[:]

_____

29.

[:]

_____

30.

[:]

_____

Write the time on the digital clock.

31. ten fourteen

[:]

32. fifty-two minutes after eight

[:]

33. seven twenty-eight

[:]

Class Activity

▶Times Before and After the Hour

Write the time as minutes *after* an hour and minutes *before* an hour.

34.

_____

_____

35.

_____

_____

36.

_____

_____

37.

_____

_____

38.

_____

_____

39.

_____

_____

40.

_____

_____

41.

_____

_____

42.

_____

_____

Tell Time

Dear Family,

In math class, your child is beginning a unit about time. This topic is directly connected to home and community and involves skills your child will use often in everyday situations.

Students are reading time to the hour, half-hour, quarter-hour, five minutes, and minute, as well as describing the time before the hour and after the hour.

For example, you can read 3:49 both as after and before the hour.

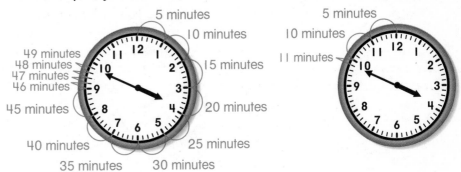

Forty-nine minutes after three

Eleven minutes before four

Students use calendars and clocks to find elapsed time and to solve problems involving elapsed time in days, weeks, months, hours, and minutes.

At the end of the unit, students will link the movement of the minute hand around a clock to angle measures in degrees. They will divide the 360° rotation of a circle by 60 minutes to find that each minute on a clock represents a 6° rotation. They will use this fact to solve word problems involving elapsed time, problems which give them practice multiplying and dividing by 6.

Help your child read time and find elapsed time. Ask your child to estimate how long it takes to do activities such as eating a meal, traveling to the store, or doing homework. Have your child look at the clock when starting an activity and then again at the end of the activity. Ask how long the activity took.

Talk to your child about events that will be happening over the next year and ask how many days or months there are until those events. Talk about past events in the year and ask your child how many days or months it has been since those events happened.

If you have any questions or comments, please call or write to me.

Sincerely,
Your child's teacher

Carta a la familia

Estimada familia:

En la clase de matemáticas su niño empieza una unidad sobre la hora. Este tema se relaciona directamente con la casa y la comunidad, y trata de destrezas que su niño usará a menudo en situaciones de la vida diaria.

Los estudiantes leen la hora, la media hora, el cuarto de hora, cinco minutos y un minuto; también describen la hora antes y después de la hora en punto.

Por ejemplo, se puede leer 3:49 de dos maneras:

Las tres y cuarenta y nueve   Las cuatro menos once

Los estudiantes usan calendarios y relojes para hallar el tiempo transcurrido y para resolver problemas de tiempo transcurrido en días, semanas, meses, horas y minutos.

Al final de la unidad, los estudiantes harán la conexión entre el movimiento del minutero del reloj y las medidas de ángulos en grados. Dividirán la rotación de 360° de un círculo entre 60 minutos para hallar que cada minuto del reloj representa una rotación de 6°. Luego usarán este dato para resolver problemas verbales que tratan de tiempo transcurrido, lo que a su vez les deja practicar la multiplicación y la división por 6.

Ayude a su niño a leer la hora y hallar el tiempo transcurrido. Pídale que estime cuánto le lleva hacer actividades como comer una comida, ir a la tienda o hacer la tarea. Pídale que se fije en la hora antes de empezar una actividad y luego otra vez al completar la actividad. Pídale que le diga cuánto tiempo le llevó hacer la actividad.

Háblele a su niño acerca de sucesos que ocurrirán durante el año que viene y pregúntele cuántos días o meses faltan para que sucedan. Háblele de sucesos pasados del año y pregúntele cuántos días o meses hace que pasaron estos sucesos.

Si tiene alguna pregunta o comentario, por favor comuníquese conmigo.

Atentamente,
El maestro de su niño

►Features of Calendars

January

Sun	Mon	Tues	Wed	Thurs	Fri	Sat
	1	2	3	4	5	6
7	8	9	10	11	12	13
14	15	16	17	18	19	20
21	22	23	24	25	26	27
28	29	30	31			

February

Sun	Mon	Tues	Wed	Thurs	Fri	Sat
				1	2	3
4	5	6	7	8	9	10
11	12	13	14	15	16	17
18	19	20	21	22	23	24
25	26	27	28			

March

Sun	Mon	Tues	Wed	Thurs	Fri	Sat
				1	2	3
4	5	6	7	8	9	10
11	12	13	14	15	16	17
18	19	20	21	22	23	24
25	26	27	28	29	30	31

April

Sun	Mon	Tues	Wed	Thurs	Fri	Sat
1	2	3	4	5	6	7
8	9	10	11	12	13	14
15	16	17	18	19	20	21
22	23	24	25	26	27	28
29	30					

May

Sun	Mon	Tues	Wed	Thurs	Fri	Sat
		1	2	3	4	5
6	7	8	9	10	11	12
13	14	15	16	17	18	19
20	21	22	23	24	25	26
27	28	29	30	31		

June

Sun	Mon	Tues	Wed	Thurs	Fri	Sat
					1	2
3	4	5	6	7	8	9
10	11	12	13	14	15	16
17	18	19	20	21	22	23
24	25	26	27	28	29	30

July

Sun	Mon	Tues	Wed	Thurs	Fri	Sat
1	2	3	4	5	6	7
8	9	10	11	12	13	14
15	16	17	18	19	20	21
22	23	24	25	26	27	28
29	30	31				

August

Sun	Mon	Tues	Wed	Thurs	Fri	Sat
			1	2	3	4
5	6	7	8	9	10	11
12	13	14	15	16	17	18
19	20	21	22	23	24	25
26	27	28	29	30	31	

September

Sun	Mon	Tues	Wed	Thurs	Fri	Sat
						1
2	3	4	5	6	7	8
9	10	11	12	13	14	15
16	17	18	19	20	21	22
23	24	25	26	27	28	29
30						

October

Sun	Mon	Tues	Wed	Thurs	Fri	Sat
	1	2	3	4	5	6
7	8	9	10	11	12	13
14	15	16	17	18	19	20
21	22	23	24	25	26	27
28	29	30	31			

November

Sun	Mon	Tues	Wed	Thurs	Fri	Sat
				1	2	3
4	5	6	7	8	9	10
11	12	13	14	15	16	17
18	19	20	21	22	23	24
25	26	27	28	29	30	

December

Sun	Mon	Tues	Wed	Thurs	Fri	Sat
						1
2	3	4	5	6	7	8
9	10	11	12	13	14	15
16	17	18	19	20	21	22
23	24	25	26	27	28	29
30	31					

Class Activity

Name _____ Date _____

Vocabulary

month   day
week   elapsed time

▶ Use a Calendar

Use the calendars on pages 407–408 to complete exercises 1–3.

1. What is the fourth **month** of the year?

   _____

2. What is the date of the twenty-second **day** of the third month?

   _____

3. What day of the **week** is the third day of the seventh month?

   _____

▶ Elapsed Time on a Calendar

Write the elapsed time.

4. August 1 to November 1 is _____ months.

5. 7:00 A.M. May 2 to 7:00 A.M. May 19 is _____ days.

Write the month.

6. Eight months after March _____

7. Six months before December _____

Write the date.

8. Seven days after the third of July _____

9. Two weeks after November 2 _____

10. Four days before June 10 _____

11. One week before August 23 _____

Name _____ **Date** _____

Class Activity

► Solve Problems About Elapsed Time on a Calendar

Solve.

Show your work.

12. Garnetta worked on her project from October 4 to October 11. She then had 4 more days to complete it. How many days did she work on her project?

_____

13. David's family left for their vacation on June 3. After 2 weeks, they returned home. What date did they arrive home?

_____

14. Randi planted flower seeds in the house on January 15. On May 15, she planted the small plants outside. Three months later, they bloomed. How many months did it take the seeds to grow into blooming plants?

_____

15. Irene went to the aquarium on July 16. Bruce went to the aquarium 1 week later. Chantal went to the aquarium 4 days after Bruce. On what date did Chantal go to the aquarium?

_____

16. Marilyn went to the History Museum on August 5. Alison went 1 week later. If Charlie went to the History Museum 3 days before Alison, what date did he go?

_____

Elapsed Time

Class Activity

▶ **Elapsed Time in Minutes and Hours**

17. Find the elapsed time.

Start Time	End Time	Elapsed Time
4:00 P.M.	7:00 P.M.	
7:45 A.M.	8:15 A.M.	
2:17 P.M.	7:17 P.M.	
11:00 A.M.	2:00 P.M.	
11:55 A.M.	4:25 P.M.	

18. Find the end time.

Start Time	Elapsed Time	End Time
1:00 P.M.	2 hours	
4:15 A.M.	4 hours	
4:55 P.M.	18 minutes	
2:15 A.M.	1 hour and 15 minutes	
11:55 A.M.	2 hours and 5 minutes	

19. Find the start time.

Start Time	Elapsed Time	End Time
	3 hours	4:15 P.M.
	15 minutes	2:45 P.M.
	2 hours and 35 minutes	11:55 A.M.
	1 hour and 20 minutes	3:42 A.M.

Class Activity

▶ Solve Problems About Elapsed Time on a Clock

Solve. Use your clock if you need to.

Show your work.

20. Loretta left her friend's house at 3:45. She had been there for 2 hours and 20 minutes. What time did she get there?

_____

21. Berto spent from 3:45 P.M. to 4:15 P.M. doing math homework and from 4:30 P.M. to 5:10 P.M. doing social studies homework. How much time did he spend on his math and social studies homework?

_____

22. Ed arrived at a biking trail at 9:00 A.M. He biked for 1 hour and 45 minutes. He spent 20 minutes riding home. What time did he get home?

_____

23. Mario finished swimming at 10:45. He swam for 1 hour and 15 minutes. What time did he start?

_____

24. Vasco finished cleaning his room at 4:30. It took him 25 minutes. What time did he start?

_____

25. Eric has basketball practice from 3:30 P.M. to 4:15 P.M. He has violin practice at 5:30. Today basketball practice ended 30 minutes late and it takes Eric 15 minutes to walk to violin practice. Will he be on time? Explain.

_____

▶Rotations of the Minute Hand

The clocks on this page show the movement of the minute hand.

1. The minute hand has traveled one quarter of the way around the clock.

_____ minutes have passed. The minute hand has rotated _____ degrees.

2. The minute hand has traveled halfway around the clock.

_____ minutes have passed. The minute hand has rotated _____ degrees.

3. The minute hand has traveled three quarters of the way around the clock.

_____ minutes have passed. The minute hand has rotated _____ degrees.

4. The minute hand has traveled all the way around the clock.

_____ minutes have passed. The minute hand has rotated _____ degrees.

Find how many minutes have passed and how many degrees the minute hand has rotated.

5.

minutes: _____
degrees: _____

6.

minutes: _____
degrees: _____

7.

minutes: _____
degrees: _____

8.

minutes: _____
degrees: _____

Vocabulary

degrees

▶Degrees of Rotation in 1 Minute

The minute hand rotates 6 degrees (°) in 1 minute.
Complete the sentence.

9. Between 12:00 and 12:08, the minute hand rotates _____ degrees.

10. Between 12:00 and 12:07, the minute hand rotates _____ degrees.

11. Between 12:00 and 12:10, the minute hand rotates _____ degrees.

▶Degrees of Rotation Is a Number of Minutes

Complete the sentence.

12. From 4:16 to 4:25, _____ minutes pass. The minute hand rotates

     _____ degrees.

13. From 2:43 to 2:48, _____ minutes pass. The minute hand rotates

     _____ degrees.

14. From 8:55 to 9:01, _____ minutes pass. The minute hand rotates

     _____ degrees.

15. From 12:59 to 1:01, _____ minutes pass. The minute hand rotates

     _____ degrees.

▶Find End Times Using Clock Angles

Solve.

16. A clock starts at 4:15. What time is it after the minute hand rotates

     18 degrees? _____

17. A clock starts at 7:57. What time is it after the minute hand rotates

     24 degrees? _____

18. A clock starts at 10:59. What time is it after the minute hand rotates

     42 degrees? _____

Clock Angles

Write each time on the digital clock. Then write how to say the time.

1.

         :

_____

2.

         :

_____

3.

         :

_____

4.

         :

_____

Write the time as minutes after an hour and minutes before an hour.

5.

_____

_____

6.

_____

_____

Name _____ **Date** _____

Solve.

7. Diego went to his grandparents' house on August 3. He stayed there until August 21. How many days did he stay at his grandparents' house?

_____

8. At 8:45 Tamara went to basketball practice. Her practice lasted 1 hour and 15 minutes. What time did she finish her practice?

_____

9. A clock shows 7:00. What time is it after the minute hand rotates 90°? Use the clock in exercise 1 if you need to.

_____

10. **Extended Response** Carla finished her homework at 8:30. She had spent 30 minutes on math and 45 minutes on a science report. Show what time she started her homework on the clock below.

Explain how you found your answer.

_____

_____

_____

_____

Show your work.

Class Activity

▶The Meaning of Fractions

Vocabulary
fraction   denominator
numerator   unit fraction

A **fraction** can be used to represent a part of a whole. The bottom number of a fraction is called the **denominator**. It tells how many equal parts the whole is divided into. The top number is the **numerator**. It tells how many of the equal parts you are talking about.

1 whole

$\dfrac{1}{3}$ ← numerator
← denominator

Shade 1 part.

▶Unit Fractions

A **unit fraction** is a fraction with a numerator of 1. The fraction strips at the right below all represent unit fractions. What patterns do you see?

| | → | | 1 | one |
| 1 whole | | Shade 1 whole. | | |

Divide the whole into 2 equal parts. → Shade 1 part. $\dfrac{1}{2}$ one half

Divide the whole into 3 equal parts. → Shade 1 part. $\dfrac{1}{3}$ one third

Divide the whole into 4 equal parts. → Shade 1 part. $\dfrac{1}{4}$ one fourth

Divide the whole into 5 equal parts. → Shade 1 part. $\dfrac{1}{5}$ one fifth

Divide the whole into 6 equal parts. → Shade 1 part. $\dfrac{1}{6}$ one sixth

Class Activity

▶Build Fractions from Unit Fractions

Write the unit fractions. Show your shaded unit fractions as a whole number times a unit fraction and as a total of unit fractions.

1.

Divide the whole into 5 equal parts. → Shade 2 parts.

$$\frac{1}{5} + \frac{1}{5} + \frac{1}{5} + \frac{1}{5} + \frac{1}{5} \qquad \frac{1}{5} + \frac{1}{5} = 2 \times \frac{1}{5} = \frac{2}{5}$$

2.

Divide the whole into 9 equal parts. → Shade 4 parts.

3.

Divide the whole into 7 equal parts. → Shade 5 parts.

4.

Divide the whole into 8 equal parts. → Shade 7 parts.

5.

Divide the whole into 6 equal parts. → Shade 3 parts.

6.

Divide the whole into 7 equal parts. → Shade 7 parts.

Fractions as Parts of a Whole

Class Activity

Name _____ **Date** _____

▶ Fractions as Parts of a Whole

Write a fraction to represent the divided 1 whole and then the shaded part.

7.

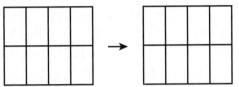

Divide a rectangle into 8 equal parts.   Shade 3 of the parts.

$1 = \dfrac{8}{8}$ _____ $\dfrac{3}{8}$ _____

8.

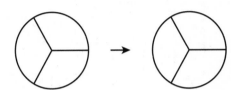

Divide a circle into 3 equal parts.   Shade 1 of the parts.

$1 =$ _____   _____

9.

Divide a square into 4 equal parts.   Shade 3 of the parts.

$1 =$ _____   _____

10.

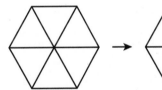

Divide a hexagon into 6 equal parts.   Shade 2 of the parts.

$1 =$ _____   _____

11.

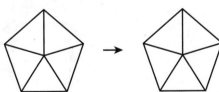

Divide a pentagon into 5 equal parts.   Shade 4 of the parts.

$1 =$ _____   _____

12.

Divide a rectangle into 7 equal parts.   Shade 5 of the parts.

$1 =$ _____   _____

Shade the given fraction of the whole.

13. $\frac{5}{6}$

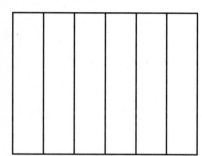

14. $\frac{2}{4}$

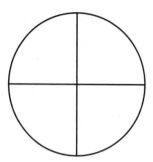

15. $\frac{3}{7}$

16. Suppose you shade one fourth of two different-size squares. Is one fourth of one square the same size as one fourth of the other square? Explain.

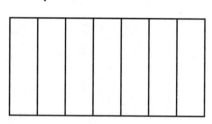

_____

_____

_____

Dear Math Students:

Today my teacher asked us to shade a square to show $\frac{1}{3}$. Here is my drawing. Is my drawing right?

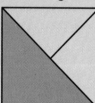

If not, make a correct drawing. Explain below.

Thank you,

The Puzzled Penguin

_____

 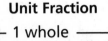

Dear Family,

In this unit, your child will be introduced to fractions. Students will build fractions from unit fractions and explore fractions as parts of a whole and parts of a set.

Unit Fraction

| ⊢——— 1 whole ——— ⊣ |

| $\frac{1}{3}$ | $\frac{1}{3}$ | $\frac{1}{3}$ |

$$\frac{1}{3} + \frac{1}{3} = \frac{2}{3}$$

Fraction of a Whole

$\frac{3}{4}$ ← numerator
← denominator

Fraction of a Set

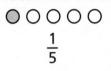

$\frac{1}{5}$

Students will find a fraction of a number.

$\frac{2}{3}$ of 12 is 8

○ ○ ○ ○
○ ○ ○ ○
○ ○ ○ ○

Students will also find equivalent fractions, and compare, add, and subtract fractions.

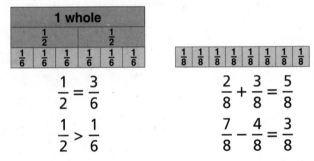

$$\frac{1}{2} = \frac{3}{6}$$

$$\frac{1}{2} > \frac{1}{6}$$

$$\frac{2}{8} + \frac{3}{8} = \frac{5}{8}$$

$$\frac{7}{8} - \frac{4}{8} = \frac{3}{8}$$

In this unit, your child will also be introduced to division with remainders.

$$8\overline{)75} \quad 9 \text{ R3}$$

Please call if you have any questions or comments.

Sincerely,
Your child's teacher

Estimada familia:

En esta unidad su niño conocerá las fracciones por primera vez. Los estudiantes formarán fracciones a partir de fracciones cuyo numerador es uno y explorarán las fracciones como partes de un todo y partes de un conjunto.

Fracción cuyo numerador es uno

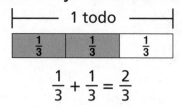

$$\frac{1}{3} + \frac{1}{3} = \frac{2}{3}$$

Fracción de un todo

$$\frac{3}{4} \begin{matrix} \leftarrow \text{numerador} \\ \leftarrow \text{denominador} \end{matrix}$$

Fracción de un conjunto

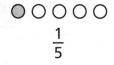

$$\frac{1}{5}$$

Los estudiantes hallarán una fracción de un número.

$$\frac{2}{3} \text{ de 12 son 8}$$

Los estudiantes también hallarán fracciones equivalentes y compararán, sumarán y restarán fracciones.

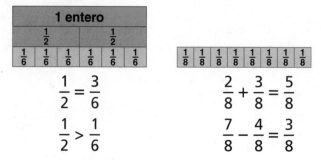

$$\frac{1}{2} = \frac{3}{6}$$

$$\frac{1}{2} > \frac{1}{6}$$

$$\frac{2}{8} + \frac{3}{8} = \frac{5}{8}$$

$$\frac{7}{8} - \frac{4}{8} = \frac{3}{8}$$

En esta unidad su niño también conocerá por primera vez la división con residuos.

$$8)\overline{75} \quad 9 \text{ R3}$$

Si tiene alguna duda o comentario, por favor comuníquese conmigo.

Atentamente,
El maestro de su niño

Fractions as Parts of a Whole

Class Activity

Name _____ Date _____

►Review Building Fractions from Unit Fractions

Write an addition equation to represent the part of
the whole that is shaded. Then show it as the product
of a whole number and a unit fraction.

1.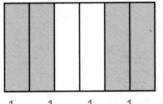

$\frac{1}{6} + \frac{1}{6} + \frac{1}{6} + \frac{1}{6} = \frac{4}{6}$

$4 \times \frac{1}{6} = \frac{4}{6}$

2.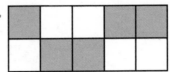

_____

_____

3.

_____

_____

Shade the given fraction of the whole.

4. $\frac{4}{6}$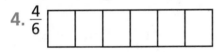

5. $\frac{1}{2}$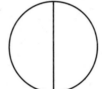

6. $\frac{6}{8}$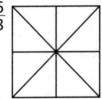

7. Complete the table.

In Words	$\frac{N}{D}$	Total and Product of Unit Fractions	Description	Drawing
two thirds			_____ parts out of _____ equal parts in a whole.	
			$\frac{2}{10}$ parts out of equal parts in a whole.	
		$\frac{1}{8} + \frac{1}{8} + \frac{1}{8} + \frac{1}{8} + \frac{1}{8} = \frac{\square}{8}$, $5 \times \frac{1}{8} = \frac{\square}{8}$	_____ parts out of _____ equal parts in a whole.	
	$\frac{3}{7}$		_____ parts out of _____ equal parts in a whole.	
two sixths			_____ parts out of _____ equal parts in a whole.	

►Fraction of a Set

Answer each question.

8. What fraction of the buttons are square?

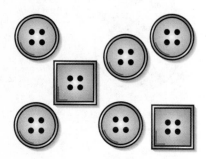

_____

9. What fraction of the balls are soccer balls?

_____

Give two answers to each question.

10. What fraction of the coins are pennies?

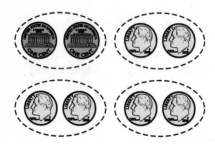

_____   _____

11. What fraction of the pieces of fruit are pears?

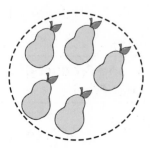

_____   _____

Shade the given fraction of each set.

12. $\dfrac{7}{11}$

13. $\dfrac{2}{9}$

14. $\dfrac{1}{5}$

▶ Solve Word Problems Involving Unit Fractions of Sets

Solve each problem.

Show your work.

1. One sixth of Kiera's cousins have red hair. Kiera has 12 cousins. How many cousins have red hair?

   _____

2. One third of the students on the bus are in the third grade. There are 15 students on the bus. How many students are in the third grade?

   _____

3. One half of Angel's crayons are sharp. Angel has 14 crayons. How many crayons are sharp?

   _____

4. One fourth of the roses in a bouquet are pink. There are 24 roses in the bouquet. How many roses are pink?

   _____

5. One tenth of the trees in the forest are oak trees. There are 90 trees in the forest. How many trees are oak trees?

   _____

6. There are 56 seals at the seashore. One eighth of the seals are swimming. How many seals are swimming?

   _____

Class Activity

▶Find a Unit Fraction of a Number

Use mental math to find the answer.

7. $\frac{1}{4} \times 8 =$ _____

8. $\frac{1}{2} \times 10 =$ _____

9. $\frac{1}{3}$ of $12 =$ _____

10. $\frac{1}{6} \times 18 =$ _____

11. $\frac{1}{5} \times 15 =$ _____

12. $\frac{1}{10}$ of $20 =$ _____

▶Equivalent Equations

The three equations below all mean the same thing.

$\frac{1}{4}$ of $12 = 3$

$\frac{1}{4} \times 12 = 3$

$12 \div 4 = 3$

Write each equation in two other ways.

13. $\frac{1}{6}$ of $12 = 2$

_____

_____

14. $\frac{1}{4} \times 24 = 6$

_____

_____

15. $21 \div 7 = 3$

_____

_____

16. $\frac{1}{5}$ of $20 = 4$

_____

_____

17. $\frac{1}{2} \times 16 = 8$

_____

_____

18. $9 \div 3 = 3$

_____

_____

Unit Fractions of Sets and Numbers

►Use a Bar Graph to Compare

Use the bar graph below to complete exercises 1–4.

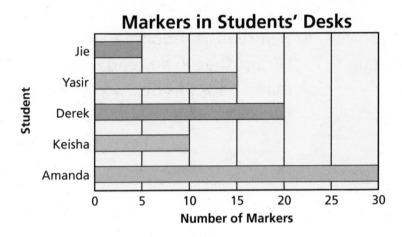

Markers in Students' Desks

Fill in the blanks.

1. Jie has _____ as many markers as Yasir has.

   Yasir has _____ as many markers as Jie has.

2. Derek has _____ as many markers as Jie has.

   Jie has _____ as many markers as Derek has.

3. Derek has _____ as many markers as Keisha has.

   Keisha has _____ as many markers as Derek has.

4. Amanda has _____ as many markers as Yasir has.

   Yasir has _____ as many markers as Amanda has.

►Solve Comparison Word Problems

Solve each problem. Then write the other comparing sentence. The first one is done for you.

5. Carmen rides the train 7 miles to work. Joe rides 6 times as far as Carmen. How far does Joe ride the train? _____42 miles_____

   Carmen rides $\frac{1}{6}$ as far as Joe.

   _____

6. Ben read 28 books last summer. His brother Ryan read $\frac{1}{7}$ as many books as Ben. How many books did Ryan read? _____

   _____

   _____

7. Kurt has 8 CDs. Julie has 4 times as many CDs as Kurt. How many CDs does Julie have? _____

   _____

   _____

   _____

8. A cheetah can run 70 miles per hour. A rabbit runs about $\frac{1}{2}$ as fast as a cheetah. How fast can a rabbit run? _____

   _____

   _____

9. The Knights won 36 basketball games last season. The Spartans won $\frac{1}{9}$ as many games. How many games did the Spartans win? _____

   _____

   _____

10. Raul's father weighs 180 pounds. Raul weighs $\frac{1}{3}$ as much as his father. How much does Raul weigh? _____

    _____

    _____

    _____

11. Lon has 9 books. Jerome has 6 times as many books as Lon has. How many books does Jerome have? _____

    _____

    _____

12. Barry's father is 48 years old. Barry is $\frac{1}{6}$ as old as his father. How old is Barry? _____

    _____

    _____

Compare with Fractions

Name **Date**

Class Activity

▶More Comparison Statements

Use the bar graph below for Exercises 1–5.

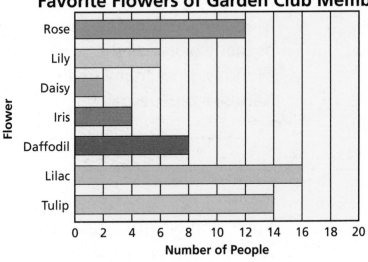

Favorite Flowers of Garden Club Members

Fill in the blanks.

1. _____ as many people like daffodils as like daisies.

   _____ as many people like daisies as like daffodils.

2. _____ as many people like lilacs as like daffodils.

   _____ as many people like daffodils as like lilacs.

3. _____ as many people like irises as like lilacs

   _____ as many people like lilacs as like irises.

4. _____ as many people like lilies as like roses.

   _____ as many people like roses as like lilies.

5. **Write Your Own** Write two comparison statements involving the number of people who like daisies.

   _____

   _____

UNIT 6 LESSON 5 Practice Fractional Comparisons **429**

Class Activity

►More Comparison Word Problems

Solve each problem. Then write the other comparing sentence.

6. Reyna caught 6 fish. Her grandfather caught 4 times as many fish as Reyna did. How many fish did Reyna's grandfather catch? _____

_____

_____

7. Kara saw 42 geese fly on Monday. On Tuesday, she saw $\frac{1}{7}$ as many geese as she saw on Monday. How many geese did Kara see on Tuesday? _____

_____

_____

8. There are 72 chairs in the lunchroom. In the basement, there are $\frac{1}{9}$ as many chairs as there are in the lunchroom. How many chairs are in the basement? _____

_____

_____

9. Rosi's dog weighs 7 pounds. Marco's dog weighs 8 times as much as Rosi's dog. What is the weight of Marco's dog? _____

_____

_____

10. Scott and his grandmother made a quilt. Scott's grandmother sewed 36 of the quilt squares. Scott sewed $\frac{1}{6}$ as many quilt squares as his grandmother. How many quilt squares did Scott sew? _____

_____

_____

11. Juanita delivered 35 newspapers. Her younger brother delivered $\frac{1}{7}$ as many newspapers as Juanita did. How many newspapers did her brother deliver? _____

_____

_____

Practice Fractional Comparisons

▶ Explore Fractional Parts of a Set

1. The Promo Company prints T-shirts for the rock band
   MathGrlzz. Complete the table to show how many
   shirts of each size and color they printed on Monday.

MathGrlzz Shirts Printed on Monday

	$\frac{1}{6}$ Yellow	$\frac{2}{6}$ Red	$\frac{3}{6}$ Blue
18 small shirts			
36 medium shirts			
54 large shirts			
48 extra large shirts			

2. The Promo Company also prints caps and hats for
   MathGrlzz. Complete the table to show how many caps
   or hats of each type and color they printed on Monday.

MathGrlzz Caps and Hats Printed on Monday

	$\frac{1}{7}$ Yellow	$\frac{4}{7}$ Red	$\frac{2}{7}$ Blue
49 baseball caps			
21 knit caps			
35 floppy hats			
14 straw hats			

Name _____   **Date** _____

Class Activity

▶Solve Problems Involving a Fraction of a Set

> Harry made 27 birds out of clay. He painted $\frac{4}{9}$ of the birds blue and the rest white.

3. How many birds did he paint blue? _____   *Show your work.*

4. How many birds did he paint white? _____

5. What fraction of the birds did he paint white?

   _____

6. Tameka wrote 24 word problems. Three eighths of the problems were subtraction problems. How many subtraction problems did Tameka write?

   _____

7. Marcel had 15 carrot sticks in his lunch. He gave $\frac{2}{5}$ of the carrot sticks to Joni. How many carrot sticks did Marcel give to Joni?

   _____

8. Karen baked 48 muffins. She gave $\frac{5}{8}$ of the muffins to her cousin. How many muffins did Karen give to her cousin?

   _____

9. There are 36 trees in a section of woods. Four ninths of the trees are oak trees. How many oak trees are there?

   _____

Find a Fraction of a Set or a Number

▶Write a Rule

10. Write a rule for finding a fraction of a set or a number.

_____

_____

_____

_____

_____

_____

▶Use a Rule

Use your rule to find each amount.

11. $\frac{2}{4}$ of 12 _____

12. $\frac{2}{6}$ of 30 _____

13. $\frac{5}{7}$ of 35 _____

14. $\frac{2}{2} \times 16$ _____

15. $\frac{4}{6} \times 36$ _____

16. $\frac{5}{9}$ of 81 _____

17. $\frac{7}{8} \times 56$ _____

18. $\frac{2}{3} \times 30$ _____

19. $\frac{5}{6}$ of 18 _____

20. $\frac{3}{8}$ of 32 _____

21. $\frac{7}{10} \times 40$ _____

22. $\frac{3}{4}$ of 24 _____

Name _____ **Date** _____

Going Further

►Solve a Problem by Acting It Out

1. Olivia picked 28 daisies. She gave $\frac{5}{7}$ of the daisies to her aunt. Olivia kept the rest of the daisies. How many daisies did Olivia keep?

_____

2. Cesar bought 16 baseball cards. He kept $\frac{5}{8}$ of the cards. He gave the rest of the cards to his friend. How many cards did Cesar give to his friend?

_____

3. Pavel's father bought a box of 18 pencils. He gave $\frac{2}{9}$ of the pencils to Pavel and $\frac{2}{9}$ of the pencils to Pavel's sister Helena. How many pencils were left?

_____

4. Akio had 21 stickers. He gave $\frac{3}{7}$ of the stickers to Rich and $\frac{1}{7}$ of the stickers to Imani. Akio kept the rest of the stickers. How many stickers did Akio keep?

_____

5. Gianna had 25 postcards. She gave $\frac{1}{5}$ of the postcards to her sister. She gave $\frac{1}{4}$ of the remaining postcards to her brother. Gianna kept the rest of the postcards. How many postcards did she keep?

_____

6. Mr. Redbird caught 32 fish. He gave $\frac{1}{4}$ of the fish to his brother. He kept $\frac{3}{4}$ of the remaining fish for his family. He gave the rest of the fish to his neighbor. How many fish did Mr. Redbird give to his neighbor?

_____

Find a Fraction of a Set or a Number

▶ Read a Circle Graph

Kari has 36 animals in her beanbag collection. This **circle graph** shows the fraction of the whole collection for each type of animal. For example, $\frac{1}{6}$ of the animals in her collection are rabbits.

Kari's Beanbag Animal Collection

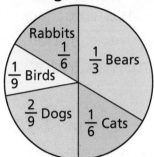

1. Complete the table.

Type of Animal	Fraction of Whole Collection	Number of Animals
Birds		
Rabbits		
Bears		
Cats		
Dogs		

Complete.

2. What type of beanbag animal does Kari have the most of?

_____

3. What type of beanbag animal does Kari have the least of?

_____

4. What fraction of the collection are the birds and dogs combined?

_____

5. What fraction of the collection are the bears and cats combined?

_____

Class Activity

▶Label and Use a Circle Graph

Ms. Timmer's class made a graph to show what color jackets students were wearing that day. There are 24 students who wore jackets.

Jacket Colors in Ms. Timmer's Class

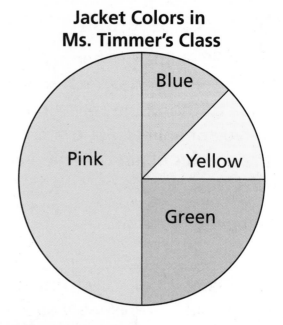

6. In each section of the circle graph, write the fraction for the color.

7. Complete the table.

Jacket Color	Fraction of All Students	Number of Students
Pink		
Blue		
Yellow		
Green		

Complete.

8. Which color jacket did most of the students wear?

_____

9. What fraction of the class wore yellow or blue jackets?

_____

10. How many more students wore green jackets than yellow jackets?

_____

11. What fraction of the class wore blue, yellow, or green jackets?

_____

▶Make Fraction Strips

Fraction Strips

Class Activity

Vocabulary

equivalent fractions

▶ Halves, Fourths, Eighths, and Sixteenths

Two fractions are **equivalent fractions** if they name the same portion of a whole.

Use your halves, fourths, eighths, and sixteenths strips to answer questions 1–5.

1. If you put your halves strip over your fourths strip, you can see that 2 fourths are the same as 1 half.

$\frac{1}{2}$		$\frac{1}{2}$	
$\frac{1}{4}$	$\frac{1}{4}$	$\frac{1}{4}$	$\frac{1}{4}$

   Complete these two equations:

   _____ fourths = 1 half $\frac{\square}{4} = \frac{1}{2}$

2. How many eighths are in a half? _____

   Complete these two equations:

   _____ eighths = 1 half $\frac{\square}{8} = \frac{1}{2}$

3. How many sixteenths are in a half? _____

   Complete these two equations:

   _____ sixteenths = 1 half $\frac{\square}{16} = \frac{1}{2}$

4. How many eighths are in one fourth? _____

   Complete these two equations:

   _____ eighths = 1 fourth $\frac{\square}{8} = \frac{1}{4}$

5. How many sixteenths are in one fourth? _____

   Complete these two equations:

   _____ sixteenths = 1 fourth $\frac{\square}{16} = \frac{1}{4}$

Class Activity

▶Thirds, Sixths, and Twelfths

Use your thirds, sixths, and twelfths strips to answer questions 6–9.

6. How many sixths are in one third? _____

   Complete these two equations:

   _____ sixths = 1 third $\dfrac{\square}{6} = \dfrac{1}{3}$

7. How many twelfths are in one third? _____

   Complete these two equations:

   _____ twelfths = 1 third $\dfrac{\square}{12} = \dfrac{1}{3}$

8. How many sixths are in two thirds? _____

   Complete these two equations:

   _____ sixths = 2 thirds $\dfrac{\square}{6} = \dfrac{2}{3}$

9. How many twelfths are in two thirds? _____

   Complete these two equations:

   _____ twelfths = 2 thirds $\dfrac{\square}{12} = \dfrac{2}{3}$

10. Use all your fraction strips to find 4 more pairs of
    equivalent fractions. Write an equation for each pair
    of equivalent fractions you find.

▶Play *Spinning a Whole*

Play *Spinning a Whole* with your partner. Write down anything interesting you discover while playing the game.

Rules for *Spinning a Whole*

Number of players: 2 or 3
What You Will Need: a Gameboard for Halves or Thirds and matching pair of spinners for each player, paper clip, ruler

1. On each turn, a player chooses and spins one of the two spinners.

2. Using the labeled fraction bars as a guide, the player marks and shades a section of the whole to represent the fraction the spinner landed on.

   • On a player's first turn, the player starts at the left end of the whole.

   • On other turns, the player starts at the right end of the last section shaded.

3. If a player spins a fraction greater than the unshaded portion of the whole, the player does not shade anything on his or her turn.

4. The first player to fill his or her whole bar completely and exactly wins.

Play *Spinning a Whole*

Game Board for Halves

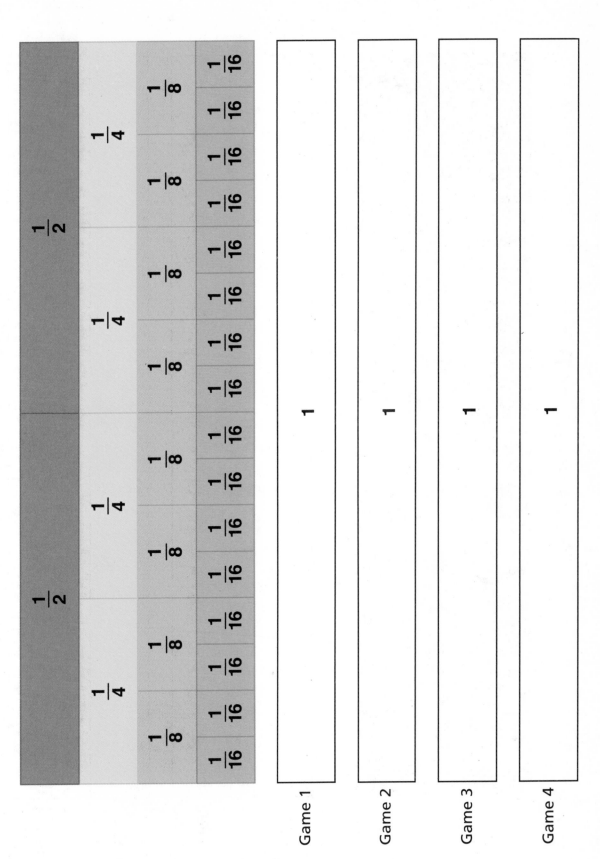

Game 1

Game 2

Game 3

Game 4

Game Board for Thirds

$\frac{1}{3}$	$\frac{1}{6}$	$\frac{1}{12}$
		$\frac{1}{12}$
	$\frac{1}{6}$	$\frac{1}{12}$
		$\frac{1}{12}$
$\frac{1}{3}$	$\frac{1}{6}$	$\frac{1}{12}$
		$\frac{1}{12}$
	$\frac{1}{6}$	$\frac{1}{12}$
		$\frac{1}{12}$
$\frac{1}{3}$	$\frac{1}{6}$	$\frac{1}{12}$
		$\frac{1}{12}$
	$\frac{1}{6}$	$\frac{1}{12}$

Game 1 — 1

Game 2 — 1

Game 3 — 1

Game 4 — 1

Spinners for Halves

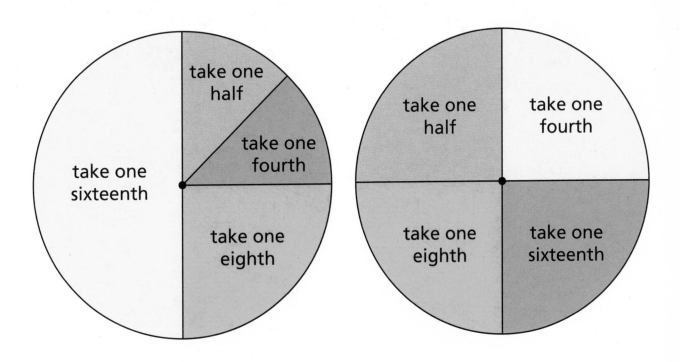

Spinners for Thirds

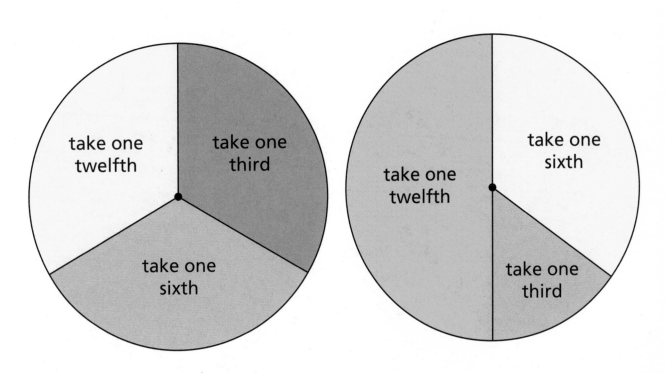

Spinners for Halves and Thirds

Multiplication Table Rows

	1	2	3	4	5	6	7	8	9	10
1	1	2	3	4	5	6	7	8	9	10
2	2	4	6	8	10	12	14	16	18	20
3	3	6	9	12	15	18	21	24	27	30
4	4	8	12	16	20	24	28	32	36	40
5	5	10	15	20	25	30	35	40	45	50
6	6	12	18	24	30	36	42	48	54	60
7	7	14	21	28	35	42	49	56	63	70
8	8	16	24	32	40	48	56	64	72	80
9	9	18	27	36	45	54	63	72	81	90
10	10	20	30	40	50	60	70	80	90	100

Equivalent Fraction Box

× 1	× 2	× 3	× 4	× 5	× 6	× 7	× 8	× 9	× 10

=	=	=	=	=	=	=	=	=	=

× 1	× 2	× 3	× 4	× 5	× 6	× 7	× 8	× 9	× 10

Equivalence Chains

Class Activity

Vocabulary

equivalent

▶ Model Equivalence Chains

1. Show that $\frac{2}{7} = \frac{6}{21}$ by 3-fracturing each part of the second model.

▶ Identify Equivalent Fractions

Write the multiplier in the box. Are the fractions equivalent? Write yes or no. If the fractions are equivalent, write the common multiplier.

2. $\frac{2}{7}$ ×☐ $\frac{6}{21}$ ×☐ _____

3. $\frac{1}{5}$ ×☐ $\frac{4}{25}$ ×☐ _____

4. $\frac{3}{4}$ ×☐ $\frac{6}{8}$ ×☐ _____

5. $\frac{5}{8}$ ×☐ $\frac{15}{24}$ ×☐ _____

6. $\frac{4}{9}$ ×☐ $\frac{40}{90}$ ×☐ _____

7. $\frac{7}{8}$ ×☐ $\frac{42}{56}$ ×☐ _____

▶ Make Equivalence Chains

Make an equivalence chain starting with the fraction given.

8. $\frac{1}{2} =$

9. $\frac{2}{3} =$

10. **On the Back** Explain the meaning of equivalent fractions. Draw a picture to help explain.

Name _____ **Date** _____

_____

_____

_____

_____

_____

_____

_____

_____

_____

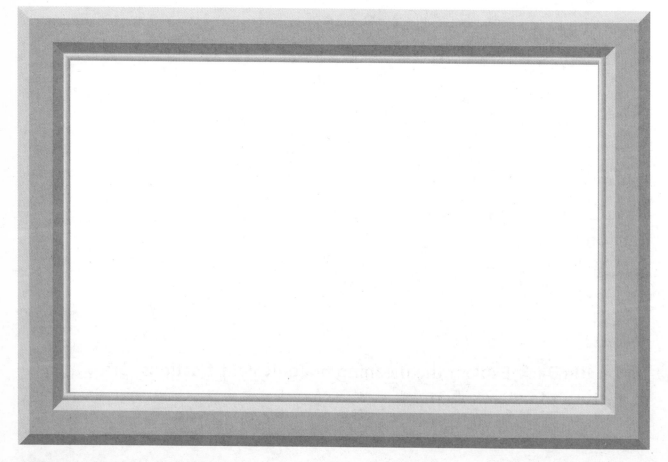

Equivalence Patterns

▶Fracturing a Fraction

Equivalent fractions show the same amount, but they are divided into a different unit fraction. Fracturing a fraction gives us an equivalent fraction with more unit fractions, but the unit fractions are smaller.

Complete to write the equivalent fractions shown on the fraction strips.

Fewer but larger unit fractions

More but smaller unit fractions

1. 5-fracture each third

$$\frac{\boxed{2}}{\boxed{3}} = \frac{\boxed{2} \times 5}{\boxed{3} \times 5} = \frac{\boxed{}}{\boxed{}}$$

2. 3-fracture each fourth

$$\frac{\boxed{}}{\boxed{}} = \frac{\boxed{} \times 3}{\boxed{} \times 3} = \frac{\boxed{}}{\boxed{}}$$

3. 7-fracture each half

$$\frac{\boxed{}}{\boxed{}} = \frac{\boxed{} \times 7}{\boxed{} \times 7} = \frac{\boxed{}}{\boxed{}}$$

4. 2-fracture each sixth

$$\frac{\boxed{}}{\boxed{}} = \frac{\boxed{} \times 2}{\boxed{} \times 2} = \frac{\boxed{}}{\boxed{}}$$

5. 3-fracture each eighth

$$\frac{\boxed{}}{\boxed{}} = \frac{\boxed{} \times 3}{\boxed{} \times 3} = \frac{\boxed{}}{\boxed{}}$$

▶Show that Fractions are Equivalent

Shade the fraction strips to show that each pair of fractions is equivalent. Then fill in the missing multipliers in the answer boxes.

6. $\dfrac{1}{2}$ and $\dfrac{5}{10}$

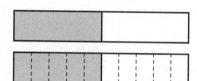

$$\frac{1}{2} = \frac{1 \times \boxed{5}}{2 \times \boxed{5}} = \frac{5}{10}$$

7. $\dfrac{1}{4}$ and $\dfrac{2}{8}$

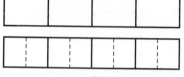

$$\frac{1}{4} = \frac{1 \times \boxed{}}{4 \times \boxed{}} = \frac{2}{8}$$

8. $\dfrac{2}{3}$ and $\dfrac{6}{9}$

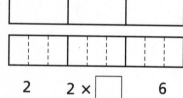

$$\frac{2}{3} = \frac{2 \times \boxed{}}{3 \times \boxed{}} = \frac{6}{9}$$

9. $\dfrac{3}{5}$ and $\dfrac{6}{10}$

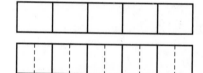

$$\frac{3}{5} = \frac{3 \times \boxed{}}{5 \times \boxed{}} = \frac{6}{10}$$

Complete to show that the fractions are equivalent.

10. $\dfrac{5}{8}$ and $\dfrac{15}{24}$

$$\frac{5}{8} = \frac{5 \times \boxed{}}{8 \times \boxed{}} = \frac{15}{24}$$

11. $\dfrac{4}{9}$ and $\dfrac{28}{63}$

$$\frac{4}{9} = \frac{4 \times \boxed{}}{9 \times \boxed{}} = \frac{28}{63}$$

Find the missing numbers.

12. $\dfrac{3}{8} = \dfrac{3 \times \boxed{}}{8 \times \boxed{}} = \dfrac{9}{\boxed{}}$

13. $\dfrac{2}{5} = \dfrac{2 \times \boxed{}}{5 \times \boxed{}} = \dfrac{\boxed{}}{40}$

14. $\dfrac{5}{9} = \dfrac{5 \times \boxed{}}{9 \times \boxed{}} = \dfrac{35}{\boxed{}}$

15. $\dfrac{4}{7} = \dfrac{4 \times \boxed{}}{7 \times \boxed{}} = \dfrac{\boxed{}}{35}$

16. $\dfrac{5}{6} = \dfrac{5 \times \boxed{}}{6 \times \boxed{}} = \dfrac{25}{\boxed{}}$

17. $\dfrac{3}{4} = \dfrac{3 \times \boxed{}}{4 \times \boxed{}} = \dfrac{24}{\boxed{}}$

Find Equivalent Fractions by Multiplying

Vocabulary

simplify

▶Simplify Fractions with Fraction Strips

Fracturing a fraction gives us an equivalent fraction with more unit fractions. **Simplifying** a fraction is just the opposite. It gives us an equivalent fraction with fewer unit fractions.

Write the simpified fraction shown on the second fraction strip.

4-group the twelfths to make thirds

1.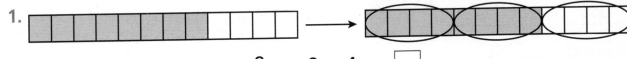

$$\frac{8}{12} = \frac{8 \div 4}{12 \div 4} = \frac{\square}{\square}$$

2-group the tenths to make fifths

2.

$$\frac{4}{10} = \frac{4 \div 2}{10 \div 2} = \frac{\square}{\square}$$

8-group the sixteenths to make halves

3.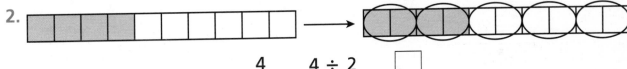

$$\frac{8}{16} = \frac{8 \div 8}{16 \div 8} = \frac{\square}{\square}$$

6-group the eighteenths to make thirds

4.

$$\frac{12}{18} = \frac{12 \div 6}{18 \div 6} = \frac{\square}{\square}$$

5-group the twenty-fifths to make fifths

5.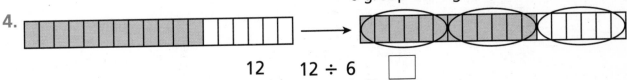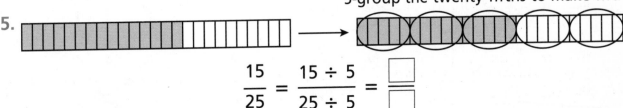

$$\frac{15}{25} = \frac{15 \div 5}{25 \div 5} = \frac{\square}{\square}$$

Name _____

Date _____

Class Activity

▶Simplify Fractions

Shade the fraction strips to show that the fractions are equivalent. Group the top unit fractions to make the bottom unit fractions. Then fill in the missing divisors.

6. $\dfrac{14}{21}$ and $\dfrac{2}{3}$

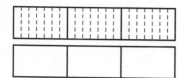

$$\dfrac{14}{21} = \dfrac{14 \div \boxed{7}}{21 \div \boxed{7}} = \dfrac{2}{3}$$

7. $\dfrac{12}{16}$ and $\dfrac{3}{4}$

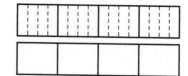

$$\dfrac{12}{16} = \dfrac{12 \div \boxed{}}{16 \div \boxed{}} = \dfrac{3}{4}$$

8. $\dfrac{9}{15}$ and $\dfrac{3}{5}$

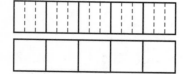

$$\dfrac{9}{15} = \dfrac{9 \div \boxed{}}{15 \div \boxed{}} = \dfrac{3}{5}$$

9. $\dfrac{16}{18}$ and $\dfrac{8}{9}$

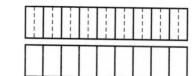

$$\dfrac{16}{18} = \dfrac{16 \div \boxed{}}{18 \div \boxed{}} = \dfrac{8}{9}$$

Simplify the fraction.

10. $\dfrac{14}{21} = \dfrac{14 \div \boxed{}}{21 \div \boxed{}} = \dfrac{\boxed{}}{3}$

11. $\dfrac{21}{28} = \dfrac{21 \div \boxed{}}{28 \div \boxed{}} = \dfrac{\boxed{}}{4}$

12. $\dfrac{63}{81} = \dfrac{63 \div \boxed{}}{81 \div \boxed{}} = \dfrac{7}{\boxed{}}$

13. $\dfrac{16}{18} = \dfrac{16 \div \boxed{}}{18 \div \boxed{}} = \dfrac{8}{\boxed{}}$

14. $\dfrac{30}{42} = \dfrac{30 \div \boxed{}}{42 \div \boxed{}} = \dfrac{\boxed{}}{7}$

15. $\dfrac{20}{24} = \dfrac{20 \div \boxed{}}{24 \div \boxed{}} = \dfrac{5}{\boxed{}}$

16. $\dfrac{10}{20} = \dfrac{10 \div \boxed{}}{20 \div \boxed{}} = \dfrac{1}{\boxed{}}$

17. $\dfrac{20}{25} = \dfrac{20 \div \boxed{}}{25 \div \boxed{}} = \dfrac{\boxed{}}{5}$

18. $\dfrac{27}{36} = \dfrac{27 \div \boxed{}}{36 \div \boxed{}} = \dfrac{3}{\boxed{}}$

Find Equivalent Fractions by Dividing

▶Use Fraction Strips to Add

Equivalent Fraction Strips

▶Add Fractions Using Fraction Strips

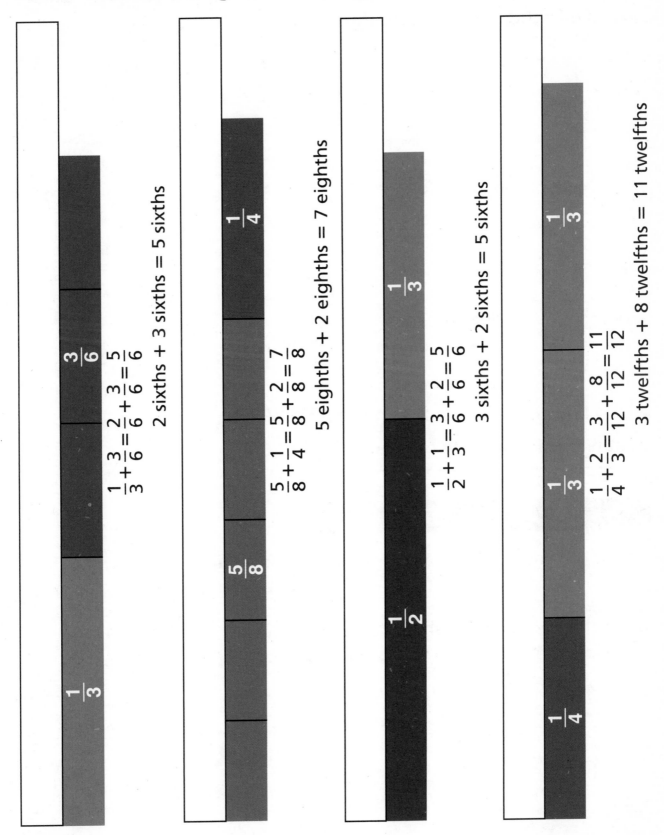

$\frac{1}{3} + \frac{3}{6} = \frac{2}{6} + \frac{3}{6} = \frac{5}{6}$

2 sixths + 3 sixths = 5 sixths

$\frac{5}{8} + \frac{1}{4} = \frac{5}{8} + \frac{2}{8} = \frac{7}{8}$

5 eighths + 2 eighths = 7 eighths

$\frac{1}{2} + \frac{1}{3} = \frac{3}{6} + \frac{2}{6} = \frac{5}{6}$

3 sixths + 2 sixths = 5 sixths

$\frac{1}{4} + \frac{2}{3} = \frac{3}{12} + \frac{8}{12} = \frac{11}{12}$

3 twelfths + 8 twelfths = 11 twelfths

▶ Add Fractions Made from the Same Unit Fraction

Circle the fractions on the strip. Then add.

1.

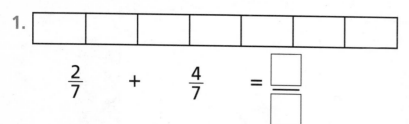

$\dfrac{2}{7}$ + $\dfrac{4}{7}$ = $\dfrac{\square}{\square}$

2 sevenths + 4 sevenths = 6 _____

Complete.

2. $\dfrac{3}{6} + \dfrac{2}{6} = \dfrac{\square}{\square}$

3. $\dfrac{1}{5} + \dfrac{3}{5} = \dfrac{\square}{\square}$

4. $\dfrac{3}{8} + \dfrac{2}{8} = \dfrac{\square}{\square}$

5. Which number does not change when you add fractions with the same denominator? Why?

_____

▶ Add Fractions Made from Different Unit Fractions

Use the fraction strips to complete exercises 6–8.

6. How can you rename $\dfrac{4}{6}$ and $\dfrac{1}{4}$ so they can be added?

_____

7. Use the fraction strips above to show how to rename the fractions so they can be added.

8. $\dfrac{4}{6}$ + $\dfrac{1}{4}$

$\dfrac{\square}{12}$ + $\dfrac{\square}{12}$ = $\dfrac{\square}{12}$

8 twelfths + 3 twelfths = _____

Add. Use the fraction strips to help you.

9. $\frac{3}{7} + \frac{2}{7} =$ _____

10. $\frac{3}{9} + \frac{5}{9} =$ _____

11. $\frac{6}{11} + \frac{2}{11} =$ _____

12. $\frac{4}{12} + \frac{7}{12} =$ _____

13. $\frac{2}{3} + \frac{2}{9} =$ _____

14. $\frac{5}{8} + \frac{3}{16} =$ _____

15. $\frac{3}{4} + \frac{3}{12} =$ _____

16. $\frac{2}{3} + \frac{1}{5} =$ _____

17. $\frac{1}{4} + \frac{1}{6} =$ _____

18. $\frac{3}{6} + \frac{1}{4} =$ _____

19. $\frac{1}{2} + \frac{2}{5} =$ _____

20. $\frac{1}{3} + \frac{2}{4} =$ _____

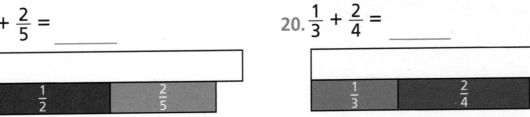

21. **On the Back** Explain how you found the answer to exercise 18.

_____

_____

_____

_____

_____

_____

_____

_____

_____

_____

_____

_____

_____

_____

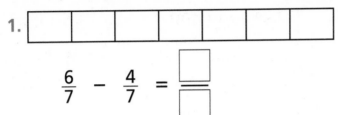

Class Activity

▶ Subtract Fractions Made from the Same Unit Fraction

Circle $\frac{6}{7}$ of the fraction strip. Then subtract $\frac{4}{7}$.

1.

$$\frac{6}{7} - \frac{4}{7} = \frac{\square}{\square}$$

6 sevenths − 4 sevenths = _____

Complete.

2. $\frac{5}{8} - \frac{2}{8} =$ _____

3. $\frac{9}{10} - \frac{5}{10} =$ _____

4. $\frac{11}{12} - \frac{7}{12} =$ _____

5. Which number does not change when you subtract fractions with the same denominator?

_____

▶ Subtract Fractions Made from Different Unit Fractions

Use the fraction strip to complete exercises 6–8.

Find $\frac{1}{2} - \frac{1}{6}$.

6. How can you rename $\frac{1}{2}$ so $\frac{1}{6}$ can be subtracted?

_____

7. Use the fraction strip above to show how to rename $\frac{1}{2}$ so that $\frac{1}{6}$ can be subtracted.

8. $\quad \frac{1}{2} - \frac{1}{6}$

$$\frac{\square}{6} - \frac{1}{6} = \frac{\square}{\square}$$

[_____] sixths − one sixth = _____

9. Show $\frac{3}{4} - \frac{3}{8}$ on the fraction strip to the right.

▶Compare Fractions

10. Which is greater, $\frac{3}{6}$ or $\frac{2}{6}$? Explain how you know.

_____

_____

11. Which is greater, $\frac{1}{3}$ or $\frac{1}{4}$? Explain how you know.

_____

_____

12. Which is greater, $\frac{2}{3}$ or $\frac{2}{4}$? Explain how you know.

_____

_____

Compare these fractions. Write >, <, or = in the ◯.

13. $\frac{1}{5}$ ◯ $\frac{1}{4}$

14. $\frac{1}{2}$ ◯ $\frac{1}{4}$

15. $\frac{4}{8}$ ◯ $\frac{2}{8}$

16. $\frac{4}{7}$ ◯ $\frac{4}{9}$

17. $\frac{3}{12}$ ◯ $\frac{3}{11}$

18. $\frac{4}{10}$ ◯ $\frac{4}{5}$

19. $\frac{6}{8}$ ◯ $\frac{7}{8}$

20. $\frac{5}{5}$ ◯ $\frac{6}{6}$

21. $\frac{7}{8}$ ◯ $\frac{7}{9}$

**Use fraction strips to compare these fractions.
Write >, <, or = in the ◯.**

22. $\frac{4}{6}$ ◯ $\frac{1}{3}$

23. $\frac{2}{7}$ ◯ $\frac{1}{6}$

24. $\frac{9}{10}$ ◯ $\frac{4}{5}$

25. $\frac{1}{2}$ ◯ $\frac{5}{8}$

26. $\frac{5}{6}$ ◯ $\frac{9}{12}$

27. $\frac{5}{9}$ ◯ $\frac{2}{3}$

Write the fractions in order from least to greatest.

28. $\frac{1}{2}, \frac{1}{4}, \frac{1}{3}$

_____

29. $\frac{3}{5}, \frac{2}{5}, \frac{4}{5}$

_____

► Add, Compare, and Subtract Fractions

Add, compare, and subtract each pair of fractions.

Add	Compare	Subtract
30. $\frac{3}{8} + \frac{5}{8} =$ _____	$\frac{3}{8}$ ◯ $\frac{5}{8}$	
31. $\frac{1}{4} + \frac{1}{3} =$ _____	$\frac{1}{4}$ ◯ $\frac{1}{3}$	
32. $\frac{1}{3} + \frac{1}{2} =$ _____	$\frac{1}{3}$ ◯ $\frac{1}{2}$	
33. $\frac{5}{6} + \frac{1}{3} =$ _____	$\frac{5}{6}$ ◯ $\frac{1}{3}$	
34. $\frac{1}{2} + \frac{2}{4} =$ _____	$\frac{1}{2}$ ◯ $\frac{2}{4}$	

Class Activity

Name _____ Date _____

► **Fractions in Word Problems**

Solve.

Show your work.

35. Layton ate $\frac{1}{6}$ of the cake. Kyra ate $\frac{3}{6}$ of the cake. Who ate more cake? How much more?

_____

36. Jorie ate $\frac{5}{6}$ of her popsicle. Nat ate $\frac{3}{4}$ of his popsicle. Who ate more? How much more?

_____

37. One fourth of the cars in the parking lot are red. Three eighths of the cars are blue. Are there more red cars or more blue cars?

_____

38. The red squirrel ate $\frac{2}{3}$ of the acorns. The gray squirrel ate $\frac{1}{4}$ of the acorns. What fraction of the acorns did they eat altogether?

_____

39. Camille has two cats, Cole and Nicky. Every day, Cole eats $\frac{1}{3}$ of a can of food. Nicky eats $\frac{4}{6}$ of a can of food. How much of the can do the two cats eat together?

_____

40. Oakton School and Pine School use the same amount of paper. Oakton recycles $\frac{3}{4}$ of its paper. Pine recycles $\frac{2}{4}$ of its paper. How much more of its paper does Oakton recycle than Pine recycles?

_____

Compare and Subtract Fractions

▶Compare Fractions on a Number Line

Circle the lengths to show each fraction. Then compare them. Write <, >, or = in the ◯.

1. $\frac{3}{6}$ ◯ $\frac{5}{6}$

    0   1
    |——+———+———+———+———+———+——>
    $\frac{0}{6}$ $\frac{1}{6}$ $\frac{2}{6}$ $\frac{3}{6}$ $\frac{4}{6}$ $\frac{5}{6}$ $\frac{6}{6}$

2. $\frac{3}{8}$ ◯ $\frac{2}{8}$

    0   1
    |——+———+———+———+———+———+———+———+——>
    $\frac{0}{8}$ $\frac{1}{8}$ $\frac{2}{8}$ $\frac{3}{8}$ $\frac{4}{8}$ $\frac{5}{8}$ $\frac{6}{8}$ $\frac{7}{8}$ $\frac{8}{8}$

3. $\frac{2}{5}$ ◯ $\frac{1}{3}$

    $\frac{0}{3}$ $\frac{1}{3}$ $\frac{2}{3}$ $\frac{3}{3}$

    $\frac{0}{5}$ $\frac{1}{5}$ $\frac{2}{5}$ $\frac{3}{5}$ $\frac{4}{5}$ $\frac{5}{5}$

4. $\frac{2}{3}$ ◯ $\frac{1}{2}$

    $\frac{0}{3}$ $\frac{1}{3}$ $\frac{2}{3}$ $\frac{3}{3}$

    $\frac{0}{2}$ $\frac{1}{2}$ $\frac{2}{2}$

5. $\frac{1}{4}$ ◯ $\frac{2}{8}$

    $\frac{0}{4}$ $\frac{1}{4}$ $\frac{2}{4}$ $\frac{3}{4}$ $\frac{4}{4}$

    $\frac{0}{8}$ $\frac{1}{8}$ $\frac{2}{8}$ $\frac{3}{8}$ $\frac{4}{8}$ $\frac{5}{8}$ $\frac{6}{8}$ $\frac{7}{8}$ $\frac{8}{8}$

6. $\frac{2}{3}$ ◯ $\frac{5}{6}$

    $\frac{0}{3}$ $\frac{1}{3}$ $\frac{2}{3}$ $\frac{3}{3}$

    $\frac{0}{6}$ $\frac{1}{6}$ $\frac{2}{6}$ $\frac{3}{6}$ $\frac{4}{6}$ $\frac{5}{6}$ $\frac{6}{6}$

7. $\frac{1}{4}$ ◯ $\frac{3}{6}$

    $\frac{0}{4}$ $\frac{1}{4}$ $\frac{2}{4}$ $\frac{3}{4}$ $\frac{4}{4}$

    $\frac{0}{6}$ $\frac{1}{6}$ $\frac{2}{6}$ $\frac{3}{6}$ $\frac{4}{6}$ $\frac{5}{6}$ $\frac{6}{6}$

8. $\frac{1}{3}$ ◯ $\frac{2}{4}$

    $\frac{0}{3}$ $\frac{1}{3}$ $\frac{2}{3}$ $\frac{3}{3}$

    $\frac{0}{4}$ $\frac{1}{4}$ $\frac{2}{4}$ $\frac{3}{4}$ $\frac{4}{4}$

Class Activity

▶ Add and Subtract Fractions on a Number Line

Circle the lengths on the number lines to add or subtract.

9. $\frac{3}{6} + \frac{2}{6} =$ _____

0   1

| $\frac{0}{6}$ | $\frac{1}{6}$ | $\frac{2}{6}$ | $\frac{3}{6}$ | $\frac{4}{6}$ | $\frac{5}{6}$ | $\frac{6}{6}$ |

10. $\frac{3}{6} - \frac{2}{6} =$ _____

0   1

| $\frac{0}{6}$ | $\frac{1}{6}$ | $\frac{2}{6}$ | $\frac{3}{6}$ | $\frac{4}{6}$ | $\frac{5}{6}$ | $\frac{6}{6}$ |

11. $\frac{2}{5} + \frac{2}{5} =$ _____

0   1

| $\frac{0}{5}$ | $\frac{1}{5}$ | $\frac{2}{5}$ | $\frac{3}{5}$ | $\frac{4}{5}$ | $\frac{5}{5}$ |

12. $\frac{4}{5} - \frac{3}{5} =$ _____

0   1

| $\frac{0}{5}$ | $\frac{1}{5}$ | $\frac{2}{5}$ | $\frac{3}{5}$ | $\frac{4}{5}$ | $\frac{5}{5}$ |

13. $\frac{1}{8} + \frac{3}{8} =$ _____

0   1

| $\frac{0}{8}$ | $\frac{1}{8}$ | $\frac{2}{8}$ | $\frac{3}{8}$ | $\frac{4}{8}$ | $\frac{5}{8}$ | $\frac{6}{8}$ | $\frac{7}{8}$ | $\frac{8}{8}$ |

14. $\frac{7}{8} - \frac{5}{8} =$ _____

0   1

| $\frac{0}{8}$ | $\frac{1}{8}$ | $\frac{2}{8}$ | $\frac{3}{8}$ | $\frac{4}{8}$ | $\frac{5}{8}$ | $\frac{6}{8}$ | $\frac{7}{8}$ | $\frac{8}{8}$ |

15. $\frac{2}{6} + \frac{3}{6} =$ _____

0   1

| $\frac{0}{6}$ | $\frac{1}{6}$ | $\frac{2}{6}$ | $\frac{3}{6}$ | $\frac{4}{6}$ | $\frac{5}{6}$ | $\frac{6}{6}$ |

16. $\frac{4}{5} - \frac{2}{5} =$ _____

0   1

| $\frac{0}{5}$ | $\frac{1}{5}$ | $\frac{2}{5}$ | $\frac{3}{5}$ | $\frac{4}{5}$ | $\frac{5}{5}$ |

Fractions on a Number Line and Fractions and Decimals

Class Activity

Name _____ Date _____

Vocabulary
decimal
decimal point

►Relate Fractions and Decimals

Fractions can be written as **decimals**.

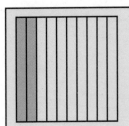

	Fraction		Decimal	
	write:	**read:**	**write:**	**read:**
	$\frac{2}{10}$	two tenths	**0.2**	two tenths

↑ — **decimal point**

	Fraction		Decimal	
	write:	**read:**	**write:**	**read:**
	$\frac{2}{100}$	two hundredths	**0.02**	two hundredths

	Fraction		Decimal	
	write:	**read:**	**write:**	**read:**
	$\frac{30}{100}$	thirty hundredths	**0.30**	thirty hundredths

Write each fraction as a decimal.

17. $\frac{1}{10}$ = _____

18. $\frac{5}{10}$ = _____

19. $\frac{9}{10}$ = _____

20. $\frac{34}{100}$ = _____

21. $\frac{50}{100}$ = _____

22. $\frac{6}{100}$ = _____

Write each decimal as a fraction.

23. 0.8 = _____

24. 0.5 = _____

25. 0.7 = _____

26. 0.09 = _____

27. 0.65 = _____

28. 0.40 = _____

29. **On the Back** Explain how to write $\frac{3}{100}$ as a decimal.

▶Use Models to Visualize Mixed Numbers and Improper Fractions

Write the mixed number and improper fraction that the drawing shows.

1.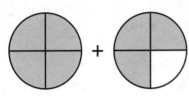

$1 + \dfrac{3}{4} = 1\dfrac{3}{4}$

$\dfrac{4}{4} + \dfrac{3}{4} = \dfrac{7}{4}$

2.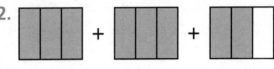

$1 + \underline{} + \underline{} = \underline{}$

$\dfrac{3}{3} + \underline{} + \underline{} = \underline{}$

3.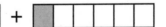

$1 + \underline{} + \underline{} + \underline{} = \underline{}$

$\dfrac{3}{3} + \underline{} + \underline{} + \underline{} = \underline{}$

4.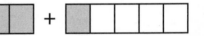

$1 + \underline{} = \underline{}$

$\underline{} + \underline{} = \underline{}$

5.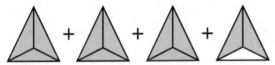

$1 + \underline{} = \underline{}$

$\underline{} + \underline{} = \underline{}$

6.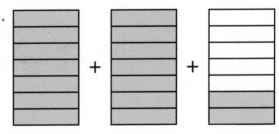

$1 + \underline{} + \underline{} = \underline{}$

$\dfrac{7}{7} + \underline{} + \underline{} = \underline{}$

Class Activity

▶ Mixed Numbers and Improper Fractions on a Number Line

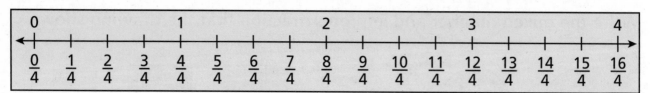

Use the number line to write the improper fraction,
mixed number, or whole number.

7. $\dfrac{13}{4} =$ _____

8. $\dfrac{7}{4} =$ _____

9. $\dfrac{10}{4} =$ _____

10. $\dfrac{16}{4} =$ _____

11. $1\dfrac{1}{4} =$ _____

12. $2\dfrac{1}{4} =$ _____

13. $3\dfrac{1}{4} =$ _____

14. $2\dfrac{3}{4} =$ _____

▶ Practice with Mixed Numbers and Improper Fractions

Write the improper fraction or mixed number.

15. $2\dfrac{3}{5} =$ _____

16. $\dfrac{8}{6} =$ _____

17. $1\dfrac{2}{7} =$ _____

18. $\dfrac{11}{9} =$ _____

$\dfrac{5}{5} + \dfrac{5}{5} + \dfrac{3}{5} = \dfrac{13}{5}$

19. $1\dfrac{5}{8} =$ _____

20. $3\dfrac{1}{2} =$ _____

21. $\dfrac{19}{4} =$ _____

22. $\dfrac{7}{5} =$ _____

23. $\dfrac{10}{3} =$ _____

24. $2\dfrac{1}{6} =$ _____

25. $1\dfrac{3}{9} =$ _____

26. $\dfrac{11}{7} =$ _____

Improper Fractions and Mixed Numbers

Class Activity

▶Explore Division with Remainders

Solve.

1. Hassan is making party decorations for the classroom. He needs 5 inches of string for each one. He has 15 inches of string. How many decorations can Hassan make?

_____

2. Ana is also making decorations. She needs 5 inches of string per decoration. She has 16 inches of string. How many decorations can she make? How many inches of string will be left over?

_____

3. Glenna is making copies of a story she wrote. She needs 4 pieces of paper per copy. She has 34 pieces of paper. How many copies can Glenna make?

_____

4. Owen needs to pack 44 snacks into boxes. He can fit 8 snacks in each box. How many boxes does Owen need to pack all of the snacks?

_____

5. Ty plans to write 60 math problems. He can fit 8 problems on a page. How many pages will Ty need for all 60 math problems?

_____

6. The Science Club is renting vans for 37 people to take a field trip. Each van holds 8 people. How many vans are needed?

_____

7. A truck company will carry 65 tons of gravel today. Each truck can hold 9 tons. How many trucks will be needed to carry the gravel?

_____

8. Hector needs to put 9 flowers in each vase. He has 59 flowers in all. How many vases can Hector fill? How many flowers will be left over?

_____

▶Practice Dividing with Remainders

Write the answer.

9. 3)17   10. 6)26   11. 8)27   12. 7)39

13. 6)40   14. 9)56   15. 5)48   16. 2)15

17. 5)33   18. 8)45   19. 7)44   20. 3)29

21. 4)30   22. 9)71   23. 3)31   24. 8)63

25. 2)17   26. 4)27   27. 5)37   28. 6)56

29. 7)54   30. 8)54   31. 9)73   32. 10)55

                                        Introduce Division with Remainders

▶Express the Remainder as a Fraction

**Write the answer with a remainder and then as
a mixed number.**

1. $6\overline{)56}$ 2. $8\overline{)49}$ 3. $3\overline{)17}$ 4. $7\overline{)68}$

5. $9\overline{)42}$ 6. $5\overline{)48}$ 7. $8\overline{)30}$ 8. $7\overline{)18}$

9. $4\overline{)22}$ 10. $7\overline{)36}$ 11. $6\overline{)28}$ 12. $9\overline{)88}$

13. $8\overline{)75}$ 14. $5\overline{)49}$ 15. $9\overline{)38}$ 16. $7\overline{)58}$

17. $2\overline{)19}$ 18. $3\overline{)26}$ 19. $6\overline{)53}$ 20. $8\overline{)54}$

▶Interpret Remainders

Solve.

21. At the end of each day, the 3 bakers at Ben's Bakery each take home an equal amount of leftover cake. On Tuesday, 7 cakes were left over. How much cake will each baker take home?

_____

22. A delivery man has 78 jugs of water in his truck. He will leave 9 jugs of water at each delivery stop. How many stops will he make? How many jugs will be left in his truck?

_____

23. Today 6 people went on a picnic in the park. They agreed to share 14 cups of lemonade equally. How much lemonade will each person get to drink?

_____

24. Ben's Bakery has 54 cupcakes. The bakery packs cupcakes in boxes of 8 each. How many boxes will be filled? How many cupcakes will be left over?

_____

25. Mr. Calvert has 7 cats. Each week, he divides 38 cans of cat food equally among his cats. How many cans of cat food does each cat eat per week?

_____

26. There are 89 goldfish in the fishpond. They will be put in fish tanks for the winter. If each fish tank holds 9 fish, how many tanks are needed?

_____

27. Thirty-nine people are traveling to the basketball game. If each van holds 9 people, how many vans will be needed?

_____

28. Jamal has 41 CDs. Each shelf in his CD rack holds 6 CDs. How many shelves does he need to hold all his CDs?

_____

Understand Remainders

▶More Division Word Problems with Remainders

Solve.

1. Eileen is putting popcorn balls into bags for a party. She has 51 popcorn balls. Each bag holds 6. How many bags can Eileen fill completely? How many popcorn balls will be left over?

2. Luis is making hot chocolate for 8 friends. The friends would like to share it equally. If Luis makes 25 cups of hot chocolate, how much hot chocolate can each friend have?

3. Rey is filling the fish tanks at the zoo. He has 63 gallons of water. Each tank holds 10 gallons. How many tanks can Rey fill? How much water will be left over?

4. Lisa is putting cans on shelves in the grocery store. There are 37 cans. Each shelf holds 8 cans. How many shelves can Lisa fill? How many cans will be left over?

5. Mrs. Lin ordered 34 mini-pizzas for her niece's party. Nine girls are coming to the party. How many mini-pizzas can each girl have if the pizzas are shared equally?

6. Crystal needs to pack 40 pieces of clothing into her dresser drawers. If each drawer holds 7 pieces of clothing, how many dresser drawers does she need to fit all her clothing?

7. Sunny has 43 rings. She can put 8 rings in a jewelry box. How many jewelry boxes does Sunny need to store all the rings?

8. Emilio is arranging daisies in vases. He has 54 daisies. Each vase will hold 7 daisies. How many vases can Emilio fill?

▶Practice Dividing with Remainders

Write the answer with a remainder and as a mixed number.

9. 23 ÷ 7 _____   10. 31 ÷ 6 _____   11. 75 ÷ 9 _____

_____   _____   _____

12. 63 ÷ 8 _____   13. 44 ÷ 9 _____   14. 52 ÷ 7 _____

_____   _____   _____

15. 85 ÷ 9 _____   16. 17 ÷ 5 _____   17. 38 ÷ 7 _____

_____   _____   _____

18. 46 ÷ 6 _____   19. 67 ÷ 8 _____   20. 57 ÷ 7 _____

_____   _____   _____

21. 43 ÷ 5 _____   22. 37 ÷ 4 _____   23. 79 ÷ 8 _____

_____   _____   _____

Practice Division with Remainders

1. Write a fraction to represent the part of the whole that is shaded.

_____

2. What fraction of the circles are shaded?

_____

Use mental math to find the answer.

3. $\frac{1}{5} \times 40 =$ _____

4. $\frac{3}{4}$ of 24 = _____

**Use the fraction strips to show the fractions are equivalent.
Then fill the missing numbers in the boxes.**

5. $\frac{4}{5}$ and $\frac{8}{10}$

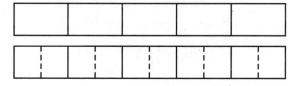

$$\frac{4}{5} = \frac{4 \times \square}{5 \times \square} = \frac{8}{10}$$

6. $\frac{9}{12}$ and $\frac{3}{4}$

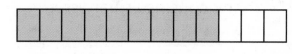

$$\frac{9}{12} = \frac{9 \div \square}{12 \div \square} = \frac{3}{4}$$

Complete.

7. $\dfrac{3}{8} = \dfrac{3 \times \square}{8 \times \square} = \dfrac{15}{\square}$

8. $\dfrac{8}{12} = \dfrac{8 \div \square}{12 \div \square} = \dfrac{2}{\square}$

9. Compare. Write >, <, or = in the ◯.

$\frac{1}{5}$ ◯ $\frac{1}{4}$

10. Write the answer with a remainder and as a mixed number.

$6\overline{)38}$

Write the mixed number or improper fraction.

11. $\frac{15}{4} =$ _____

12. $2\frac{7}{8} =$ _____

Add or subtract.

13. $\frac{2}{7} + \frac{3}{7} =$ _____

14. $\frac{6}{9} - \frac{3}{9} =$ _____

Add or subtract. Use the fraction strips to help you.

15. $\frac{1}{6} + \frac{3}{12} =$ _____

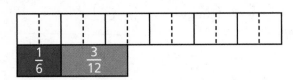

16. $\frac{2}{3} - \frac{4}{9} =$ _____

17. Use the bar graph to fill in the blanks.

Vanessa has _____ as many cousins as Andrew.

Andrew has _____ as many cousins as Vanessa.

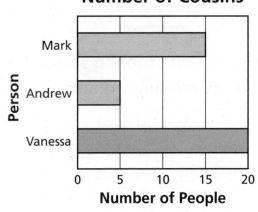

Number of Cousins

Solve.

18. Harris has 41 books. Each shelf in his bookshelf holds 6 books. How many shelves does he need to hold all his books?

_____

19. A store has 63 caps. $\frac{2}{9}$ of the caps are blue. How many blue caps does the store have?

_____

20. **Extended Response** Use the circle graph to answer the question.

A bakery made 36 batches of cookies in all. How many batches of coconut cookies were made?

_____

Explain how you found your answer.

_____

_____

_____

Batches of Cookies Baked

Vocabulary

net
cube

►Make a Cube

Cut around the outside of the first **net**. Fold to make a
cube. Which of the other two nets will make a **cube**?
Cut out the nets to test your prediction.

1.

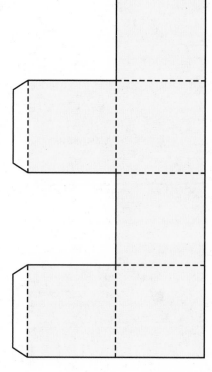

2.

3.

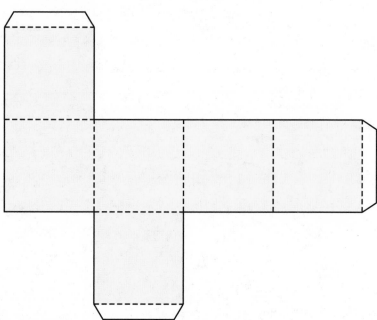

Explore Cubes

Name _____   **Date** _____

▶Identify Cube Nets

Circle the nets that you think will form a cube. Cut out the ones you circled and test your predictions.

4.

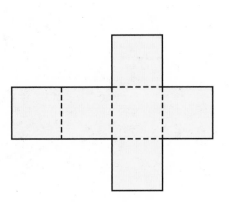

5.

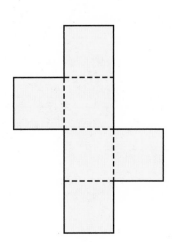

6.

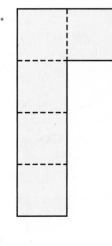

7.

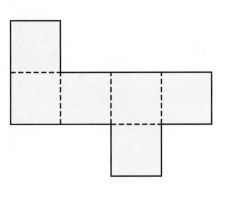

8.

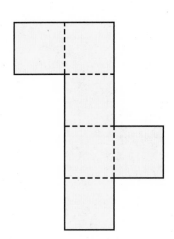

9.

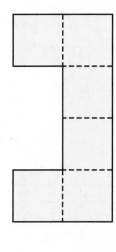

Explore Cubes

▶ Create a Cube Net

10. Draw a net that will form a cube when it is folded.
    Then, cut it out and form the cube.

Explore Cubes

Dear Family,

Your child is exploring three-dimensional or solid figures.

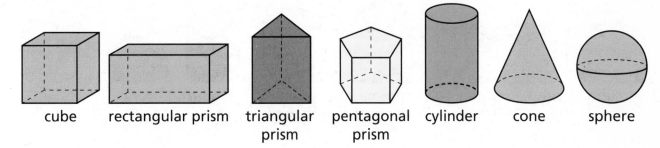

cube   rectangular prism   triangular prism   pentagonal prism   cylinder   cone   sphere

Your child will be making most of these solid figures by cutting out, folding, and taping a two-dimensional net of the object. This is a net for a triangular prism.

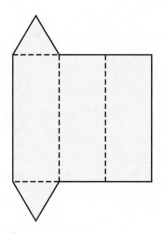

At home, point out different solid figures and discuss them with your child. Ask questions, such as: What is the name of that solid figure? What do you think it would look like from the side, top, back, or front? How is it different from another solid figure?

Encourage your child to build solid figures from cubes, clay, or folded paper.

When you are shopping with your child, discuss the different solid figures used for packaging. Ask your child to consider why particular solid figures are used for certain products.

If you have any questions or comments, please call or write to me.

Sincerely,
Your child's teacher

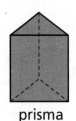Estimada familia:

Su niño está explorando figuras tridimensionales o cuerpos geométricos.

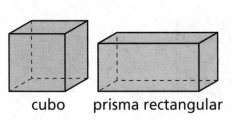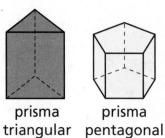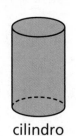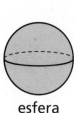

cubo prisma rectangular prisma triangular prisma pentagonal cilindro cono esfera

Su niño va a construir estos cuerpos geométricos cortando, doblando y pegando con cinta adhesiva una red bidimensional del objeto. Ésta es una red para un prisma triangular.

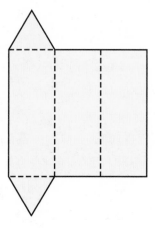

En casa señale diferentes cuerpos geométricos y coméntelos con su niño. Hágale preguntas como: ¿Cómo se llama este cuerpo geométrico? ¿Cómo crees que se vería desde el lado, desde arriba, desde atrás o desde adelante? ¿Cómo se diferencia de otro cuerpo geométrico?

Anime a su niño a que construya cuerpos geométricos usando cubos, arcilla o papel doblado.

Cuando uaya de compras con su niño, comente con él o con ella los distintos cuerpos geométricos que se usan para los envases. Pídale que piense por qué se usan determinados cuerpos geométricos para ciertos productos.

Si tiene alguna duda o comentario, por favor comuníquese conmigo.

Atentamente,
El maestro de su niño

Explore Cubes

▶Cube Models From Drawings

Use cubes to build a model from each drawing.

1.

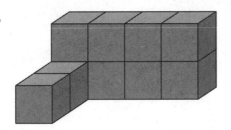

2.

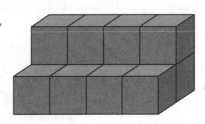

3.

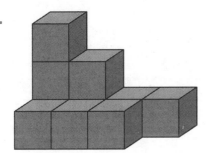

4.

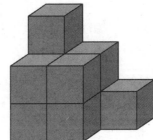

5.

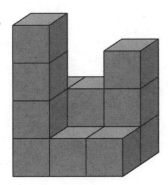

6.

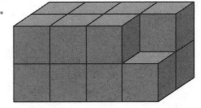

►Views of Three-Dimensional Objects

7. Label the front, back, left, and right edges of a sheet of paper. Build a model to match the picture.

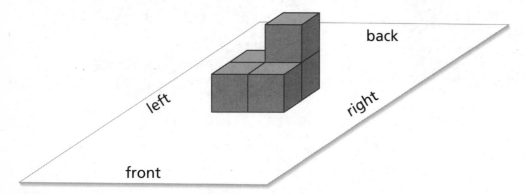

8. Using your model, label the drawings below as the *front, back, right,* or *left* views of the building. Each drawing will have two labels.

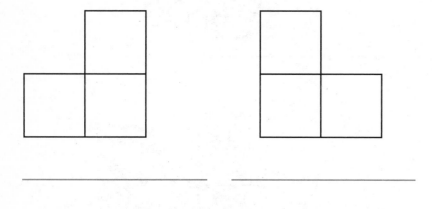

_____   _____

_____   _____

9. Draw the top view of the model from exercise 7.

10. Build a model to match the drawing below. Place it on a sheet of paper with edges labeled *front, back, right,* and *left.*

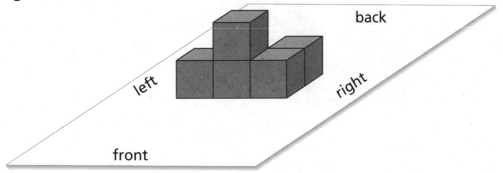

11. Using your model, label the views below as *front, back, right,* or *left.* One drawing will have two labels.

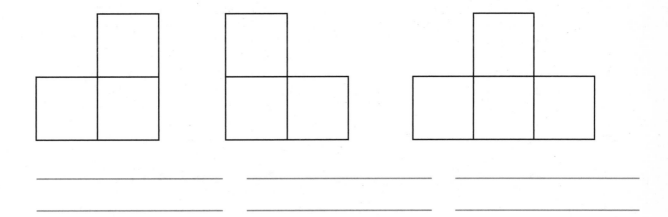

_____   _____   _____

_____   _____   _____

12. Draw the top view of the model from exercise 10.

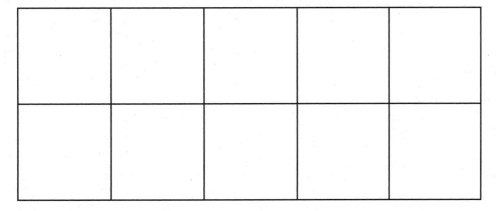

Name _____   **Date** _____

13. Build a model from the drawing below and place it on a sheet of paper with edges labeled *front, back, right,* and *left.*

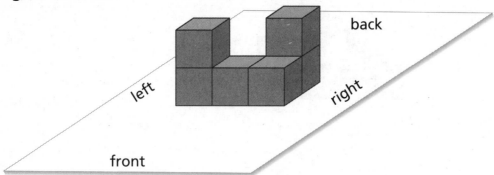

14. Using your model, label the views below as *front, back, left,* or *right.* Each drawing will have two labels.

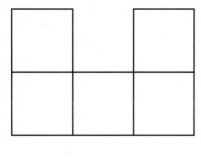

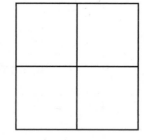

_____   _____

_____   _____

15. Draw the top view of the model from exercise 13.

Two-Dimensional Pictures of Three-Dimensional Buildings

►Make Models From Views

Each exercise shows three views of the same model.

Use the views to build a model on a sheet of paper with edges labeled *front, back, right,* and *left.* Compare your model with your partner's.

16.

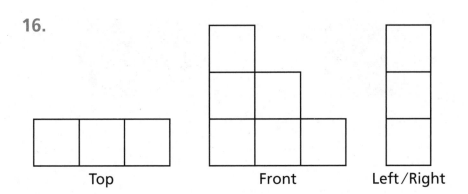

Top   Front   Left/Right

17.

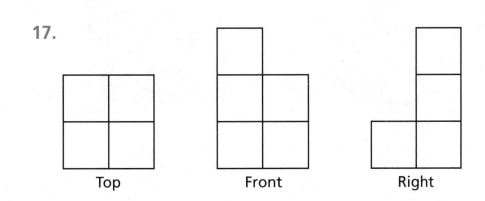

Top   Front   Right

Name _____ Date _____

Going Further

Copyright © Houghton Mifflin Company. All rights reserved.

▶ Volume of 3-D Objects

The **volume** of a three-dimensional figure is the number of cubic units that fit inside it.

Find the volume of each figure in cubic units. Build them with cubes if you need to do so.

1 cubic unit

1.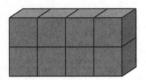

_____

2.

_____

3.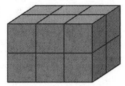

_____

4.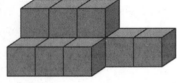

_____

5.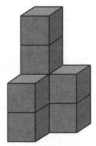

_____

6.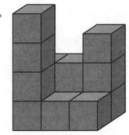

_____

Two-Dimensional Pictures of Three-Dimensional Buildings

Class Activity

Name _____ Date _____

▶Prism Nets

Cut out each net and form the solid figure.

1.

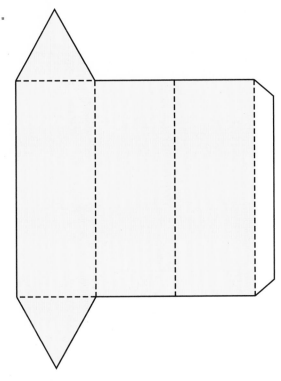

2.

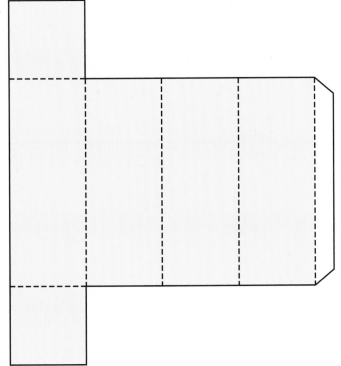

Explore Prisms, Cylinders, and Square Pyramids

Class Activity

▶Cylinder Net

Cut out each net and form the solid figure.

5.

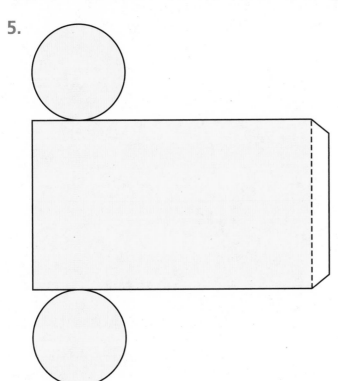

▶Square Pyramid Net

6.

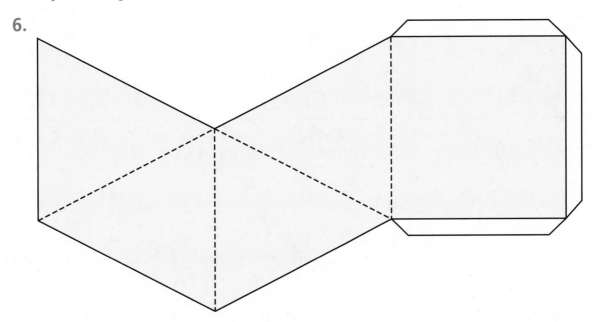

Explore Prisms, Cylinders, and Square Pyramids

Class Activity

►**Build a Cone**

Cut out the net and form the solid figure.

1.

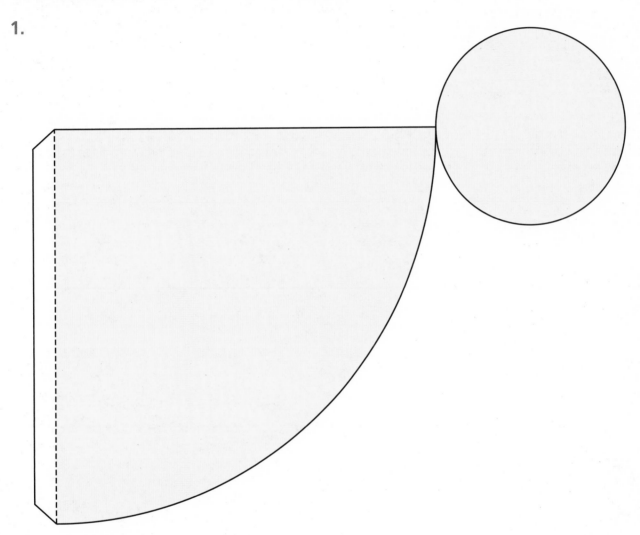

Explore Cones

Vocabulary

edge   face

vertex   vertices

► **Sort 3-D Figures**

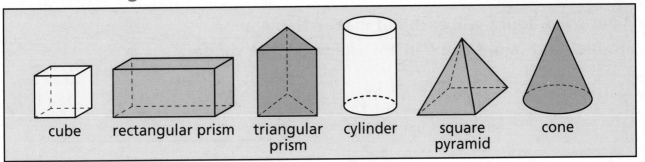

cube   rectangular prism   triangular prism   cylinder   square pyramid   cone

Use the figures above to complete exercises 2–3. Use the words edge, face, and vertex (or vertices).

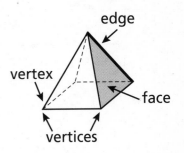

edge

vertex

face

vertices

2. Choose your own sorting rule to sort the solid figures shown into two groups.

My sorting rule is _____

_____.

The figures in one group are _____

_____.

The figures in the other group are _____

_____

3. Choose a different sorting rule to sort the solid figures shown into two groups.

My sorting rule is _____

_____.

The figures in one group are _____

_____.

The figures in the other group are _____

_____.

► Packages

What solid figure will each net make? Name a product that might come in a package of that shape.

4.

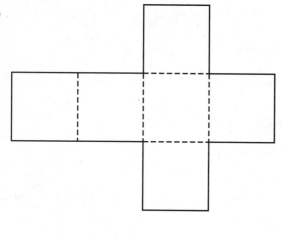

_____

5.

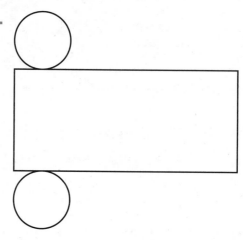

_____

6.

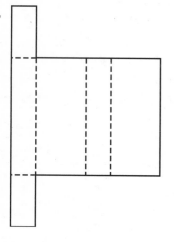

_____

7.

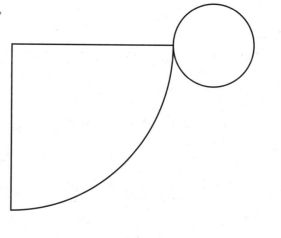

_____

8. Choose a product and design a package for it. You can copy one of the nets above onto inch grid paper or create your own net for your package. Include your product's name and information on the net, color it, and then fold it to create your package.

Explore Cones

Vocabulary
circle
radius
diameter
circumference

▶ Characteristics of a Circle

1. Place a pencil inside one end of a paper clip. Hold the pencil point in place on a sheet of paper. Place another pencil inside the other end of the paper clip. Ask a partner to hold your paper still while you draw a **circle** by moving the second pencil.

2. Draw and label a **radius** on your circle.

3. How does the length of the radius compare to the length of the paper clip?

   _____

4. Draw and label a **diameter** on your circle.

5. How does the length of the diameter compare to the length of the paper clip?

   _____

   _____

6. Find the **circumference** of this circle. Describe your method.

   _____

   _____

   _____

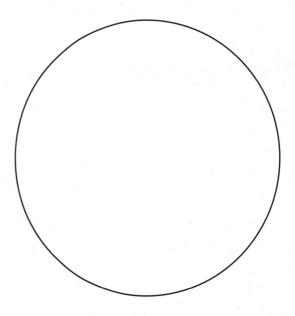

Vocabulary

sphere

►Characteristics of a Sphere

This is a **sphere** .

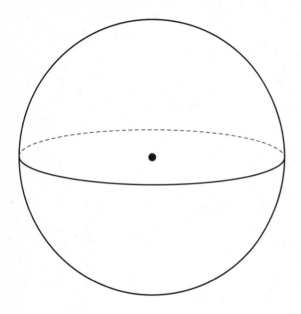

7. How is a sphere similar to a circle?

_____

_____

_____

8. How is a sphere different from a circle?

_____

_____

9. Draw and label a radius on the sphere.

10. Draw and label a diameter on the sphere.

1. Draw a net that will form a cube when folded.

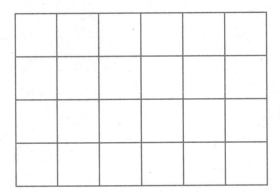

2. Study the model below. Draw the front, back, right, left, and top views.

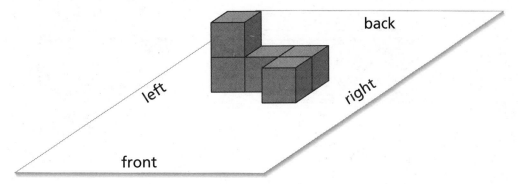

_____ _____ _____

_____ _____

Name the solid figure.

3.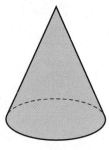

_____

4.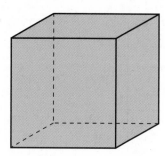

_____

5.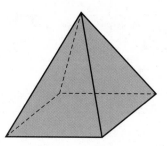

_____

6.

_____

7.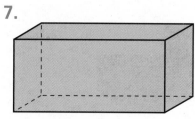

_____

8.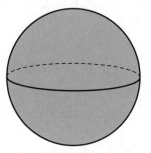

_____

9. Name the solid figure that the net will form.

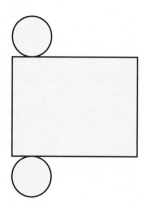

_____

10. Extended Response Name and describe this prism. Tell what you know about its faces, edges, and vertices.

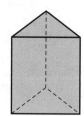

_____

_____

_____

_____

_____

Class Activity

▶Estimate and Measure Length

Estimate the length of each line segment in inches.
Then measure it to the nearest inch.

inch

1.

Estimate: _____ Actual: _____

2.

Estimate: _____ Actual: _____

Estimate the length of each line segment in inches.
Then measure it to the nearest $\frac{1}{2}$ inch.

3.

Estimate: _____ Actual: _____

4.

Estimate: _____ Actual: _____

Estimate the length of each line segment in inches.
Then measure it to the nearest $\frac{1}{4}$ inch.

5.

Estimate: _____ Actual: _____

6.

Estimate: _____ Actual: _____

▶ Draw Line Segments

Draw a line segment that has the given length.

7. 5 inches

8. $4\frac{1}{2}$ inches

9. $4\frac{3}{4}$ inches

10. $3\frac{1}{4}$ inches

11. 2 inches

12. $1\frac{1}{4}$ inches

13. $1\frac{1}{2}$ inches

14. $3\frac{3}{4}$ inches

15. Draw a rectangle that is 1 inch wide and 3 inches long.

Dear Family,

In this unit, students explore ways to measure things using the customary and metric systems of measurement.

The units of measurement we will be working with include:

U.S. Customary System

Length
1 foot (ft) = 12 inches (in.)
1 yard (yd) = 3 feet (ft)
1 mile (mi) = 5,280 feet (ft)

Capacity
1 cup (c) = 8 fluid ounces (oz)
1 pint (pt) = 2 cups (c)
1 quart (qt) = 2 pints (pt)
1 gallon (gal) = 4 quarts (qt)

Weight
1 pound (lb) = 16 ounces (oz)

Metric System

Length
1 meter (m) = 10 decimeters (dm)
1 meter (m) = 100 centimeters (cm)
1 decimeter (dm) = 10 centimeters (cm)

Capacity
1 liter (L) = 1,000 milliliters (mL)

Mass
1 kilogram (kg) = 1,000 grams (g)

Students also read, write, and compare temperatures in degrees Fahrenheit and degrees Celsius.

You can help your child become familiar with these units of measurement by working with measurements together. For example, you might estimate and measure the length of something in inches and convert the measurement to feet. You might use a measuring cup to explore how the cup can be used to fill pints, quarts, or gallons of liquid. From inside, you could read the temperature on an outdoor thermometer and decide if it is hot, warm, cool, or cold outside.

Thank you for helping your child learn important math skills. Please call if you have any questions or comments.

Sincerely,
Your child's teacher

Carta a la familia

Estimada familia:

En esta unidad los estudiantes descubren cómo medir cosas utilizando tanto el sistema medidas usuales como el sistema métrico decimal.

Las unidades de medida con las que trabajaremos incluirán:

Sistema usual
Longitud
1 pie (pie) = 12 pulgadas (pulg) 1 yarda (yd) = 3 pies (pies) 1 milla (mi) = 5,280 pies (pies)
Capacidad
1 taza (taza) = 8 onzas líquidas (oz) 1 pinta (pt) = 2 tazas (tazas) 1 cuarto de galón (ct) = 2 pintas (pt) 1 galón (gal) = 4 cuartos de galón (ct)
Peso
1 libra (lb) = 16 onzas (oz)

Sistema métrico decimal
Longitud
1 metro (m) = 10 decímetros (dm) 1 metro (m) = 100 centímetros (cm) 1 decímetro (dm) = 10 centímetros (cm)
Capacidad
1 litro (L) = 1,000 mililitros (mL)
Masa
1 kilogramo (kg) = 1,000 gramos (g)

Los estudiantes también leen, escriben y comparan temperaturas en grados Farenheit y en grados centígrados.

Puede ayudar a su niño a que se familiarice con estas unidades métricas trabajando juntos con las medidas. Por ejemplo, pueden estimar y medir la longitud de algo en pulgadas y convertir la medida a pies. Podrían usar una taza medidora para aprender cómo se pueden llenar pintas, cuartos de galón o galones con la taza y un líquido. Desde el interior de la casa podrían leer la temperatura en un termómetro exterior y decidir si la temperatura exterior es caliente, cálida, fresca o fría.

Gracias por ayudar a su niño a aprender destrezas matemáticas importantes.

Si tiene alguna duda o comentario, por favor comuníquese conmigo.

Atentamente,
El maestro de su niño

Customary Units of Length

Class Activity

▶Convert Customary Units of Length

> 1 foot (ft) = 12 inches (in.)
> 1 yard (yd) = 3 ft or 36 in.
> 1 mile (mi) = 5,280 ft or 1,760 yd

Complete.

1. 1 foot 3 inches = _____ inches

2. 1 yard 3 inches = _____ inches

3. 2 feet 5 inches = _____ inches

4. 1 yard 1 foot = _____ inches

5. 1 yard 9 inches = _____ inches

6. 2 feet 7 inches = _____ inches

7. 1 yard 2 feet = _____ inches

8. 2 feet 11 inches = _____ inches

9. 1 foot 10 inches = _____ inches

10. 2 yards = _____ inches

11. 3 feet = 1 _____

12. 6 feet = _____ yards

13. 27 feet = _____ yards

14. 2 feet = _____ inches

15. 32 feet = _____ yards _____ feet or _____ yards

16. 16 feet = _____ yards _____ foot or _____ yards

17. 29 feet = _____ yards _____ feet or _____ yards

18. 25 feet = _____ yards _____ foot or _____ yards

Solve.

19. Marcus has 27 feet of rope to make rope swings. He needs 6 yards of rope for each swing. How many rope swings can he make? How many feet of rope will be left over?

20. Cassidy has 50 inches of ribbon. She wants to divide it equally among her 6 nieces. How many inches of ribbon can each niece have? Give the answer as a mixed number.

▶ **Find Benchmarks**

Write the answer.

21. This line segment is 1 **inch** long.
    Put two fingers on the line segment. Then hold up
    your fingers. Write the name of an object that is
    about 1 inch (or two finger widths) long.

    _____

22. One **foot** is equal to 12 inches. Spread both hands
    on a ruler to show 1 foot. Write the name of an
    object that is about 1 foot (or both hands) long.

    _____

23. One **yard** is equal to 3 feet or 36 inches. How
    many 12-inch lengths are in 1 yard? Write the
    name of an object that is about 1 yard long.

    _____

24. One **mile** is 5,280 feet or 1,760 yards. In describing
    a long distance, why would it make sense to use
    miles instead of feet or yards?

    _____

▶ **Choose Appropriate Units**

**Choose the unit you would use to measure each.
Write *inch*, *foot*, *yard*, or *mile*.**

25. the width of a piece of notebook paper _____

26. the length of a classroom board _____

27. the height of the school _____

28. the distance you travel to school _____

Vocabulary
inch
foot
yard
mile

Class Activity

Vocabulary

centimeter (cm)

▶Estimate and Measure Length

Estimate the length of each line segment in centimeters. Then measure it to the nearest centimeter.

⊢——⊣ 1 cm

1. ⊢————⊣

Estimate: _____ Actual: _____

2. ⊢—————————⊣

Estimate: _____ Actual: _____

3. ⊢———————————⊣

Estimate: _____ Actual: _____

4. ⊢———————————————⊣

Estimate: _____ Actual: _____

5. ⊢—————————————⊣

Estimate: _____ Actual: _____

6. Estimate the length of these items in your classroom. Then measure to the nearest centimeter. Record your information in the chart.

	Estimate (cm)	Actual (cm)
pair of scissors		
gluestick		
pencil		
marker		

Class Activity

▶ Convert Metric Units of Length

Complete the tables.

7.

m	cm
1	100
2	
	300
	400
5	
	600
7	
8	
	900
	1,000

8.

m	dm
1	10
2	
	30
	40
5	
6	
7	
	80
	90
10	

9.

dm	cm
10	100
20	
	300
40	
50	
	600
	700
80	
	900
	1,000

Compare. Write >, <, or = in the ◯ .

10. 120 cm ◯ 1 m

11. 10 dm ◯ 100 cm

12. 3 m ◯ 3,000 cm

13. 6 m ◯ 600 dm

Centimeters, Decimeters, and Meters

Name _____

Date _____

Complete the tables.

14.

cm	dm
10	1
20	
30	
40	
	5
	6
	7
80	
	9
	10

15.

cm	m
100	1
	2
	3
400	
500	
600	
	7
	8
900	
1,000	

16.

dm	m
10	1
20	
	3
	4
50	
	6
70	
80	
	9
	10

Compare. Write >, <, or = in each ◯ .

17. 30 dm ◯ 2 m

18. 200 cm ◯ 2 m

19. 70 cm ◯ 70 dm

20. 1 m ◯ 50 cm

21. 800 cm ◯ 7 m

22. 5 dm ◯ 60 cm

▶ Find Benchmarks

23. This line segment is 1 **centimeter** long. Use your little finger to show 1 centimeter. Write an object that is about 1 cm (or your little finger width) long.

    _____

24. One **decimeter** is equal to 10 cm. This line segment is 1 decimeter long. Spread your hand to show 1 decimeter. Write an object that is about 1 dm (or your hand spread out) long.

    _____

25. One **meter** is equal to 100 cm. How many decimeters are in one meter? Write an object or distance that is about 1 meter long.

    _____

26. One **kilometer** is 1,000 meters. It takes about 10 minutes to walk a kilometer. Write the name of a place that is about 1 km from your house.

    _____

▶ Choose the Appropriate Unit

Choose the unit you would use to measure each. Write *centimeter, decimeter, meter,* or *kilometer*.

27. the width of your classroom _____

28. the distance you fly on an airplane _____

29. the length of a pencil _____

30. the length of your fingernail _____

Centimeters, Decimeters, and Meters

Class Activity

▶Estimate and Find the Perimeter

Estimate the perimeter in inches. Then measure each side to the nearest $\frac{1}{4}$ inch and find the perimeter.

1.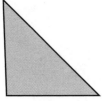

_____

2.

_____

3.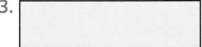

_____

4.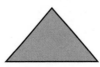

_____

5.

_____

6.

_____

7.

_____

8.

_____

Class Activity

▶ Add Customary Units of Length

Add.

9. $3\frac{1}{2}$ inches + 4 inches

_____

10. $8\frac{1}{4}$ inches + $2\frac{1}{4}$ inches

_____

11. $5\frac{1}{2}$ inches + $8\frac{1}{2}$ inches

_____

12. $3\frac{1}{4}$ inches + $2\frac{3}{4}$ inches

_____

13. $4\frac{1}{2}$ inches + $5\frac{1}{4}$ inches

_____

14. $7\frac{1}{4}$ inches + $\frac{1}{2}$ inches

_____

15. $4\frac{1}{2}$ inches + $5\frac{3}{4}$ inches

_____

16. $5\frac{1}{2}$ inches + $5\frac{3}{4}$ inches

_____

17. $3\frac{3}{4}$ inches + $5\frac{3}{8}$ inches

_____

18. $4\frac{5}{8}$ inches + $6\frac{3}{4}$ inches

_____

Solve.

19. Mia wants to make a friendship bracelet. She needs three pieces of string that are each $9\frac{3}{4}$ inches long. How many inches of string does she need in all?

$9\frac{3}{4}$ in. $9\frac{3}{4}$ in. $9\frac{3}{4}$ in.

20. Larry measured his living room. Then he wrote down the measurements. What is the perimeter of his living room in feet?

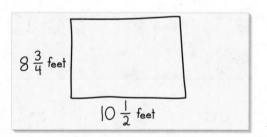

$8\frac{3}{4}$ feet

$10\frac{1}{2}$ feet

_____

_____

Class Activity

▶ **Units of Capacity**

Vocabulary

cup (c)
fluid ounce (fl oz)
quart (qt)   gallon (gal)

---

1 cup 🥤 = 8 fluid ounces   4 cups 🥤🥤🥤🥤 = 1 quart

2 cups 🥤🥤 = 1 pint   4 quarts = 1 gallon

Solve.

1. Regina drank 2 cups of milk. Rex drank 8 fluid ounces of milk. Who drank more milk?

   _____

2. Fran spilled a half-gallon of water. Mark spilled 3 quarts. Who spilled more water?

   _____

3. Would you rather have a pint and a half of your favorite drink or 4 cups?

   _____

4. Would you rather have a cup or a fourth of a pint of a drink you don't like?

   _____

5. There are 2 quarts of tomato juice in the refrigerator. Mrs. Chavez needs $\frac{3}{4}$ of a gallon to make a stew. Does she have enough? Explain.

   _____
   _____

6. Juana has a 12-cup punch bowl. She uses a 1-quart container to fill it. How many times must she pour a quart into the bowl to fill it? Explain.

   _____
   _____

Class Activity

▶ **Convert Units of Capacity**

| 1 cup (c) = 8 fluid ounces (fl oz) |
| 2 cups (c) = 1 pint (pt) |
| 4 cups (c) = 1 quart (qt) |
| 16 cups (c) = 1 gallon (gal) |

Complete the table.

	Number of cups	Number of pints	Number of quarts	Number of half-gallons	Number of gallons
Cup					
Pint					
Quart					
Half-Gallon					
Gallon					

Complete.

7. 8 cups = _____ pints

8. $\frac{1}{2}$ cup = _____ fluid ounces

9. 9 pints = _____ quarts

10. _____ pints = 18 quarts

11. _____ quarts = 4 gallons

12. 8 quarts = _____ gallons

13. 16 fluid ounces = 1_____

14. 8 pints = 1 _____

15. _____ cups = 3 pints

16. 5 pints = _____ quarts

17. _____ fluid ounces = $\frac{1}{2}$ gallon

18. _____ quarts = 8 $\frac{1}{4}$ gallons

Class Activity

▶ Establish Benchmarks

Complete.

19. This container holds 1 cup. Write the name of another container that holds about 1 cup.

_____

20. This container holds 1 pint. Write the name of another container that holds about 1 pint.

_____

21. This container holds 1 quart. Write the name of another container that holds about 1 quart.

_____

22. This container holds 1 gallon. Write the name of another container that holds about 1 gallon.

_____

▶ Choose Units

Choose the best unit to use to measure how much each item can hold. Write *cup, pint, quart,* or *gallon.*

23. a carton of heavy cream

_____

24. a swimming pool

_____

25. a flower vase

_____

26. a wash tub

_____

27. **On the Back** Think of a container. Choose the unit you would use to measure its capacity. Draw the container and write the name of the unit you chose. Explain why you chose that unit.

Customary Units of Capacity

Class Activity

Vocabulary

liter (L)
milliliter (mL)

▶ Convert Metric Units of Capacity

| 1 liter (L) = 1,000 milliliters (mL) |

Complete.

1. 2 L = _____ mL

2. 15,000 mL = _____ L

3. $\frac{1}{2}$ L = _____ mL

4. _____ L = 250 mL

5. _____ L = 4,000 mL

6. 4,000 mL = _____ L

▶ Benchmarks for a Liter and a Milliliter

Write the answer.

7. This bottle holds 1 **liter**.

Name another container that
holds about 1 liter.

_____

8. This eyedropper holds 1 **milliliter**.

Name another container that
holds about 1 milliliter.

_____

▶ Choose the Appropriate Unit

**Choose the unit you would use to measure the
capacity of each. Write *mL* or *L*.**

9. a kitchen sink _____

10. a soup spoon _____

11. a teacup _____

12. a washing machine _____

Circle the better estimate.

13. a juice container   1 L   1 mL

14. a bowl of soup   500 L   500 mL

▶ **Solve Problems Involving Capacity**

Solve.

15. Diane has 39 cups of lemonade to divide equally among 4 tables. How much lemonade should she put at each table?

_____

16. A recipe calls for 3 pints of milk. How many times must you fill a 1-cup measuring cup to make 3 pints?

_____

17. Mr. Valle made 26 cups of barbeque sauce. He wants to divide it equally among 3 friends. How much sauce will each friend get?

_____

18. Rebecca has 33 cups of ice. Each pitcher of iced tea needs 4 cups of ice. How many pitchers can Rebecca fill? How much ice will be left over?

_____

19. One bottle of water has a red label and holds 2 liters. Another bottle of water has a blue label and holds 1,500 milliliters. What color is the label on the larger bottle?

_____

20. Camilla poured 2,300 milliliters of punch into a punch bowl. Then José poured 3 more liters of punch into the bowl. How many milliliters of punch are in the bowl altogether?

_____

21. A bowl of punch has 2L of lemon-lime soda and 600 mL of lemonade. How many more mL of lemon-lime soda does the punch have?

_____

22. A pudding recipe makes 6 cups of pudding. Will a 1-quart container be large enough to hold the pudding? Why or why not?

_____

23. Would you rather have 500 milliliters of your favorite drink or $\frac{1}{4}$ liter?

24. A bottle holds 750 mL. How many liters will 2 bottles hold?

_____

► Use Improper Fractions and Mixed Numbers in Measurements

Write the improper fraction or mixed number for each measurement.

1. $\frac{7}{2}$ c = _____

2. $\frac{9}{5}$ L = _____

3. $\frac{18}{4}$ m = _____

4. $1\frac{3}{8}$ qt = _____

5. $1\frac{3}{4}$ ft = _____

6. $3\frac{2}{3}$ gal = _____

7. $4\frac{1}{2}$ in. = _____

8. $\frac{16}{7}$ pt = _____

9. $3\frac{7}{8}$ c = _____

10. $2\frac{5}{6}$ mi = _____

11. $3\frac{1}{3}$ yd = _____

12. $\frac{19}{12}$ ml = _____

13. $\frac{17}{9}$ km = _____

14. $2\frac{1}{4}$ in. = _____

15. $\frac{21}{5}$ qt = _____

Name _____   **Date** _____

Class Activity

▶ Fractions as Lengths

Write the length of each line segment using a fraction.

16.

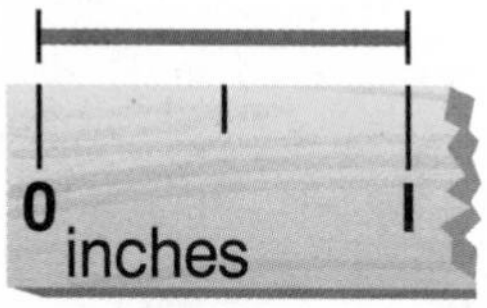

0 inches |

_____

17.

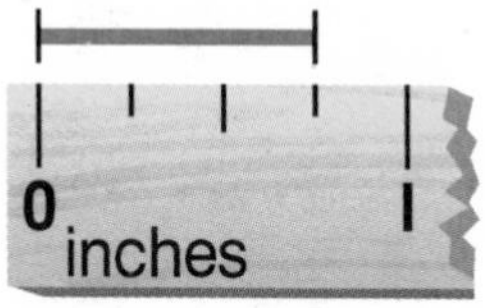

0 inches |

_____

18.

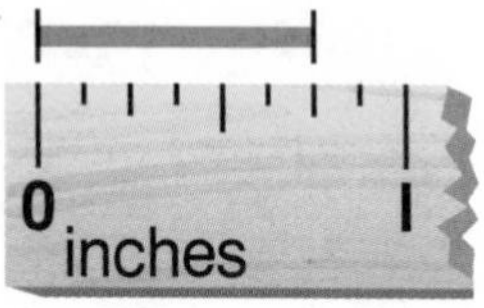

0 inches |

_____

Write the length of each line segment using an improper fraction and a mixed number.

19.

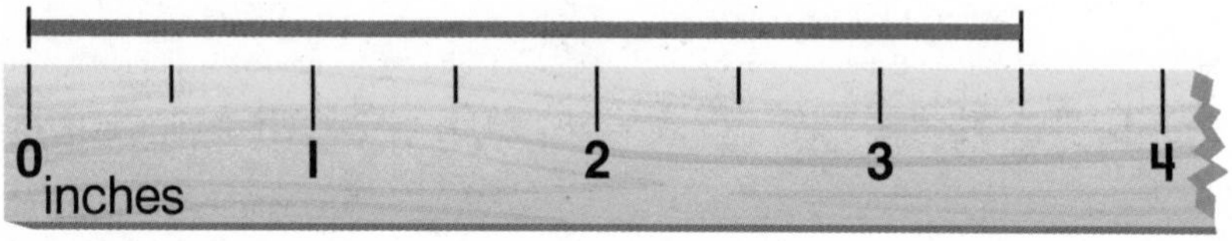

0 inches   1   2   3   4

_____

20.

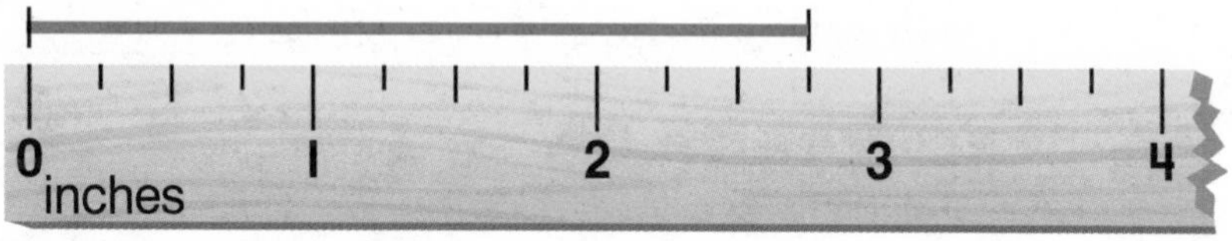

0 inches   1   2   3   4

_____

21.

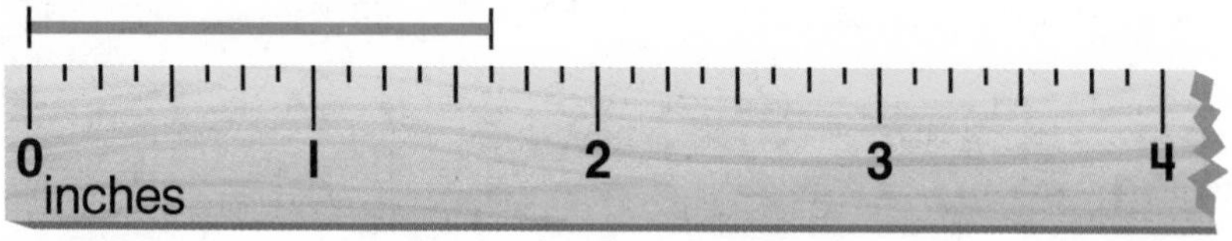

0 inches   1   2   3   4

_____

22.

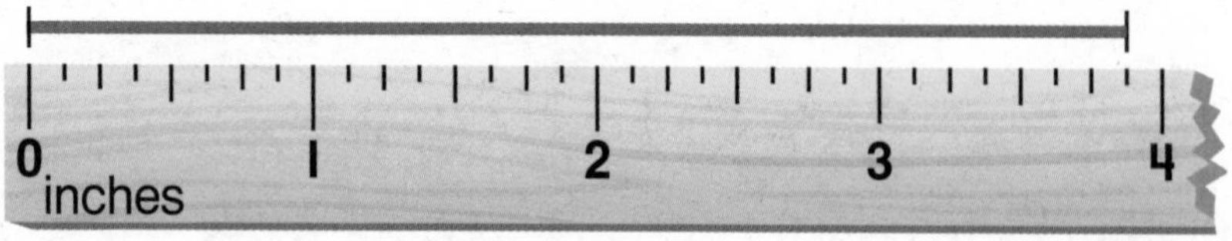

0 inches   1   2   3   4

_____

Improper Fractions and Mixed Numbers in Measurements

Name _____ **Date** _____

Class Activity

►Review Measurement Equivalencies

Complete.

1.

Inches	Feet
12	1
1	$\frac{1}{12}$
2	
4	

2.

Feet	Yards
	1
1	
2	
4	

3.

cm	m
	1
1	
87	
158	

4.

Cup	Pint
	1
1	
	2
3	

5.

Pint	Quart
	1
1	
6	
	$1\frac{1}{2}$

6.

Quart	Gallon
4	1
1	
2	
	$1\frac{1}{2}$

7. 1,500 mL = _____

8. 7L = _____

9. 16 cups = _____ pints = _____ quarts = 1 gallon

10. 1 cup = _____ pint = _____ quart = _____ gallon

11. 6 c = _____ pt = _____ qt = _____ gal

12. 48 c = _____ pt = _____ qt = _____ gal

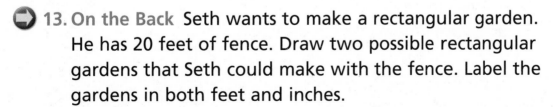

13. **On the Back** Seth wants to make a rectangular garden. He has 20 feet of fence. Draw two possible rectangular gardens that Seth could make with the fence. Label the gardens in both feet and inches.

Measurement Equivalencies and Fractions **527**

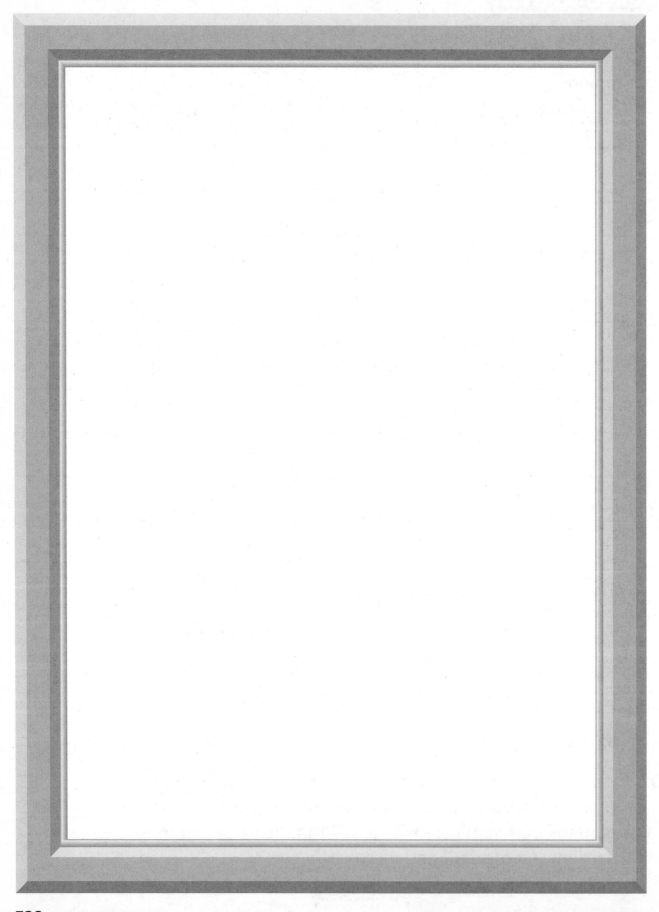

▶ Ounces or Pounds

Complete.

1.

Ounces	Pounds
16	1
1	
	2
	3
8	
4	

2.

Pounds	Ounces
$1\frac{1}{2}$	
$2\frac{3}{4}$	
4	
	68
$4\frac{1}{2}$	
	76

3. 2 lb = _____ oz

4. 60 oz = _____ lb

5. 10 lb = _____ oz

6. _____ lb = 12 oz

7. 2 oz = _____ lb

8. 40 oz = _____ lb

▶ **Establish Benchmarks for a Pound and an Ounce**

9. This weighs about 1 **ounce**.

Name another item that weighs about 1 ounce.

_____

10. This weighs about 1 **pound**.

Name another item that weighs about 1 pound.

_____

▶Choose the Appropriate Unit

**Choose the unit you would use to measure the
weight of each. Write *pound* or *ounce*.**

11. a backpack full of books

_____

12. a couch

_____

13. a peanut

_____

14. a pencil

_____

Circle the better estimate.

15. a student desk   3 lb   30 lb

16. a television   20 oz   20 lb

17. a hamster   5 oz   5 lb

18. a slice of cheese   1 lb   1 oz

Solve.

19. Kiko bought 2 pounds of
peaches, 8 ounces of cherries,
12 ounces of plums, and $1\frac{1}{4}$
pounds of apples. What was the
total weight of her purchases?

_____

_____

20. A pound of potatoes was used
to make some soup. If the soup
is divided evenly among 8
people, how many ounces of
potatoes will each person get?

_____

21. Would you rather have a pound
and a half of your favorite nuts
or 20 ounces?

_____

22. Gregory bought $1\frac{1}{4}$ pounds of
nails at 10¢ an ounce. How
much did he pay?

_____

Customary Units of Weight and Metric Units of Mass

Class Activity

Vocabulary

gram (g)
kilogram (kg)

▶Grams and Kilograms

Complete.

23.

Grams	Kilograms
1,000	1
1	
	2
	3
500	
40	

24.

Kilograms	Grams
$1\frac{1}{2}$	
$\frac{200}{1,000}$	
	250
$5\frac{3}{4}$	
6	
$6\frac{1}{2}$	6,500

25. 2 kg = _____ g

26. 750 g = _____ kg

27. 10 kg = _____ g

28. _____ kg = 500 g

▶Benchmarks for a Gram and a Kilogram

Write the answer.

29. A paper clip has a mass of about 1 **gram**.

Name another item with a mass of about 1 gram.

_____

30. A book has a mass of about 1 **kilogram**.

Name another item with a mass of about 1 kilogram.

_____

Customary Units of Weight and Metric Units of Mass **531**

Class Activity

►Choose the Appropriate Unit

Choose the unit you would use to measure the mass of each. Write *gram* or *kilogram*.

31. an elephant

_____

32. a crayon

_____

33. a stamp

_____

34. a dog

_____

Circle the better estimate.

35. a pair of sunglasses   150 g   150 kg

36. a horse   6 kg   600 kg

37. a watermelon   40 g   4 kg

38. a quarter   500 g   5 g

Solve.

39. The mass of a small penguin is 1 kilogram 800 grams. How many grams less than 2 kilograms is that?

_____

40. Would you rather have $\frac{1}{2}$ kilogram or 400 grams of your favorite candy?

_____

41. Rolls of coins are sometimes weighed to check how many are inside. A penny weighs about 3 g. About how many grams would a dollars worth of pennies weigh?

_____

42. Jenna wants to put 200 grams of peanuts in each of 5 small cups for party favors. Would a 1-kg bag of peanuts be enough to fill the cups? Explain

_____

_____

Customary Units of Weight and Metric Units of Mass

▶Temperature in Fahrenheit

Circle the better estimate of the temperature.

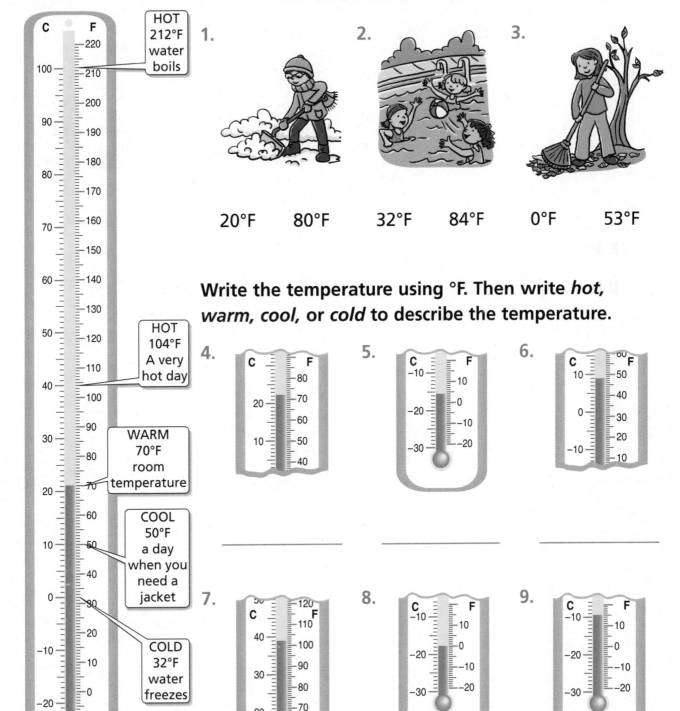

HOT
212°F
water
boils

HOT
104°F
A very
hot day

WARM
70°F
room
temperature

COOL
50°F
a day
when you
need a
jacket

COLD
32°F
water
freezes

COLD
−10°F
a very
cold day

1.

20°F   80°F

2.

32°F   84°F

3.

0°F   53°F

**Write the temperature using °F. Then write *hot,
warm, cool,* or *cold* to describe the temperature.**

4.

5.

6.

_____   _____   _____

7.

8.

9.

_____   _____   _____

► **Temperature in Celsius**

Circle the better estimate of the temperature.

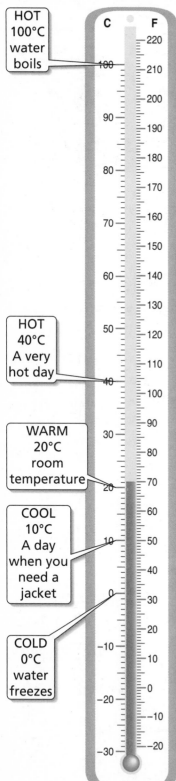

HOT
100°C
water
boils

HOT
40°C
A very
hot day

WARM
20°C
room
temperature

COOL
10°C
A day
when you
need a
jacket

COLD
0°C
water
freezes

10.

50°C   11°C

11.

30°C   100°C

12.

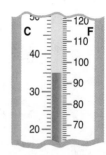

22°C   0°C

Write the temperature using °C. Then write *hot*, *warm*, *cool*, or *cold* to describe the temperature.

13.

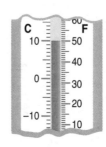

_____

14.

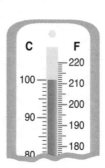

_____

15.

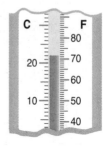

_____

16.

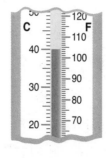

_____

17.

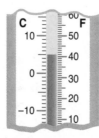

_____

18.

_____

1. Estimate the length of the line segment in inches. Then measure it to the nearest $\frac{1}{4}$ inch.

Estimate: _____ Actual: _____

2. Estimate the length of the line segment to the nearest centimeter. Then measure it to the nearest centimeter.

Estimate: _____ Actual: _____

Complete.

3. 2 feet 3 inches = _____ inches   4. 24 feet = _____ yards

5. 1 yard 2 feet = _____ inches   6. 2 meters = _____ centimeters

7. 400 centimeters = _____ meters   8. 5 pints = _____ cups

9. 13 quarts = _____ gallons   10. 8 quarts = _____ pints

11. 1 liter = _____ milliliters   12. 24 ounces = _____ pounds

13. 2 pounds = _____ ounces   14. 2,000 grams = _____ kilograms

Solve.

15. What is the perimeter of a rectangle that is $1\frac{1}{4}$ inches long and $3\frac{1}{8}$ inches wide?

_____

Write the temperature. Then write *hot, warm, cool,* or *cold* to describe the temperature.

16.  _____°F _____

17.  _____°C _____

Solve.

18. Bert has 56 gallons of water for the pet shop's fish tanks. Each tank holds 6 gallons of water. How many tanks can Bert fill? How much water will be left?

_____

19. A ten-gallon fish tank needs to have half of its water replaced every two weeks. How many quarts of water need to be replaced every two weeks?

_____

20. **Extended Response** A large loaf of bread contains 40 slices of bread. Each slice weighs 1 ounce. How many pounds does the loaf of bread weigh? Explain how you found the answer.

_____

_____

_____

Test

Name _____ **Date** _____

Class Activity

▶**Read a Map**

Each square on the **map** is 1 block. You can travel up, down, right, or left along the lines on the map.

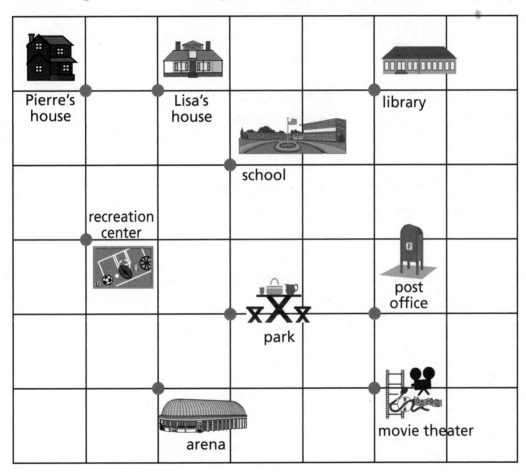

1. How many blocks is the school from the park?

_____

2. How many blocks is the library from the post office?

_____

3. Whose house is closer to the library, Pierre's or Lisa's?

_____

By how much? _____

Name _____ **Date** _____

Class Activity

Vocabulary

route

▶Follow Directions

Use the map on page 537 to answer the questions.

4. Pierre was at the park. He walked 1 block up and 2 blocks left. Where is he now?

   _____

5. Lisa was at her house. She walked 2 blocks right, 3 blocks down, and 1 block right. Where is she now?

   _____

6. Sarah was at school. She walked 2 blocks left and 1 block down. Where is she now?

   _____

7. Lucio was at the arena. He walked 1 block up, 3 blocks right, and 3 blocks up. Where is he now?

   _____

▶Describe Routes

8. On the map, draw a **route** with a colored pencil from the school to the arena.

9. Describe your route.

   _____

10. How many blocks long is your route?

   _____

11. On the map, draw another route with a different colored pencil from the school to the arena.

12. Describe your route.

   _____

13. Which of your routes is longer?

   _____

Directions and Maps

►Make a Map

14. Draw a map of an amusement park. Include a waterfall, treasure chest, bumper cars, a snack bar, and other places such as raging rapids, scrambler, pirates cove, or sunken ship. Place each point for the place where two grid lines intersect on the map.

►**Use Your Map**

Use the map you created on page 539 to complete the following.

15. Draw a route on your map with a colored pencil from the snack bar to the bumper cars.

16. Describe this route.

_____

_____

17. Draw a route on your map with a different colored pencil from the snack bar to the water fall.

18. Describe this route.

_____

_____

19. Which place is further from the snack bar, the bumper cars or the waterfall?

_____

Choose two places on your map.

20. Name the two places and describe a route from one to the other.

_____

_____

21. Describe a different route from one place to the other.

_____

_____

22. Is the second route longer, shorter, or equal in distance to your first route?

_____

Dear Family,

Your child is working on a geometry unit about coordinate grids.

Students first work on grids without number labels. Then they make a map by adding features (places or objects) where two grid lines intersect. They describe routes on the map as up, down, right, and left in blocks or units.

Students then progress to coordinate grids — grids with number labels for each horizontal and vertical line. They describe locations on grids using ordered pairs. For example, this coordinate grid shows the point (2, 3). The first number in the ordered pair shows how far to the right the point is from 0. The second number shows how far up the point is from 0.

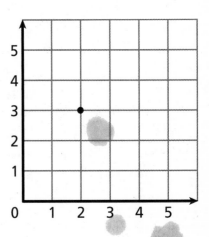

In the last lesson, students draw triangles and quadrilaterals on coordinate grids. They also use grid lines to measure the length of line segments and to draw rectangles from specific descriptions. The rectangle shown here is a possible response to the following description: The width of the rectangle is 3 units shorter than its length.

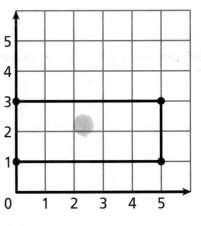

If you have any questions or comments, please call or write to me.

Sincerely,
Your child's teacher

Estimada familia:

Su niño está trabajando en una unidad de geometría sobre las cuadrículas de coordenadas.

Al principio, los estudiantes trabajan con cuadrículas que no están rotuladas con números. Agregan puntos (que representan lugares u objetos) donde se cruzan dos rectas para hacer un mapa. Describen las rutas en el mapa en términos de bloques o unidades hacia arriba, hacia abajo, hacia la derecha o hacia la izquierda.

Luego, los estudiantes usan cuadrículas de coordenadas, o sea, cuadrículas rotuladas con números en la recta horizontal y vertical. Describen ubicaciones en las cuadrículas usando pares ordenados. Por ejemplo, esta cuadrícula de coordenadas muestra el punto (2, 3). El primer número del par ordenado muestra a qué distancia a la derecha de 0 está el punto, y el segundo número muestra a qué distancia vertical está de 0.

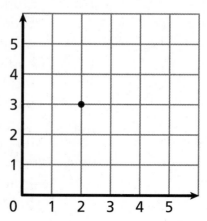

En la última lección los estudiantes trazan triángulos y cuadriláteros en cuadrículas de coordenadas. También usan las rectas de la cuadrícula para medir la longitud de segmentos de recta y trazan rectángulos a partir de descripciones específicas. El rectángulo que se muestra aquí es una respuesta posible a la siguiente descripción: el rectángulo tiene 3 unidades menos de ancho que de largo.

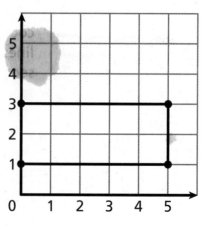

Si tiene alguna duda o pregunta, por favor comuníquese conmigo.

Atentamente,
El maestro de su niño

Directions and Maps

Class Activity

Name _____ **Date** _____

▶Coordinate Grids

You can use **ordered pairs** to find and name points on a **coordinate grid**.

Hector's Backyard

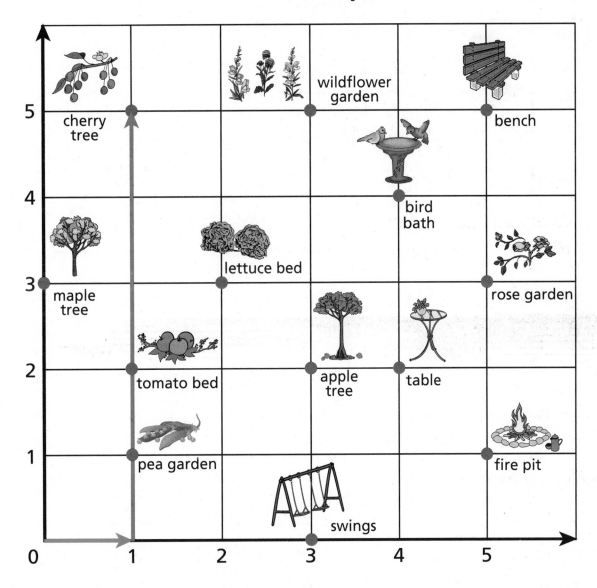

The cherry tree is located at (1, 5). To find (1, 5), start at 0. The first number tells how many spaces to the **right**, so move 1 space to the right. The second number tells how many spaces **up**, so move 5 spaces up.

(right, up)

▶Locate Points

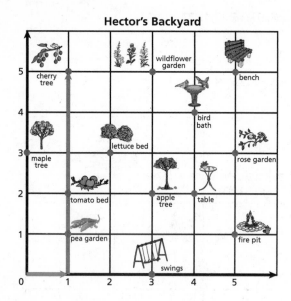

Hector's Backyard

Use each ordered pair to find places in Hector's backyard. Name what you find at each point.

1. (3, 5) _____   **2.** (4, 2) _____

3. (1, 2) _____   **4.** (5, 5) _____

5. (3, 0) _____   **6.** (0, 3) _____

▶Write Ordered Pairs

Write the ordered pair for the location of each place in Hector's backyard.

7. lettuce bed (_____, _____)   **8.** rose garden (_____, _____)

9. fire pit (_____, _____)   **10.** bird bath (_____, _____)

11. apple tree (_____, _____)   **12.** maple tree (_____, _____)

13. Draw a new place at the intersection of two grid lines on the map of Hector's backyard.
Write the ordered pair for its location. (_____, _____)

▶**Solve Problems With Ordered Pairs**

Use the coordinate grid below for exercises 14–18.

Fair Ground

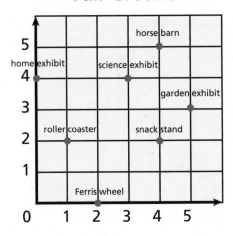

14. Larry went to the fair with his sister, Marissa. First they went to (1, 2). Where did they go first?

_____

15. Larry and Marissa went to (3, 4). What is located at (3, 4)?

_____

16. In the afternoon, Larry went to the home exhibit and Marissa went to the Ferris wheel. Write the ordered pairs for each location.

home exhibit (_____, _____)   Ferris wheel (_____, _____)

17. What do the points for the Ferris wheel and home exhibit have in common?

_____

18. Larry said he would meet Marissa at the horse barn at (5, 4). What mistake did he make? What is the correct ordered pair?

_____

▶Figures on Grids

Use the coordinate grid below for exercises 19–22.

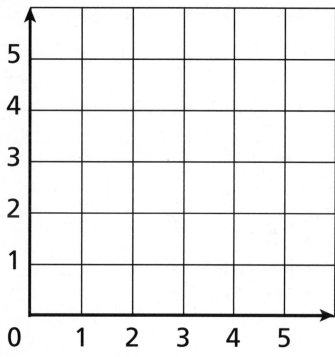

19. Graph each ordered pair. Label the point with the given letter.

Point A (1, 1), Point B (1, 4), Point C (2, 4), Point D (2, 1)

20. Draw a line segment to connect the points in order that you marked for exercise 19. Name the figure you drew.

_____

21. Graph each ordered pair. Label the point with the given letter.

Point E (3, 3), Point F (3, 5), Point G (5, 5), Point H (5, 3)

22. Draw a line segment to connect the points in order that you marked for exercise 21. Name the figure you drew.

_____

▶Triangles on Coordinate Grids

1. Mark a point on this coordinate grid to form the third vertex of a right triangle. Join the three points with line segments to make a right triangle.

2. Write the ordered pair for each vertex.

(____, ____) (____, ____) (____, ____)

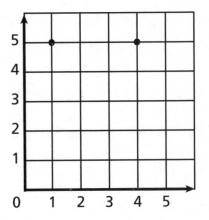

3. Mark a point on this coordinate grid to form the third vertex of an obtuse triangle. Join the three points to make an obtuse triangle.

4. Write the ordered pair for each vertex.

(____, ____) (____, ____) (____, ____)

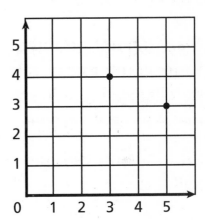

5. Draw a triangle on this coordinate grid. Place each vertex at the intersection of two grid lines.

6. Write the ordered pair for each vertex.

(____, ____) (____, ____) (____, ____)

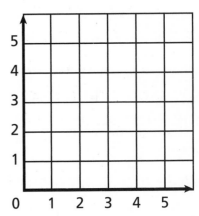

▶Quadrilaterals on Coordinate Grids

7. Mark a point on this coordinate grid to form the fourth vertex of a square. Join the four points with line segments to make a square.

8. Write the ordered pair for each vertex.

(____, ____) (____, ____)

(____, ____) (____, ____)

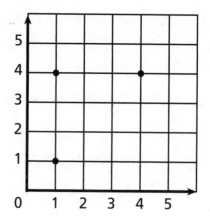

9. Mark a point on this coordinate grid to form the fourth vertex of a parallelogram. Join the four points to make a parallelogram.

10. Write the ordered pair for each vertex.

(____, ____) (____, ____)

(____, ____) (____, ____)

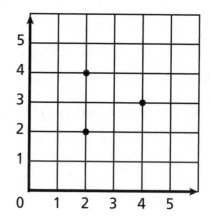

11. Draw a quadrilateral on this coordinate grid. Place each vertex at the intersection of two grid lines.

12. Write the ordered pair for each vertex.

(____, ____) (____, ____)

(____, ____) (____, ____)

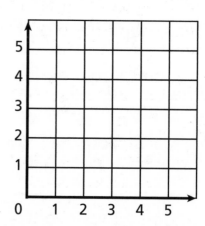

Explore Line Segments and Figures on a Coordinate Grid

▶Distance Between Points

The distance between two parallel line segments on a grid is 1 unit.

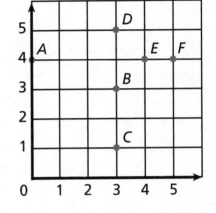

13. Draw a horizontal line segment from *A* to *E*. How long is the line segment?

_____

14. Draw a horizontal line segment from *E* to *F*. How long is the line segment?

_____

15. How long is the line segment from *A* to *F*?

_____

16. Draw a vertical line segment from *D* to *B*. How long is the line segment?

_____

17. Draw a vertical line segment from *B* to *C*. How long is the line segment?

_____

18. How long is the line segment from *D* to *C*?

_____

19. Draw a horizontal line segment with endpoints at the intersection of grid lines.

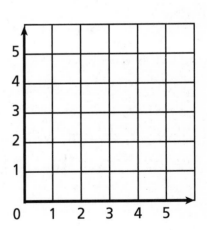

20. How long is your horizontal line segment?

_____

21. Draw a vertical line segment with endpoints at the intersection of grid lines.

22. How long is your vertical line segment?

_____

Class Activity

►Dimensions of Rectangles

23. How long is the width of this rectangle?

_____

24. How long is the length of this rectangle?

_____

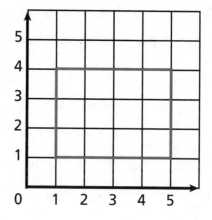

25. Draw a rectangle with a length that is 2 units longer than its width.

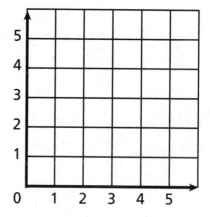

26. Draw a rectangle with a width that is 3 units shorter than its length.

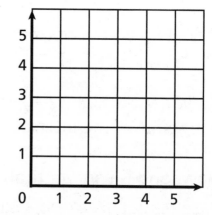

Use the coordinate grid below to complete exercises 1–4.

Greenville

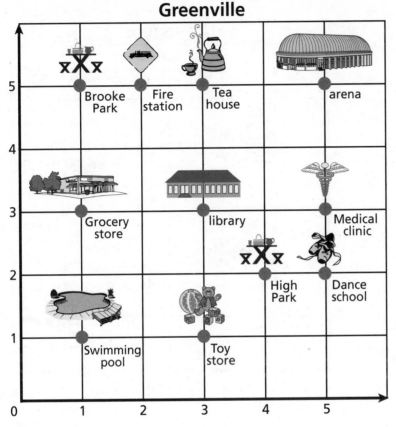

1. Lita started at the toy store. She walked 2 blocks right and 1 block up. Where is she?

_____

2. Lyle was at Brooke Park. He walked 1 block down, 3 blocks right, and 2 blocks down. Where is he?

_____

3. Chen was at the arena. He walked 1 block down, 3 blocks left, 3 blocks down, and 1 block left. Where is he?

_____

4. Michaela wants to go from Brooke Park to the Dance school. Describe a route that she can take.

_____

Use the coordinate grid below to complete exercises 5–10.

Name the animals you find at the point for each ordered pair.

5. (1, 2) _____

6. (5, 0) _____

Write the ordered pair for the location of the animals.

7. Sharks (_____, _____)

8. Dolphins (_____, _____)

9. Mato went to the aquarium. The first place he went to was at (5, 5). Which place did he go to first?

_____

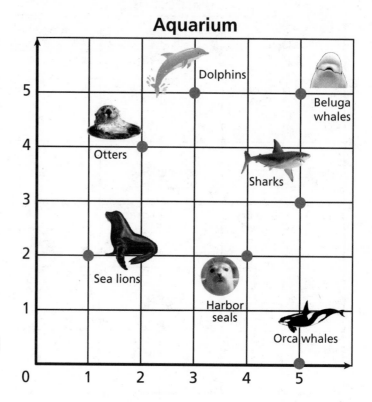

Aquarium

10. Extended Response After watching the sea lions being fed, Mato went to see the otters and the harbor seals. Write the ordered pair for each animal.

otters (_____, _____)   harbor seals (_____, _____)

What is the order of the numbers in an ordered pair? Why does the order matter? Use the example of the otters and harbor seals in your explanation.

_____

_____

_____

_____

Glossary

acute angle An angle whose measure is less than 90°.

acute triangle A triangle in which the measure of each angle is less than 90°.

addend A number to be added.

Example: $8 + 4 = 12$

addend   addend

addition A mathematical operation that combines two or more numbers.

Example: $23 + 52 = 75$

addend   addend   sum

adjacent (sides) Two sides that meet at a point.

Example: Sides *a* and *b* are adjacent.

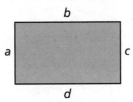

A.M. The time period between midnight and noon.

angle A figure formed by two rays or two line segments that meet at an endpoint.

area The number of square units in a region

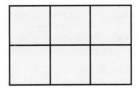

The area of the rectangle is 6 square units.

array An arrangement of objects, pictures, or numbers in columns and rows.

Associative Property of Addition (Grouping Property of Addition) The property which states that changing the way in which addends are grouped does not change the sum.

Example: $(2 + 3) + 1 = 2 + (3 + 1)$

$$5 + 1 = 2 + 4$$
$$6 = 6$$

Associative Property of Multiplication (Grouping Property of Multiplication) The property which states that changing the way in which factors are grouped does not change the product.

Example: $(2 \times 3) \times 4 = 2 \times (3 \times 4)$

$$6 \times 4 = 2 \times 12$$
$$24 = 24$$

Glossary (Continued)

axis (plural: **axes**) A reference line for a graph. A bar graph has 2 axes; one is horizontal and the other is vertical.

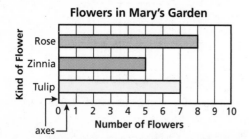

Flowers in Mary's Garden

axes

B

bar graph A graph that uses bars to show data. The bars may be horizontal or vertical.

Canned Goods at Turner's Market

base (of a geometric figure) The bottom side of a 2-D figure or the bottom face of a 3-D figure.

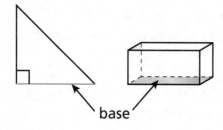

base

C

calculator A tool used to perform mathematical operations.

capacity The amount a container can hold.

---

cell A rectangle in a table where a column and row meet.

Coin Toss

	Heads	Tails
Sam	11	6
Zoe	9	10

} cell

centimeter (cm) A metric unit used to measure length.

100 cm = 1 m

circle A plane figure that forms a closed path so that all points on the path are the same distance from a point called the center.

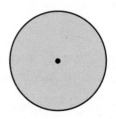

circle graph A graph that represents data as parts of a whole.

Jacket Colors in Ms. Timmer's Class

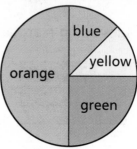

blue

yellow

orange

green

circumference The distance around a circle, about $3\frac{1}{7}$ times the diameter.

column A vertical group of cells in a table.

Coin Toss

	Heads	Tails
Sam	11	6
Zoe	9	10

column

Commutative Property of Addition (Order Property of Addition) The property which states that changing the order of addends does not change the sum.

Example: 3 + 7 = 7 + 3

10 = 10

Commutative Property of Multiplication (Order Property of Multiplication) The property which states that changing the order of factors does not change the product.

Example: 5 × 4 = 4 × 5

20 = 20

comparison bars Bars that represent the larger amount, smaller amount, and difference in a comparison problem.

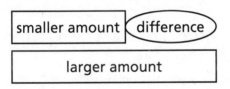

In Volume 2, we use comparison bars for multiplication.

cone A solid figure that has a circular base and comes to a point called the vertex.

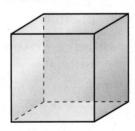

congruent figures Figures that have the same size and shape.

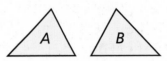

Triangles A and B are congruent.

coordinates The numbers in an ordered pair that locate a point on a coordinate grid. The first number is the distance across and the second number is the distance up.

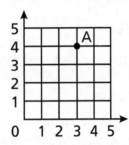

The coordinates 3 and 4 in the ordered pair (3, 4) locate Point A on the coordinate grid.

coordinate grid A grid formed by two perpendicular number lines in which every point is assigned an ordered pair of numbers.

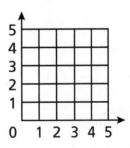

cube A solid figure that has six square faces of equal size.

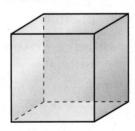

Glossary (Continued)

cup (c) A customary unit of measurement used to measure capacity.

   2 cups = 1 pint
   4 cups = 1 quart
  16 cups = 1 gallon

cylinder A solid figure with two congruent circular or elliptical faces and one curved surface.

data Pieces of information.

decimal A number with one or more digits to the right of a decimal point.

Examples: 1.23 and 0.3

decimal point The dot that separates the whole number from the decimal part.

    1.23

    ↑
decimal point

decimeter (dm) A metric unit used to measure length

1 decimeter = 10 centimeters

degree (°) A unit for measuring angles or temperature.

degrees Celsius (°C) The metric unit for measuring temperature.

degrees Fahrenheit (°F) The customary unit of temperature.

denominator The bottom number in a fraction that shows the total number of equal parts in the whole.

Example: $\frac{1}{3}$ ←— denominator

diagonal A line segment that connects two corners of a figure and is not a side of the figure.

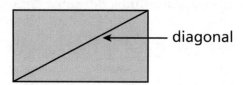

diameter A line segment that connects two point on a circle and also passes through the center of the circle. The term is also used to describe the length of such a line segment.

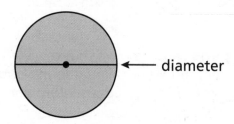

difference The result of subtraction or of comparing.

digit Any of the symbols 0, 1, 2, 3, 4, 5, 6, 7, 8, 9.

dividend The number that is divided in division.

Examples:

    $12 \div 3 = 4$ $3\overline{)12}^{\,4}$

    ↑   ↑
 dividend   dividend

division The mathematical operation that separates an amount into smaller equal groups to find the number of groups or the number in each group.

Example: $12 \div 3 = 4$ is a division number sentence.

divisor The number that you divide by in division.

Example: $12 \div 3 = 4$ $3\overline{)12}^{\,4}$

      ↑   ↑
   divisor divisor

E

edge The line segment where two faces of a solid figure meet.

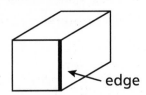

edge

elapsed time The time that passes between the beginning and the end of an activity.

endpoint The point at either end of a line segment or the beginning point of a ray.

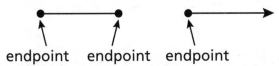

endpoint   endpoint   endpoint

equation A mathematical sentence with an equals sign.

Examples: $11 + 22 = 33$
$75 - 25 = 50$

equilateral triangle A triangle whose sides are all the same length.

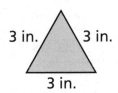

3 in.   3 in.

3 in.

equivalent Equal, or naming the same amount.

equivalent fractions Fractions that name the same amount.

Example: $\frac{1}{2}$ and $\frac{2}{4}$

equivalent fractions

estimate About how many or about how much.

even number A whole number that is a multiple of 2. The ones digit in an even number is 0, 2, 4, 6, or 8.

event In probability, a possible outcome.

expanded form A number written to show the value of each of its digits.

Examples:
$347 = 300 + 40 + 7$
$347 = 3$ hundreds $+ 4$ tens $+ 7$ ones

expression A combination of numbers, variables, and/or operation signs. An expression does not have an equals sign.

Examples: $4 + 7$ $a - 3$

F

face A flat surface of a solid figure.

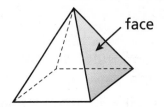

face

factors Numbers that are multiplied to give a product.

Example: $4 \times 5 = 20$

factor   factor   product

flip To reflect a figure over a line. The size and shape of the figure remain the same.

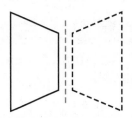

foot (ft) A customary unit used to measure length.

1 foot = 12 inches

Glossary (Continued)

formula An equation with variables that describes a rule.

The formula for the area of a rectangle is:

$A = l \times w$

where A is the area, l is the length, and w is the width.

fraction A number that names part of a whole or part of a set.

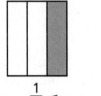

$\frac{1}{3}$ ← fraction → $\frac{2}{3}$

front-end estimation A method of estimating that keeps the largest place value in a number and drops the rest.

Example: 527   →   500
           + 673   →   + 600
                      1,100

The 5 in 527 is the "front end" number
The 6 in 673 is the "front end" number

function table A table of ordered pairs that shows a function.

For every input number, there is only one possible output number.

Rule: add 2	
Input	Output
1	3
2	4
3	5
4	6

G

gallon (gal) A customary unit used to measure capacity.

1 gallon = 4 quarts = 8 pints = 16 cups

gram (g) A metric unit of mass, about 1 paper clip.

1,000 grams = 1 kilogram

greater than (>) A symbol used to compare two numbers.

Example: 6 > 5
          6 is greater than 5.

group To combine numbers to form new tens, hundreds, thousands, and so on.

growing pattern A number or geometric pattern that increases.

Examples: 2, 4, 6, 8, 10…
          1, 2, 5, 10, 17…

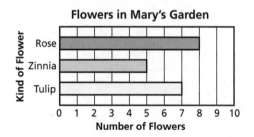

H

height A measurement of vertical length, or how tall something is.

horizontal Extending in two directions, left and right.

horizontal bar graph A bar graph with horizontal bars.

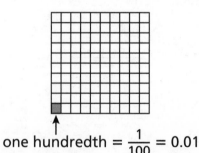
Flowers in Mary's Garden

hundredth One of the equal parts when a whole is divided into 100 equal parts.

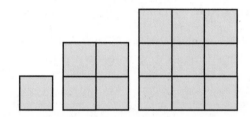

one hundredth = $\frac{1}{100}$ = 0.01

I

improper fraction A fraction in which the numerator is equal to or is greater than the denominator. Improper fractions are equal to or greater than 1. $\frac{5}{5}$ and $\frac{8}{3}$ are improper fractions.

inch (in.) A customary unit used to measure length.

12 inches = 1 foot

isosceles triangle A triangle that has at least two sides of the same length.

K

key A part of a map, graph, or chart that explains what symbols mean.

kilogram (kg) A metric unit of mass.

1 kilogram = 1,000 grams

kilometer (km) A metric unit of length.

1 kilometer = 1,000 meters

L

less than (<) A symbol used to compare numbers.

Example: 5 < 6
5 *is less than* 6.

line A straight path that goes on forever in opposite directions.

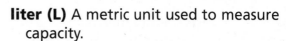

line graph A graph that uses a straight line or a broken line to show changes in data.

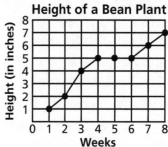

line of symmetry A line on which a figure can be folded so that the two halves match exactly.

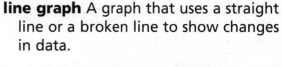

line plot A way to show data using a number line.

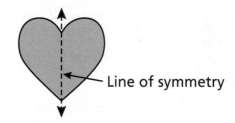

line segment A part of a line. A line segment has two endpoints.

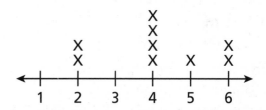

liter (L) A metric unit used to measure capacity.

1 liter = 1,000 milliliters

Glossary **S7**

Glossary (Continued)

M

mass The amount of matter in an object.

mean (average) The sum of the values in a set of data divided by the number of pieces of data in the set.

Example: 3 + 5 + 4 + 8 = 20
20 ÷ 4 = 5   5 is the mean

mental math A way to solve problems without using pencil and paper, or a calculator.

meter (m) A metric unit used to measure length.

1 meter = 100 centimeters

method A procedure, or way, of doing something.

mile (mi) A customary unit of length.

1 mile = 5,280 feet

milliliter (mL) A metric unit used to measure capacity.

1,000 milliliters = 1 liter

mixed number A whole number and a fraction.

$1\frac{3}{4}$ is a mixed number.

mode The number that occurs most often in a set of data.

In this set of numbers {3, 4, 5, 5, 5, 7, 8}, 5 is the mode.

multiple A number that is the product of the given number and another number.

multiplication A mathematical operation that combines equal groups.

Example: 4 × 3 = 12

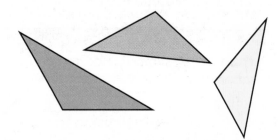

factor   factor   product

3 + 3 + 3 + 3 = 12

4 times

N

net A flat pattern that can be folded to make a solid figure.

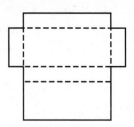

This net can be folded into a rectangular prism.

number line A line on which numbers are assigned to lengths.

numerator The top number in a fraction that shows the number of equal parts counted.

Example: $\frac{1}{3}$ ◄—— numerator

O

obtuse angle An angle that measures more than 90° but less than 180°.

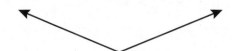

obtuse triangle A triangle with one angle that measures more than 90°.

odd number A whole number that is not a multiple of 2. The ones digit in an odd number is 1, 3, 5, 7, or 9.

opposite sides Sides that are across from each other; they do not meet at a point.

Example: Sides *a* and *c* are opposite.

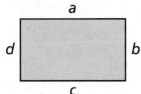

ordered pair A pair of numbers such as (3, 4) in which one number is considered to be first and the other number second. They can name a point on a coordinate grid.

ordinal numbers Numbers used to show order or position.

Example: first, second, fifth

ounce (oz) A customary unit used to measure weight.

16 ounces = 1 pound

P

parallel lines Two lines that are everywhere the same distance apart.

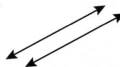

parallelogram A quadrilateral with both pairs of opposite sides parallel.

partner One of two numbers that add to make a total.

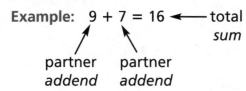

Example: $9 + 7 = 16$ ←—— total
sum

partner partner
addend *addend*

perimeter The distance around the outside of a figure.

perpendicular Two lines or line segments that cross or meet to form right angles.

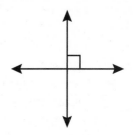

pictograph A graph that uses pictures or symbols to represent data.

Favorite Ice Cream Flavors

Peanut Butter Crunch

Cherry Vanilla

Chocolate

Each 🍦 = 3

pint (pt) A customary unit used to measure capacity.

1 pint = 2 cups

place value The value assigned to the place that a digit occupies in a number.

9 6 2
↑ ↑ ↑
hundreds tens ones

place value drawing A drawing that represents a number. Hundreds are represented by boxes, tens by vertical lines, and ones by small circles.

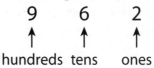

962

plane figure A closed figure that has two dimensions.

Glossary (Continued)

P.M. The time period between noon and midnight.

pound (lb) A customary unit used to measure weight.

1 pound = 16 ounces

prism A solid figure with two parallel congruent bases, and rectangles or parallelograms for faces. A prism is named by the shape of its bases.

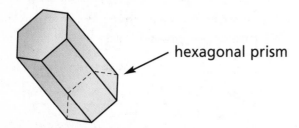

hexagonal prism

probability The chance of an event occurring.

product The answer when you multiply numbers.

Example: 4 × 7 = 28

factor   factor   product

proof drawing A drawing used to show that an answer is correct.

$$\begin{array}{r} 249 \\ + 386 \\ \hline 11 \\ 635 \end{array}$$

pyramid A solid figure with one base and whose other faces are triangles with a common vertex. A pyramid is named by the shape of its base.

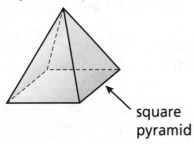

square pyramid

quadrilateral A figure with four sides.

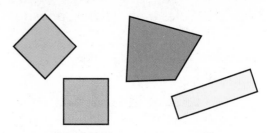

quart (qt) A customary unit used to measure capacity.

1 quart = 4 cups

quotient The answer when you divide numbers.

Examples:

35 ÷ 7 = 5 $7\overline{)35}$ ← quotient

quotient

radius A line segment that connects the center of a circle to any point on the circle. The term is also used to describe the length of such a line segment.

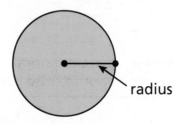

radius

range The difference between the greatest number and the least number in a set of data.

In this set of numbers {12, 15, 18, 19, 20}, the range is 20 − 12 or 8

ray A part of a line that has one endpoint and goes on forever in one direction.

rectangle A parallelogram that has 4 right angles.

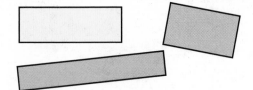

rectangular prism A prism with six rectangular faces.

rectangular pyramid A pyramid with a rectangular base and four triangular faces.

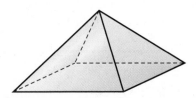

repeating pattern A pattern consisting of a group of numbers, letters, or figures that repeat.

Examples: 1, 2, 1, 2, …
A, B, C, A, B, C, …

rhombus A parallelogram with congruent sides.

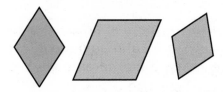

right angle An angle that measures 90°.

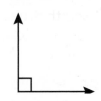

right triangle A triangle with one right angle.

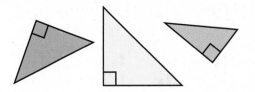

round To find about how many or how much by expressing a number to the nearest ten, hundred, thousand, and so on.

route The path taken to get to a location.

row A horizontal group of cells in a table.

Coin Toss

	Heads	Tails
Sam	11	6
Zoe	9	10

} row

S

scale An arrangement of numbers in order with equal intervals.

scalene triangle A triangle with sides of three different lengths.

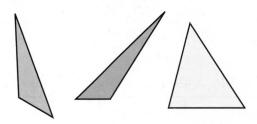

Glossary (Continued)

shrinking pattern A number or geometric pattern that decreases.

Examples: 15, 12, 9, 6, 3,…
25, 20, 16, 13, 11,…

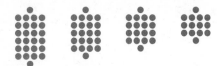

side (of a figure) A line segment that makes up a figure.

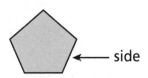

simplify To write an equivalent fraction with a smaller numerator and denominator.

slide To move a figure along a line in any direction. The size and shape of the figure remain the same.

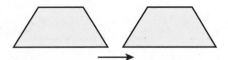

solid figure A figure that has three dimensions.

sphere A solid figure shaped like a ball.

square A rectangle with four sides of the same length.

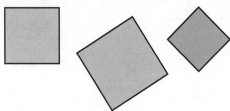

square number A product of a whole number and itself.

Example: 4 × 4 = 16

square number

square pyramid A pyramid with a square base and four triangular faces.

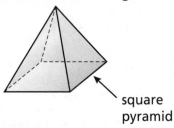

square pyramid

standard form The name of a number written using digits.

Example: 1,829

straight angle An angle that measures 180°.

subtract To find the difference of two numbers.

Example: 18 – 11 = 7

subtraction A mathematical operation on a sum (total) and an addend, which can be called the difference.

Example: 43 – 40 = 3

sum The answer when adding two or more addends.

Example: 37 + 52 = 89

addend   addend   sum
partner   *partner*   *total*

survey A method of collecting information.

symmetry A figure has symmetry if it can be folded along a line so that the two halves match exactly.

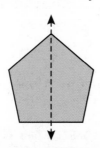

T

table An easy to read arrangement of data, usually in rows and columns.

Coin Toss

	Heads	Tails
Sam	11	6
Zoe	9	10

tally marks Short line segments drawn in groups of 5. Each mark including the slanted marks stands for 1 unit.

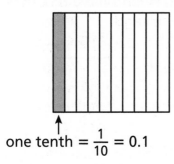 means 13

tenth One of the equal parts when a whole is divided into ten equal parts.

one tenth = $\frac{1}{10}$ = 0.1

thermometer A tool for measuring temperature.

total The answer when adding two or more addends. The sum of two or more numbers.

Example: 672 + 228 = 900

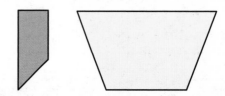

partner   partner   total
addend   addend   sum

trapezoid A quadrilateral with exactly one pair of parallel sides.

triangular prism A solid figure with two triangular faces and three rectangular faces.

Example:

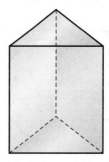

triangular pyramid A pyramid whose base is a triangle.

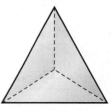

turn To rotate a figure around a point. The size and shape of the figure remains the same.

Glossary (Continued)

U

ungroup To open up 1 in a given place to make 10 of the next smaller place value in order to subtract.

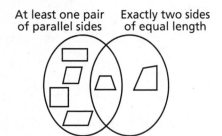

unit fraction A fraction with a numerator of 1.

V

Venn diagram A diagram that uses circles to show the relationship among sets of objects.

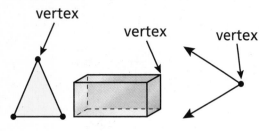

vertex A point where sides, rays, or edges meet.

vertical Extending in two directions, up and down.

vertical bar graph A bar graph with vertical bars.

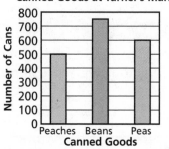

W

weight The measure of how heavy something is.

word form A name of a number written using words instead of digits.

Example: Nine hundred eighty-four

Y

yard (yd) A customary unit used to measure length.

1 yard = 3 feet = 36 inches